Torchflame Books
LARGE PRINT

PRAISE FOR ROBERT SÉAMUS MACPHERSON

"A sincere tribute to professionals who do not always receive the recognition and support they deserve, *Stewards of Humanity* is a memoir about healing through—and from—humanitarian work."

FOREWORD REVIEWS

"*Stewards of Humanity* is a fabulously well-told memoir by a soldier turned humanitarian worker who cares deeply about the troubled world in which we live."

CAROL BERGMAN, EDITOR, *ANOTHER DAY IN PARADISE; INTERNATIONAL HUMANITARIAN WORKERS TELL THEIR STORIES*, ORBIS BOOKS

"A riveting and emotional personal account of his journey…to a life of dedication to help those in need."

GENERAL TONY ZINNI, USMC (RET)

"Macpherson is a brilliant writer whose broad life experiences validates him as a major thinker, teacher, and caretaker for the plight of the victims as well as the millions of unnamed worldwide humanitarians. It is a gem of a book that will rapidly win the respect and admiration of a large audience of readers…as it should."

FREDERICK M. BURKLE, JR., MD, MPH, PHD (HON.), DTM, FAAP, FACEP

"*Stewards of Humanity* is a must-read for current and aspiring humanitarian aid workers, human rights defenders, and academics. ... This book calls us to honor those who choose to serve humanity and, through that summons, find the connection that binds us all—our responsibility to care for one another."

JANE BARRY, HUMAN RIGHTS ACTIVIST AND AUTHOR

STEWARDS OF HUMANITY

STEWARDS OF HUMANITY
LIGHTING THE DARKNESS IN HUMANITARIAN CRISIS

ROBERT SÉAMUS MACPHERSON

Torchflame Books
LARGE PRINT
Vista, CA

Copyright © 2021 Robert Ingles-Séamus Macpherson

All rights reserved. Torchflame Books supports copyright. Copyright fuels creativity, encourages diverse voices, promotes free speech, and creates a vibrant culture. Thank you for buying an authorized edition of this book and for complying with copyright laws by not reproducing, scanning, or distributing any part of it in any form without permission, except by a reviewer who wishes to quote brief passages in connection with a review written for insertion in a magazine, newspaper, broadcast, website, blog or other outlet. You are supporting independent publishing and allowing Torchflame Books to publish books for all readers.

NO AI TRAINING: Without in any way limiting the author's [and publisher's] exclusive rights under copyright, any use of this publication to "train" generative artificial intelligence (AI) technologies to generate text is expressly prohibited. The author reserves all rights to license uses of this work for generative AI training and development of machine learning language models.

ISBN: 978-1-61153-673-7

Library of Congress Control Number: 2021909103

Stewards of Humanity is published in 2025 by: Torchflame Books Large Print, an imprint of Top Reads Publishing, LLC, 1035 E. Vista Way, Suite 205, Vista, CA 92084, USA

www.torchflamebooks.com/large-print

The publisher is not responsible for websites or social media accounts (or their content) that are not owned by the publisher.

Cover Design by Elizabeth Turnbull

Interior Design by Jori Hanna

This Large Print Edition is set in 16-point Iowan Old Style type. This book is about the remarkable and courageous effort of humanitarian aid workers amid war, genocide, and starvation. The description of some of these events are vivid and may be unsettling.

*For Maisie Martyn-Sterling Macpherson,
who gave me the gift of life and the courage to face it.*

*For Veronica,
without whom, I would not be here.
For my children, Jennifer and Bud,
who never lost faith in me.
For Marjorie Macpherson,
thank you.*

*For Peter Bell,
who opened the door
that allowed me to walk with the Stewards.
For Karen Henson Robbins,
friend, mentor, and muse*

ACKNOWLEDGMENTS

This book is a collection of stories about the humanitarian efforts of extraordinary people. Over the two decades I worked in the aid community, I met many individuals who risked a great deal to save the lives of others. Although I must limit the number of events I describe, each person touched me deeply with their compassion, decency, and willingness to step outside the bounds of normalcy and walk into the worlds of disaster, violence, and deprivation.

Watching them, I found a common trait: they waded into horrific situations armed with a willingness to confront rather than retreat from injustice. They entered worlds of unspeakable violence and disaster to assume the cause of the oppressed, and to a degree, their conditions. While exposing themselves to the same threats and violence as the people, they served; often, robbed, assaulted, killed, wounded, diseased, and jailed. They were vulnerable to anyone who had a weapon.

THE STEWARDS

Stewards of Humanity is about the remarkable and courageous effort of humanitarian aid workers, amid war, genocide, and starvation. The description of some of these events are vivid and may be unsettling.

Tom Alcedo, John Ambler, Sally Austin, Gordon Bacon, Jock Baker, Stephanie Barić, Paul Barker, Jane Barry, Nassima Be, Bob Bell, Peter Bell, Jane Benbow, Flamur Beqiri, Fr. Dan Berrigan SJ, Ray Bonavitch, Kate Bunting, Marshall Burke, Dr. Frederick (Skip) Burkle, Michelle Carter, Pat Carey, Claudia Chang, Geoffrey Chege, Megan Chisholm, Rigoberto Giron, Jennifer Cook, Bud Crandall, Lynne Cripe, Dominic Crowley, Brenda Cupper, Roméo Dallaire, Charlie Danzoll, Karen

Davies, Marc De Lamotte, George Devondorf, Michael Drinkwater, Wendy Driscoll, Barbara Durr, Lionel Dyck, Ike Evans, Scott Faiia, Kate Farnsworth, Susan Farnsworth, James Fennell, Isam Ghanim, Helene D. Gayle, Paul Giannone, Kent Glenzer, Anne Goddard, Carey Grant, Marilyn Frailey Grist, Harlan Hale, Denny Hamilton, Abdalla Himedan, John Hoare, Nancy Hofmann, Larry Holzman, Trevor Hughes, Tom Hurley, Joe Iarocci, Susan Igras, Barbara Jackson, Anuj Jain, Sherine Jayawickrama, Phil Johnston, Alex Jones, Lex Kassenberg, Manjit Kaur, Rafael Khusnutdinov, Veronica Kenny-Macpherson, Wael Kirresh, Uwe Korus, Bob Laprade, Brian Larson, Sandy Laumark, Mario Lima, Joe Lowry, Sean Lowrie, Abby Maxman, Dan Maxwell, Kathy McCaston, Kevin McCort, Mike McDonagh, Kassie McIlvaine, Elizabeth Jane McLaughlin, Peter Lochery, Kathy McCaston, Giulia Campanaro McPherson, Dominic McSorley, Carmen Michielin, Jon Mitchell, Ann Moffett, Daw Mohammed, Gordy Molitor, Barbara Monahan, Anne Morris, Musa Muhammad, Barbara Murphy, Pete Murphy, Madhuri Narayanan, Abdul Raouf Nazhand, Robin Needham, Gail Neudorf, Deb Neuman, David Newberry, Chitose Noguchi, Dennis O'Brien, Paul O'Brien, Michael O'Neill, Nick Osborne, Bennett

Pafford, Christine Persaud, Laky Pissalidis, Valerie Place, Steve Pratt, Andy Pugh, Aly Khan Rajani, Lisa Reilly, Michael Rewald, Beverly Aisha Roach, Karen Robbins, Susan Rae Roth, Leo Roozendaal, Penny Rush, John Schafer, Melissa Sharer, Norman Sheehan, Carol Sherman, Michel Simbikang, Liz Sime, Nancy Smith, Holly Solberg, Patrick Solomon, Nick Southern, Milo Stanojevich, Joan Sullivan, Chris Sykes, Joelle Tanguy, Scott Thigpen, Jennene Tierney, Kathy Tin, Lise Tonelli, Catherine Toth, Eirik Trondsen, Marge Tsitouris, Virginia Ubik, Jill Umbach, Virginia Vaughn, Carsten Voelz, Edith Wallmeier, Fr. Jack Warner SJ, Kirsten Weeks, Astrid Wein, Joanna Foote Williams, Jody Williams, Stephen Williams, Roy Williams, Ian Willis, Paul Wood, Stuart Worsley, Lora Wuennenberg, Jeannie Zielinski.

ABOUT THIS BOOK

> "Memory is many things. It is a call to resolve in us what simply will not go away.... It is a desire for completion, for the continuance of something we once had but lost too soon.
> It is always an opportunity for healing ....
> —Joan Chittister

It was a long journey from serving as a US Marine in the Vietnam War and ending my service after Somalia in 1993 to entering Sarajevo as an aid worker during the Bosnian conflict. Along the way, I met many exceptional women and men, both Marines and humanitarians who were committed to the ideals of human rights and justice. Although these principles are more readily associated with humanitarians, I found they were also the foundation for the beliefs of most Marines. Both groups shared a willingness to wade into inconceivable violence and destruction to confront the horrors of war and natural disaster.

Before my deployment to Somalia, I had no experience with the humanitarian community. As an infantry officer, I never encountered them in Vietnam, Beirut, or Iraq. In fact, if I thought about the community, I assumed they were part of the United Nations or faith-based charities.

When I arrived in Somalia, the commanding general, a US Marine, Lieutenant General Robert Johnston, assigned me to work with the United Nations and "NGOs" to coordinate the assets and capabilities of the military force with the humanitarian efforts to end starvation in Somalia. On leaving his office, I asked a close friend, "What's an NGO?" He replied, "It means non-governmental organization," which meant nothing to me. He explained, "They are non-profits who are independent of national governments and work in education, health care, human rights, wars, and natural disasters." As I continued to question him, he finally looked at me and said, "They're like those CARE guys."

As a boy in grade school in the 1950s, we all

knew about CARE packages being sent to the war-torn countries of Europe and Asia.

Later, as I watched unarmed aid workers move through Mogadishu in battered Toyota Land Cruisers, I thought they were crazy. While the military convoys were protected by armed troops and Quick Reaction Forces on standby if we were ambushed, the NGOs relied on guarantees of safe passage from the same warlords who were attacking and looting their relief supplies.

To say Somalia was chaos is charitable.

As I entered their world and started to understand their work, I realized they were neither irrational nor adrenaline junkies. They were as dedicated to humanitarianism as I was to the mission of the Marine Corps. The difference was in support and capacity. I was surrounded by women and men who were trained warfighters. We had weapons, machines, aircraft, and an esprit de corps more than two centuries old. If I were injured or wounded, my comrades would darken the sun with helicopters and assets to find and rescue me.

By comparison, the NGO community was a loosely organized group of dedicated people. They were less idealistic than my fellow service women and men. As a military force, we stood off to provide security and logistical support, but the humanitarians had to enter the worst of the devastation and misery.

I continued trying to understand them. They were dedicated, but not zealots. A few worked for religious reasons, but that was rare. They shared a common characteristic of effective leadership and a keen ability to set aside the chatter of bureaucracy and find solutions to problems that appeared insurmountable.

Yet, I could not define what made them tick. I was impressed by their diversity and the inclusion of women in primary leadership roles. In Somalia, I estimated 65 percent of the country directors and UN staff were women, while in the Marine Corps, we were just beginning to embrace women Marines as equal partners. Somalia was the first time in my professional career that I worked with so many women as primary decision makers, and it was a quantitative and necessary leap for me. I was stunned at how isolated I was from credible and meaningful gender equality.

As my association with the humanitarians deepened, I realized that my colleagues, just like my fellow Marines, did not fit into one box or category. Although their reasons and motivations for being there were varied, they were part of one organization and drawn by a single ideal: a desire to assist and serve.

After returning from Somalia, I stood in front of a formation of Marines and received a medal for my actions in Somalia. One of those acts was killing a man who attacked and killed several children in my vicinity in Mogadishu. The ceremony was meant to be an honor, but it felt empty to me. I had no regrets about what I had done and knew the medal was a sincere gesture of appreciation, but Somalia had changed me. At that time, I could not articulate what that change was, but I knew I was drawn to another path in my life.

Standing in front of my comrades with flags flying and a band playing, I thought about the humanitarians I met in Somalia. Much of their work was more desperate than my own, and they certainly faced more danger, but they seldom received any distinguishing gesture for their sacrifice. They worked quietly and purposefully, made a difference, went home, and waited for their next assignment. There were no ceremonies or medals; their only recognition was a personal sense of achievement.

Throughout my ensuing years working in the humanitarian community, I found that their sacrifices resulted in conditions more ominous than a lack of recognition. Too many are killed or wounded by direct violence, others die by suicide, and the percentages of divorce, substance abuse, and post-traumatic stress disorder are substantial.

This book is an attempt to recognize the sacrifices of women and men who quietly work in terrible situations for the sole reason to help others. These individuals are not motivated by medals, parades, or citations, but by a personal desire to serve humanity.

It was an intimidating endeavor to convey their stories amid so many complex and dangerous situations. Each remembrance reminded me of their fears, hopes, exhaustion, and joy. Most survived; some did not.

My goal was to be their storyteller. I wanted to stay above the narrative. It was their journey, not mine, and I was convinced that to do their stories justice I needed to be an observer.

I was wrong.

Nothing I wrote rang true; it was detached and cold. I struggled. I had been part of these events and lived them. Why was this so difficult? The words wouldn't fall into place. They were stilted and awkward. I quit and relegated the book to the "too hard" category.

Who needs this? I asked myself.

But the book wouldn't let me walk away. It stayed with me like a chronic and subtle pain that would not ease until I dealt with it.

I tried to ignore it until, one day, I understood. As I thought about a person and their event, I reentered their lives, I relived their grief, pleasure, pain, and loss. My throat constricted, my eyes moistened, and I felt the rolling grip of emotion grab me.

That was it.

It was all so intensely personal. It happened to me, too, and I had to allow my own emotions and experience speak for these people.

It was impossible to write about these humanitarians and do it from a distance. To speak to their deeds and selflessness, their drive to give so much and, at times, tear themselves apart, I had to reenter this wild, chaotic, and complicated fray and face my own enduring fears, prejudices, and guilt.

What I found while exploring their stories was a deeper understanding of these people who lived in extreme settings of deprivation, worked long hours surrounded by high-risk conditions, made life-and-death decisions, and struggled with the demands for additional supplies that were never enough to meet the need. Each day, they confronted the moral challenge of deciding who does and does not get assistance.

They were not saints, but women and men who possessed extraordinary passion, dedication, dignity, and decency. On the surface, they were considered "normal." They swore, had tempers, and were hard-headed. Often, they were tough to be around. While some were freewheeling, others were exasperatingly sober and focused.

I began to understand the only limits to our humanness are the boundaries we allow ourselves to imagine. I watched these Stewards connect with humanity and saw the threads of their life. Their tendrils of service were cords of selfless engagement, and guided the aid workers around them through the devastation and injustice of a crisis.

The Stewards showed me that, while our egos protect us with the belief we are removed, aloof, and separate from our responsibilities to one another, in truth, we are connected.

If we allow it, this connection will manifest itself into what we all seek: peace.

PROLOGUE

Moments before cresting the hill in Albania, Claudia casually leaned across the back seat of the vehicle and said, "Bob, I notice you don't have your seat belt on." As the leader of this five-person team from the humanitarian organization CARE, it struck me: I should set the example. When I fastened it, I felt the man sitting between Claudia and me secure his own restraint.

We were making our way through the mountains of northern Albania to the border town of Kukes. In March and April 1999, Slobodan Milošević, the President of the Federal Republic of Yugoslavia, was "cleansing" Kosovo's ethnic Albanian population from the province. In Kukes, approximately 800,000 refugees made their way to

Albania across the treacherous mountain border. CARE was about to mount a large-scale assistance program, and our team was the lead element.

Within sixty seconds after Claudia's comment, we rounded a bend on the cliff road, and I saw a gaping hole where the dirt highway used to be. The mountainside had collapsed. The recent rains and heavy traffic moving relief supplies had eroded its foundation. I thought, "The driver should slam on the brakes." Instead, the vehicle surged, and I saw him throw his hands in front of his face in panic. He had stepped on the gas pedal accidentally.

As we accelerated over the cliff, I looked out of my side window, amazed at the sheer drop. It looked like five hundred feet. "This is what it's like when people say he died in an accident," I thought. For a moment, it was peaceful. I shut my eyes and silently prayed, "I'm sorry for the bad things I've done. Forgive me and make this quick."

With the first impact, a collective pain surged through me. I heard groans, but no screaming. The sound was an acknowledgment of agony. After each collision, the vehicle ricocheted and spun until we slammed again into the side of the cliff. With each crash, I heard the pitch of metal screeching as we pounded into the mountain. As the plunge continued, I marveled, "we are not in complete free fall." A window shattered into my face, the shriek of tearing metal continuing. I imagined skin being ripped from the SUV. But I was shocked: I was still alive. I felt the seat belt and the incredible force of my rib cage pushing into the restraint with each crash.

I was strangely calm. I knew I was going to die but wondered when.

I sensed it. It was not a voice, but I could feel it. It was powerful and personal. I opened my eyes to find it. Looking around the plummeting vehicle, all I could see was tangible light. I could hear the vehicle disintegrating, but I saw brilliance. It did not hurt my eyes, and it had presence. It was not a form. It was the purest thing I had ever witnessed. I could not determine size or depth, but felt surrounded and protected by it. I wondered if I was dead, but I could still sense the impact of the vehicle plunging down the cliff.

As my eyes searched for a form, I experienced something more peaceful than anything I had ever encountered. I felt safe and comfortable, and my mind opened. For a moment, a lifetime of questioning, trivializing, and disregarding something greater than me crumbled into the absolute clarity of love. This light was real, but my mind would not accept it. "I have to be imagining this. I must be unconscious."

Suddenly, there was a crushing impact, and the left side of my body absorbed the shock and collapsed. I felt my arm, shoulder, hand, fingers, ribs, and leg fracture. I glanced to my left, and realized the vehicle had impacted on the single boulder jutting from the side of the cliff. It stopped our fall. We were still alive.

Smoke filled the vehicle, and I yelled for my colleagues to get out of the SUV. I could sense their movements but could not loosen my seat belt. My left hand was broken, but the urgency quickly overcame the pain. As I worked to release the restraint, I saw the driver slumped over the steering wheel. The automobile was on fire, and I was afraid. I did not want to burn to death.

For a moment, I considered leaving him, and rationalized he was probably dead, but I climbed over the front passenger seat and started working on his seat belt. I had trouble finding the latch because of the smoke, and the air was acrid with flames. Finally, I felt it snap open. His door was crushed, so I started pulling him across the front seat toward the broken window on the passenger's side. It was a hopeless struggle because of my injuries, his weight, and the confines of the vehicle.

Unexpectedly, I felt myself being pulled from behind and hands reached across my shoulders to remove the driver. I was gently laid on the ground and started vomiting from the smoke and pain.

I looked around and saw several Albanian truck drivers who were following us and witnessed the accident. I struggled to get to my feet and found my colleagues lying along the cliffside. They were injured but alive. I could not find Claudia. I stumbled and crawled behind a boulder and saw her. She was lying on the ground, her head in the lap of an Albanian woman who was stroking her hair. I thought she was dead and dropped to my knees and looked at the woman holding her. She could sense the question in my eyes and shrugged. I bent down and said, "Claudia, please come back. I need you." She opened her eyes and smiled. I collapsed.

I awoke on the bed of an Albanian dump truck and looked up to see Claudia. I realized my head was in her lap. There was a surge of pain through my body and I passed out. When I regained consciousness, there was a priest and a doctor standing over me. I thought it was strange to find a priest in a Muslim country. In broken English, he introduced himself, and said he was from Germany. He explained I was in a rural Albanian medical clinic and the doctor had to do urgent surgery on my left hand and arm. He needed to set bones, close lacerations and remove fingernails. He had no anesthesia but had morphine to assist with the pain. The procedures were gruesome. The morphine helped, but I passed out when he pulled the thumbnail from my left hand.

The next day, I was transported by an Albanian ambulance to a military hospital in Tirana, the capital of Albania. No one spoke English, but I gathered that the military hospital had the best facilities. During one of the days in the clinic, several Albanian men appeared with someone who could speak English. They carried several large bundles. The interpreter told me the people of the village near the accident had scoured the side of the cliff to find the luggage and equipment that was thrown from our vehicle. The bundles contained three cameras, two satellite phones, personal items, and two packages, each of which had $7,500 in one-hundred-dollar US bills. In 1999, the average wage in Albania was less than $200 per month. There was not one bill missing from the money packs.

All of my colleagues survived the accident, but the driver, Claudia, and I suffered the worst injuries. Three days after the crash, a representative from the

American Embassy arrived and told me we would be flown to the US Air Force hospital in Rhein-Main, Germany. That afternoon an ambulance arrived and carried Claudia and me to the Tirana airport. From there, we were transported by a US Air Force medical evacuation plane to Rhein-Main, and finally by ambulance to the civilian Malteser Hospital in Bonn, Germany. We spent one month there, followed by two months in a rehabilitation clinic before returning to the United States. I was with Claudia, who obtained head, neck, and upper-body injuries. The driver was in another hospital and had severe damage to his chest, back, head, and face.

The perfect end to this account would be an awakening of awareness and focused purpose.

That didn't happen.

I was unnerved by the experience and still have trouble dealing with it. The accident happened on April 7, 1999, thirty years from the day I was injured in the Vietnam War, which resulted in months in a US Naval hospital recuperating. Possibly that was a coincidence, but it is the encounter with that white brilliant presence in the crashing vehicle that challenges me. Sixty seconds before we plummet off a cliff, Claudia tells me to fasten my seat belt, and moments later I encounter something that comforts me. It was real and impossible to describe.

It scares me to accept that the presence was spiritual, so I have done nothing with it. When you are twice saved from death, you want someone or something to light a bush or announce in a booming voice, "You are still here because I want you to..." but there were no instructions. I struggle to unravel what happened. For some, the experience would be a matter of faith, and I envy them, but my ego demands to understand. What happened to me? Was it real? Why me? What am I supposed to do?

In my search for understanding, I began focusing on the words: "answerable and accountable to others." This event led me to meet and witness the lives of the women and men who comprise *Stewards of Humanity*. Writing this book was a journey that demanded I discern their actions through something greater than myself.

CHAPTER 1
A PLACE THAT LOST ITS SOUL

*"Not speaking up against pure evil
is equal to cooperating with it."*
—Constance Chuks Friday

AFTER THE COLLAPSE OF THE SOMALI government in 1991, marauding gangs and clan chiefs who identified themselves as warlords took control of the country. Without a national army and police force, each of the clans fought to control Somalia and used food as a weapon of war. A widespread famine broke out. The rival warlords would not allow food aid to reach an opposing clan's desperate population. At least 500,000 Somalis perished from hunger, and more than a million were in jeopardy of a similar fate.

The fighting in Mogadishu, the capital of Somalia and the most populous, was vicious. The gunfire was unremitting. In the streets were so many dead bodies they were counted by the hundreds. The most frequent scene was to see hungry dogs tearing at corpses. By November 1992, General Mohamed Farrah Aidid became powerful enough to consolidate the warring factions in Mogadishu. He challenged the United Nations and its secretary general, Boutros Boutros-Ghali, to remove the UN peacekeeping forces of approximately 1,000 Pakistani soldiers who arrived in July 1992, from Somalia and Mogadishu.

Boutros-Ghali realized bringing stability to Somalia would require the deployment of a large, well-trained, and equipped force. The goal of such a deployment was "to prepare the way for a return to peacekeeping and post-conflict peace-building (throughout Somalia)."[1]

With a request from the United Nations secretary general, President George H. Bush ordered US troops to Somalia. Bush described the military

---

1. United Nations, "Somalia - UNOSOM 1," Peacekeeping.un.org, January 10, 2007, accessed https://peacekeeping.un.org/mission/past/unosom1backgr2.html

mission as "God's work," and said America must act to save Somali lives.

On December 9, 1992, the first US Marines and Navy Seals landed on the beaches of Mogadishu.

I was sitting in the Marine Forces Pacific headquarters in Hawai'i, where I was the operations officer for the 90,000 Marine Force and responsible for planning the deployment of US Marines to Somalia. It was a stressful and challenging staff assignment, but I was able to go home each night, and I appreciated the time with my family. I was a US Marine with almost thirty years of experience and rose from the rank of private to colonel. As an infantry officer, I served in Vietnam, Cambodia, Korea, Cuba, Lebanon, and most recently, Operation Desert Storm in Iraq.

When Commander General Hank Stackpole walked into my office, I thought he wanted an update on the pending deployment. He asked, "How do you feel about joining the forces going to Somalia?"

I was torn. Out of the previous twenty-four months, I was deployed for nineteen of them to either hostile or family unaccompanied tours. General Stackpole knew this and told me, "It is your decision, with no pressure." We had known each other for a long time, and I knew his comment was genuine. The Marine Corps was going to establish a civil-military operations center to coordinate actions with the United Nations and humanitarian organizations to assist with the delivery of aid. He felt my personality and experience would help with blending the nonprofit groups and military efforts.

I had seen pictures of the death and starvation in Somalia on the evening news and was disturbed by the misery. I knew the capabilities of the US military would make a rapid and positive impact. That evening I discussed the assignment with my wife, who had carried the household on her shoulders for the previous years.

She thought it would be okay to be gone for several weeks.

But I had a secret. I was collapsing. There was something wrong with me. In the morning, after I closed the door to the bathroom to shave, I sat on the floor in the dark and tried to get myself together to leave the house. As I drove to work in the darkness and heard a passionate or sad song on the radio, I would cry. Each night, trying to sleep, I became drenched in sweat. I knew my marriage and family were becoming distant but felt helpless to fix it. It was not that I didn't care. I just lacked the energy to engage. I felt alone and disconnected.

I knew that returning to a complicated situation would let me bury myself beneath an effort that demanded all my concentration, and, in doing so, free me from the surrounding darkness. What I didn't know was that I had just begun a lifetime struggle to patch a wounded soul.

I arrived in Mogadishu on December 11, 1992, after a twenty-one hour, non-stop flight on a USAF C-141. The United States was anxious to get its forces on the ground as soon as possible. The US military initially deployed nearly 4,000 service members in the first lift, which later increased to more than 25,000.

Upon arrival in Mogadishu, we worked to establish a headquarters, set up communication centers, and deploy armed Marines throughout the city. Our priority was to open the Mogadishu airport to ensure a secure landing strip and allow the flow of food and equipment into the country. In December I traveled in a Marine Corps helicopter from Mogadishu to Baidoa. The news media and US intelligence organizations reported for weeks about the humanitarian crisis in Baidoa. We were the first flight to visit the site and evaluate the situation on the ground. At that time, we were inclined to believe there was a severe situation in Baidoa but were skeptical that anything could be as bad as reported by the media.

I sat on a small fold-out seat between the pilots in the cockpit of the helicopter and was afforded a 270-degree view of the ground while we moved northwest. As we skimmed across the desert at 2,000 feet, I was impressed with the landscape—it had a remarkable pinkish tint. Most of us had recently returned from Operation Desert Storm in Kuwait, Iraq, and Saudi Arabia, but this desert was different. There were green patches around springs and wells. They were not numerous, but I had the impression that there was a lot of water under the surface of the barren plain.

I had a map on my lap, but it was impossible to determine our location because the terrain had few identifying features. I had plotted the helicopter route before we departed. The only way I could fix our position was to check the navigation instruments, which provided a countdown of the miles remaining until we reached the destination, and then try to determine that distance on my map.

At approximately thirty miles from our landing site, I noticed a large body of water on the horizon. There was no water indicated on my map. The pilots saw the lake and we speculated it may have rained recently and the surface water had not evaporated. We were moving at approximately 110 miles per hour and rapidly closing on the area. It seemed to stretch in every direction. As we began to circle and descend to the landing zone, I heard one of the crew members say, "My God, it's people! They're just sitting there in the middle of the desert."

During our final descent, the pilots were concerned about a "bird strike." The sky was filled with vultures. They floated in the air like an undulating mass of darkness, moving as a single, circling entity. In the distance, I could see them drop from the sky in groups of five or six to pick off whatever they could find.

When we landed, the helicopter kicked up billowing clouds of sand and dust. Although the people nearest the landing sites were far enough removed to be safe, they were pelted by the force of a hundred mile per hour wind. And they were not moving—they simply pulled a piece of cloth over their faces or tried to shield the eyes of a child beside them. They did not have the energy to move.

After exiting the aircraft, I saw the field of humanity, but no noise. There was an occasional cry from a baby, but not another sound—no emotion, joy, anger, or expectation, only complete silence.

People sat on the ground and stared with vacant eyes. I had experienced five armed conflicts to this point, but nothing in my past prepared me for this. Starvation spread in front of me as far as I could see.

Until that moment, I understood the formalities of the directives of the UN Unified Task Force for Somalia, code named Restore Hope. We were to open the roads, ensure that food and life-sustaining supplies were safely transported throughout the country, and then go home. The mission was clear, and the needs were overwhelming, but until that point it was merely a logistical problem that needed to be solved, devoid of emotion. Suddenly, it all changed. What I saw hollowed me. I was unprepared.

CHAPTER 2
THWARTING THE DARKNESS

"[We travel] into dark woods where we find, against all odds, a [person]... with the compass, and it still points true north. That's the miracle, and it's astonishing. This shaft of light, sometimes only a glimmer, both defines and thwarts the darkness."
—Anne Lamont

IN BAIDOA, ON THAT FIRST DAY, WE WERE surrounded by 10,000 starving people. The magnitude of their misery was staggering, and its immensity overwhelmed me. I saw their suffering and tried to retreat into the survival instincts I learned in combat. When suddenly confronted with a fellow Marine killed or severely wounded in the moment of a battle, you cannot allow yourself to linger in the emotion of loss. If you do, those around you will suffer from your lack of focus. You bury it with the thought, "I will deal with this later." Looking at the human dimension of this nightmare, I knew it was too immediate and malevolent to be buried. It demanded action.

That involvement came through the Irish humanitarian organization GOAL. Soon after the coalition military forces arrived, the head of GOAL in Somalia found me in a small office I shared with several others in the UN compound in Mogadishu. His name was Dominic Crowley, a tall, lanky Irishman who spoke with a soft lilt that rounded the vowels and pulled you into his conversation. I thought he was probably in his early thirties although he looked seventy because of deep lines in his face, his eyes sagging and world-weary. He was alert, but I had seldom seen such fatigue on a person's face, even during the Vietnam War. His introduction was short and pointed, and his eyes intense. He was not impolite, but it was apparent he did not have the time or energy to build a relationship based on small talk.

"My name is Dominic. I'm responsible for GOAL. We desperately need your help." One of his programs was a therapeutic feeding center on the north side of Mogadishu. The facility administered food to malnourished women and children. He assumed I understood the term therapeutic when linked to the description of the undernourished people in Somalia, but I did not have a clue and asked him to explain. He told me the centers provided foods designed as nutritional supplements. The diet is a mixture of proteins, carbohydrates, vitamins, and minerals that provides life-saving nourishment, which gradually strengthens the body without overwhelming systems that shut down during starvation. The process is delicate, because too much food, in the beginning, will kill the person.

Dominic's problem was that gangs of men and boys from the surrounding area came to the center at night and took their food to sell on the black market. None of them were hungry.

I thought the military's engagement with this problem would build trust with the non-governmental organizations (NGOs) and demonstrate one small thing we could do to make a difference. Later that day on our way to the complex, Dominic tried to explain the number of programs his organization was attempting to maintain throughout Somalia, but much of it was lost on me because I had no experience in these types of programs.

When Dominic and I entered the center, we

were approached by a young nurse named Manjit Kaur from the United Kingdom. She was less than five feet tall and could not have weighed more than eighty pounds. In greeting, she was polite but carried the same combination of fatigue and intensity I saw in Dominic. She shook hands, said, "Please, follow me," then turned and walked away.

We walked through a small administrative area, and Dominic relayed to me that Manjit spent most of her days and nights working in the center, caring for mothers and their children. Although many of the international aid workers returned to their compounds at dark, she did not.

Walking into her building, I did not expect to find a facility built to North American or European standards, but I was shocked to find a converted cattle barn with dirt floors, open windows, and a tin roof. A single pipe provided a small trickle of water. The shed was the only place GOAL could find to use as a feeding center for the increasing influx of starving people who had made their way to Mogadishu from the surrounding countryside.

The building was repaired within the limited means available to a nonprofit. It was functional but still a barn. The worst expeditionary US Military field hospital during severe combat would be considered an excellent facility compared with this center. However, the transformation from cattle station to health center, all by hand and without any of the tools and equipment available to the military forces, was astounding. The cleanliness was amazing.

Manjit explained that the center was divided into three sections. Each area had been a cattle holding pen. As she spoke, we turned a corner into the first area for the women who had recently arrived with their children. I stopped. Nothing had prepared me for what I saw. The women were human skeletons, and there was no turning the page or looking away as you could when confronted with these images in the newspaper or on TV. I felt shame, guilt, compassion, and confusion pounding through my mind. These were the people who brought us to Somalia, and the profound depth of their suffering was, and still is, beyond my comprehension. It reminded me of the World War II newsreels of the liberation of men and women from the Nazi death camps at Auschwitz and Dachau that I saw as a kid.

Somali men and women were working with GOAL, quietly administering assistance. Like in Baidoa, no one at the facility was crying or sobbing or calling out in delirium. There were no beds, only straw mats on the ground. Flies swarmed across the women's faces, but they did not have the strength to raise a hand. Worse, they did not blink as the flies crawled across their open eyes. Two staff members did what they could, but they were tending to a score of women.

Each of the women had an intravenous tube inserted in her arm for hydration and nourishment. As I walked along the rows, only a few were able to follow me with their eyes; most of them stared into space. Some women were being spoon-fed. Others were utterly still, and I realized they were dead. The staff did not have time to remove the bodies—it had to wait until later in the day. I did not dare ask what would happen to the remains. Most of these women were unknown to the staff and few, if any, had relatives in Mogadishu. In fact, by the time these women arrived at the facility, their malnourishment rendered them unable to speak.

As devastating as this scene was, the next area, the children's ward, crushed me. I try to keep it locked in the back of mind, but when the door opens, the memories spill. I can never escape them, nor can I completely subjugate the triggers that prompt them. These memories are more than a vision. I can still taste, see, and feel that place and moment.

The children were separated because their mothers were too weak to care for them. There were no infants. They had died. Manjit told me that the children here were possibly two to five years old. To me they all looked eighteen months. Their emaciated bodies made their skulls look enormous, and their skin stretched tightly over their bones. It appeared to be a fabric only used to cover a skeleton. There was no crying. They did not have the strength to roll over, much less make a sound. Manjit answered my question before I could ask. "70 percent will die of starvation. Most will be dead by tomorrow." As I looked at her, I wondered how anyone could recover from such a prolonged association with death by starvation.

I noticed the Somali women volunteers holding and attempting to feed or hydrate some of the children. Their tenderness was striking. Every woman provided comfort. They were efficient. They knew how to lift, hold, and feed the children. I wondered how many starving youths they had tended to over the months.

When we walked to the next section of the building, Manjit told me this was the intermediate area, where the women and children who had survived and gained some strength were united with one another. They generally stayed five to eight days in the first area and would remain in the intermediate clinic for four to six days. Both women and children were still weak, but the mothers were now able to tend to their young. It seemed more women survived than children. "What happens to the children whose mothers die?" The answer was in front of me. The mothers who had lost a child simply took an infant who had lost a mother.

Manjit observed, "It seems there are enough children who are orphaned for the number of mothers who have lost a child. It balances out. Some of the women may have been related to the orphaned child, but it does not matter. It is irrelevant. Nature or God is at work."

The women held the children and cushioned them against their chests. There was no breastfeeding, but both the mother and child were comforted by each other's presence. Some of the children had begun to whimper, and a few had energy to move their hands, but again there was very little noise. The women looked better, but exhausted. Many sat staring at the child, or into space with a mixture of exhaustion, bewilderment, and grief. I could not imagine what happened to these women. Where did they come from? How long had it taken them to arrive at this clinic? What occurred along the way?

In my military uniform, well fed, with a weapon under my jacket, and the power of rank and position, I recognized I needed to let this experience wash over me like a breaking Pacific surf. I wanted to understand the intensity of my feelings. I knew nothing of survival and primal persistence. I never had to work for it. Anything that happened to me had a means or method through which I could ensure my own comfort and survival.

Upon leaving the clinic, I thought about how sheltered I had been. Although I experienced war and conflict, I traveled within a bubble. If I were injured, the Marine Corps would find and rescue me. When I went to a rest area away from combat, there were cans of Coca-Cola and other staples of American life. Wherever we were assigned, we brought our culture, language, and as much of our lifestyle with us as logistically possible. In Somalia, though, I was pushed outside my psychological comfort zone. Combat was horrendous, but I was trained for it. This was the first time I directly encountered the long-term results of armed conflict on the innocent.

These women had nothing, only the raw determination to stay alive and bring themselves and their children to this place. I realized there was a reason, far more significant than random circumstance, for me to be in this place and time. It was my first encounter with life demanding that I reach beyond a self-centered pursuit of personal comfort and satisfaction. I began to comprehend I was destined for a persistent and irreconcilable search for justice, a quest that would never be satisfied. I didn't like this feeling—it made me uncomfortable. For many years, I worked hard to bury it, but the more I tried to ignore the memories, the more insistent they became.

I walked toward the other Marines who had joined me at the site. The captain in charge asked, "What do we do? We can't allow this to continue." I thought for a moment and asked him to set up one of the bases he used for mechanized armored vehicle patrols close to the site. I wanted the center to be watched throughout the night. I did not want to put Marines inside the clinic, but I wanted their presence to be visible from the village.

As we discussed my request, the captain asked me the inevitable question, "What about the rules of engagement (ROE)?" The entire force was operating under ROE that was straightforward: any Marine had the right to use deadly force when they, or an innocent, were threatened with an action that could result in grievous harm or death.

I thought for a moment and said, "The women and children inside that clinic are both innocent and without food. They are in danger of suffering grievous harm or death, as are the people attending them, if their food and medicine are stolen. I authorize the use of deadly force to protect this clinic."

My experience at this small clinic set me on a journey to release myself from perfectionism and fear of the future. In the women and children I met, I saw our common humanity, our fragility.

Manjit Kaur and Dominic Crowley had given me a compass.

It was up to me to find true north.

CHAPTER 3
WHERE HAS HER STAR GONE?

"Heroes are ordinary people who make themselves extraordinary…"
—Gerard Way

DAILY, THE MILITARY'S CAPACITY TO ASSIST with alleviating and preventing the death and starvation in Somalia increased. However, the rapidity of that growth overwhelmed the UN's ability to direct the efforts. The coalition needed help linking the military's capabilities with the aid organizations. From the beginning of the international force's arrival in Somalia, the mission was to assist the effort, but not engage in direct action. The US Marines and Army realized they had the means to support the requirements but were not trained as humanitarians.

We needed help.

The assistance came from Mike McDonagh, the country director for the Irish NGO, Concern. Before arriving in Mogadishu, he worked in Laos providing humanitarian assistance. I met him at one of the daily UN meetings I attended in Mogadishu and was quickly impressed with his knowledge, competent demeanor, and persuasive leadership.

As a US Marine, I recognized leadership as a learned trait. Ninety-five percent of women and men recognized as true leaders learned the art over years of experience and study. I have known very few natural leaders. Mike is one of them.

He is an Irishman with a passionate, dedicated, and caring charisma that fills a room. His accent, the glint in his eye, and his unrestrained dedication to doing the right thing made him the informal leader of the 200-plus humanitarian organizations in Somalia during Operation Restore Hope.

Officially, he was the country director of Concern. Unofficially, when Mike spoke at meetings with the UN and Armed Forces, he spoke for the entire NGO community. NGOs vie for limited sources of funding from donors. The competition differs from commercial entities. It is not built on profit. It is a competition to get funding for a program to administer assistance. However, Mike spent as much time assisting other NGOs to get funding for their programs as he did for his own.

Humanitarian relief groups are generally reserved about their association with military forces. The concern is not a bias but practical consideration of operational effectiveness. Their guiding principle is that all humans are treated humanely and equally in all circumstances by saving lives and alleviating suffering. They do not take sides. If warring groups perceive favoritism of an opposing government or faction from the humanitarian community, then the security and aid of the NGOs would be threatened.

At the beginning of Restore Hope, I did not understand this. We came to Somalia to end a crisis. The remote and distant demeanor of the NGOs bothered me, as I mistook it for arrogance. Mike, taught me that the reason for such distance was not prejudice against the military, but self-preservation: What keeps NGOs safe during violence is their stringent adherence to the principles of impartiality.

Mike understood that the subtle prejudices

between the NGOs and the military needed to change to further the common good. First, to effectively work together, the armed forces had to understand the what, why, and how of NGOs. Mike's acceptance of the international forces became the single most crucial element in building a cooperative effort between the communities. We began having daily meetings to integrate the military capabilities with the needs of the humanitarian community to increase the delivery of life saving assistance.

People commonly say one person cannot make a difference. That is false. During the beginning days of Restore Hope when the starvation was incomprehensible, McDonagh's efforts to build an inclusive working relationship between the NGO community and the military was instrumental in saving lives.

On occasion, Mike invited me for an evening meal at the Concern residence, a large mansion rented from a wealthy family that fled Mogadishu during the fighting. The residence served as both an office and the living quarters for approximately fifteen members of Mike's team.

I appreciated this invitation because we Marines stationed in Somalia subsisted on prepackaged meals, ready to eat MREs, the operational food ration designed to provide the required nutrition to sustain an individual in combat. While the food can be warmed, it is usually eaten cold. The use of these rations reduced the infrastructure and funds required for the military to build mess halls and provide cooks.

A trip to the Concern house delighted me because they served fresh vegetables and a salad. Equally as important, it was a homey environment with chairs, a dining table, plates, utensils, and talk that was broader than the latest gun fight or the next day's convoy.

It was at one of these meals I first became acquainted with Valerie Place.

From the beginning, Valerie and I were friends. We had different backgrounds and experiences, but we got along well. She could be remarkably funny one moment, and deeply serious the next. We talked about my home in Hawai'i and her city of Dublin. However, we spoke mostly about Somalia and her work. She talked at length about the children and their needs. She ran a feeding center and could describe the scenes of famine in such a way that it made me feel I was standing in the middle of it. She never talked about herself. In fact, I never heard her discuss what she was going to do after Somalia. She lived in the moment. When she talked to others, she made them feel like they were the most important person on the planet, and for her, at that moment, they were.

She knew what she was doing, how it needed to be done, and why it needed to be accomplished. Her work was always within Concern's goals in Somalia. Thus, she was able to run her own activities. It was obvious that she relished this freedom, and, as she told me privately, this independence was the source of her energy. She had the liberty to truly make a difference.

In February 1993, I was on my way to the small village of Lafoole to visit a camp for displaced people that needed assistance when I received a radio call via the emergency communications center the military had established for the NGO community. Mike was on the other end of the radio, calling me from Mogadishu fifteen miles away.

"Bob, this is Mike. Valerie has been shot along the road between Mog and Baidoa. It doesn't look good for her. Here are the grid coordinates for her location." I wrote them down on a pad I carried with me in my jacket.

"Can you get us a medevac helicopter?"

The women and men who were monitoring the radio transmission in the communications center in Mogadishu radioed me within seconds after Mike had ended his transmission.

"Charlie Mike Six, this is Uniform Tango One."

"Roger. Go ahead. Over."

"Do you confirm this as a valid request? Over."

"Uniform Tango One, confirm request as good. Over."

"Charlie Mike Six, do you consider grid coordinates as good? Over."

"Uniform Tango One, good to go."

"Roger, Charlie Mike Six. On call medevac bird with chaser airborne. ETA is 12 mikes."

"Uniform Tango One, out."

By this time, the military respected the humanitarian community's ability to read maps and designate precise coordinates. In fact, we speculated they could read maps better than most members of the armed forces.

The military kept two medevac and two escort helicopters on ready for an immediate launch, twenty-four hours a day. The radio communications from the moment Mike called me until the confirmation of the mission was less than four minutes. The helicopter that came for Valerie had already been airborne after finishing a previous medevac mission, so it was able to immediately redirect to the site where Valerie was shot.

Valerie was traveling in a small convoy visiting a feeding center that was part of her projects in Somalia. Through her raw enthusiasm, she had single-handedly built a facility, which became a source of survival for starving people. On the day she was shot, she had delayed her departure to continue greeting the parents and spending time with the children. When she left to continue her journey toward Baidoa, a group of armed men ambushed her vehicle. Who were they? Why her vehicle? At that time in Somalia, it was so chaotic that a motive was impossible to determine, but I suspect it was to rob and loot. A humanitarian vehicle with its radios and equipment was a lucrative target.

I was struck by the directness of Valerie's question to her companion, Karen Davies, a photographer from Dublin, as she was lying injured on the seat of the vehicle. She looked at Karen and said, "I'm dying, Karen, aren't I?" Karen nodded, and the brilliance of Valerie Place's life died.

Her words, "I'm dying, Karen, aren't I?" still affect me deeply. I imagine my friend lying on the seat of a vehicle and dying during the carnage, and for no other reason than bad timing. After doing so much for humanity, Valerie's death didn't seem right.

Several days later, a Mass was held for Valerie. After the ceremony, I went to a quiet corner on the roof of the Concern house and looked at the desert turning pink in the late afternoon. I knew this woman. I had talked to her. She had a tough exterior but was kind and sensitive. She came to Somalia to help. It was not an adventure for her, or a resume filler. Valerie truly cared about her work. Her death deepened the darkness and futility I was beginning to feel about this mission.

The day turned dark, and I let out my exhaustion and devastation. "Hey God, let me see You do something more than having a bunch of people get on their knees and pray some mumbo-jumbo about taking care of Valerie and her family. Maybe You haven't noticed what is going on around here. Are You blind or just stupid? What do You do? This is for real. These people are being murdered and starving to death, and Your answer is to have Valerie, who was doing something about it, killed. Nice job."

Since that night, I found that God will get back to you, but when She does, be prepared. She will get your attention and answer your questions.

CHAPTER 4
A PLEDGE TO HUMANITY

"One man with courage makes a majority."
—Andrew Jackson

I'VE WONDERED WHY ONE PERSON WILL wade into chaos to assist, while another will put as much distance between themselves and mayhem as possible. In the face of danger, the human instinct is to focus on self-preservation. A distinguishing factor of people who assist in crisis is their understanding of truth. Their discussions have no exaggeration or subtle manipulation to further an agenda. They understand that every word, nuance, or description has a consequence. Not for one or two people, but for thousands, and those outcomes mean the difference between living and dying.

They are gifted with patience, simplicity, and humility. At their center is a willingness to make themselves available, without an agenda, to the promotion of human welfare. In a self-absorbed world, their pursuit of humanitarianism may appear to be a waste of time. Too often, their humility is seen as weakness, but in the end, they have what we all seek: a life that mattered. They made a difference.

Throughout December 1992, another Irishman, Norman Sheehan, continued to appear in military correspondence as an essential facilitator for the coordination needed between the military and the NGO community. I had attempted to contact him for a meeting, but it was impossible because there was no phone system, and the NGO radios were continually jammed with emergencies. Norman worked with the aid group, GOAL, and I decided to make a trip to their compound in hopes of finding him in the organization's office. As my vehicle approached the complex, several guards appeared. Generally, when they saw a coalition military vehicle, they demonstrated bravado, but after what they considered an appropriate delay, the gate would open and we would enter.

On this day, six guards took up defensive positions and aimed their Kalashnikov rifles at us. Less than a week earlier, my driver and I were involved in a vicious gunfight at the airport. Each of us had taken a life. We were suffering from the effects of the incident and were quick to defend ourselves. My companion stepped out of the vehicle and leveled his rifle at the group. The guards became more agitated. They were very young, and by watching the way they handled their weapons, they were inexperienced with carrying and using a rifle. The guards began shouting at us in Somali. They were excited and likely high on the local drug called Khat, a stimulant that increases a person's level of excitement and anxiety.

I was preparing to tell my driver to lower his rifle and withdraw when I saw Norman emerge from the GOAL office. He was casual and quiet, but purposeful in telling the gunmen to lower their weapons and for us to enter the compound. Although I did not know him, in front of the guards, he made it appear like we were good friends. He apologized to us and explained this was the best of the group he was forced to employ by the warlord, Mohamed Aidid.

I knew from our first meeting I wanted to work with him.

Over the next week we met daily. He invited other NGO leaders to join us. Other members of my team and I listened to the needs of the humanitarian community and began to support their efforts by providing the trucks, helicopters, and security required to ensure their aid could be delivered throughout the country. Norman had a keen ability to see a critical need and solicit the military's assistance.

In January 1992, a group estimated at 5,000 people gathered in a remote area in southwest Somalia. They had walked into a region without roads or infrastructure, traveling as far as they could without water or food before they could go no farther. They were starving. When a member of Norman's staff found them, he sent an emergency message to the humanitarian community. The degree of starvation was grave, but there was also a measles epidemic.

Although measles is well contained throughout the industrial world with vaccinations, in refugee situations with malnourished people it remains deadly. The death rate can run as high as 40 percent, with children the most vulnerable. The group needed food, water, and the measles vaccine immediately. However, the area was so remote it would take four days to reach them on the ground and the vaccine had to be maintained at a consistent temperature.

With Norman's guidance, the Marines were able to identify the location through satellite imagery. By now, the estimate had grown to 12,000 people clustered in the area with more arriving each day. The region was outside the fuel range of the helicopters available to the coalition, so the Marines established an expeditionary airfield approximately halfway to the position. The helicopters carrying humanitarian staff, relief supplies, and medicines could refuel at the airfield to ensure a continuous flow of necessities until the humanitarian teams could establish an adequate response. The expeditionary field was located, built, manned, and supplied with fuel and other equipment within twenty-eight hours of Norman's request for assistance. As a result of the military's support, the vaccine was delivered and the epidemic ended. The helicopters continued to transport humanitarian workers and the supplies needed to support the stranded people.

Norman and I began to spend a good deal of time assessing the humanitarian requirements throughout Somalia and possible areas to engage military support. Our association pulled me out of the insular confines of the UN and military compounds. I began to see the worst of the famine and death. No matter what road or track we travelled in Mogadishu, or throughout the country, we saw endless mounds of burial sites. I knew there was death, but driving through it was far different from flying over it. Thousands of the graves were just one to three feet in length. They were for the children. Driving through the narrow passageways in the different cities was devastating. Many of the throughways were newly developed because of the fighting, or the arrival of the coalition forces. The new tracks passed over the makeshift graves. None of the bodies were buried more than eighteen inches under the surface. Norman warned me we would hear bones cracking under the vehicle's tires.

I thought the engine would muffle the sounds, but it was impossible to ignore. It happened in every town or village. The sound was not a crack—it was a loud snap, like a tree branch suddenly breaking in an ice storm. At that moment, no one spoke. We silently rationalized the bodies had decomposed, and the bones were now part of nature. The skeletons had no life, body, or soul. This thought helped in the moment, but not forever. There are sounds in both the natural and manufactured environments that pull me back into those gruesome days.

GOAL began focusing a good deal of its humanitarian assistance on therapeutic feeding centers in Baidoa and Mogadishu. Approximately three weeks after my first visit to Baidoa, I returned with Norman to a center GOAL opened in an area hit by the worst of the starvation and disease. Although the distance was only 151 miles from Mogadishu, the trip could take as long as ten hours. Fortunately, we were traveling in a small military convoy of several Humvees with radio contact to the helicopter-borne quick reaction force (QRF). In the event of an attack on our group, the QRF would respond in a matter of minutes. Both the warlords and their gunmen knew this. Thus, our trip was unimpeded other than the occasional shot from a sniper.

Upon arrival in Baidoa, we spent the evening in a small residence that served as both the office and lodging for the GOAL staff. GOAL had five feeding centers on the outskirts of the city. The next morning, we made our way to the first compound. We were traveling in a GOAL vehicle. The Humvees were safer, but the people at the sites were in such fragile health that the arrival of soldiers in military vehicles could cause additional stress.

Because I visited the therapeutic mother and child feeding site in Mogadishu, I knew these trips would be hard. Throughout Somalia, there was no escape from the graphic and heartbreaking scenes of humans dying from starvation and disease. I assumed my exposure to starving people in Mogadishu would prepare me for these visits, but I was wrong; witnessing these deaths are encounters that stay with you for the rest of your life.

If what I witnessed in Mogadishu was shocking, the GOAL centers in Baidoa were horrific. The sites in Mogadishu were a primary focus of the international humanitarian effort, but the assistance was localized. In Baidoa, before the arrival of the coalition forces, aid supplies were routinely looted or destroyed by the warlords or marauding bandits. Increasing the amount of supplies was just the beginning of providing relief, but for many people it was too late. At the first compound, Norman asked the Somali who was head of the site how many people she was assisting daily. She answered that it was tough to count, but she estimated 1,000 men, women, and children. Norman asked her how many were dying. She told him she had lost count, but we could find an accurate number. She asked us to follow her. I thought we were going to an administrative office. Instead, we walked behind a makeshift warehouse. The large area was covered with what seemed to be an infinite number of grave mounds.

There must have been thousands. At the end of a long walk, we arrived at a new row of burial sites. Several bodies were lying in the sun. They were covered with straw. A group of ten or twelve men who spent their days digging graves were standing nearby. Our guide asked one of the men how many people they had buried that day. He told her during their shift they placed twenty-three. It struck me that he said during their shift. She told us they had to have a day team and a night team to keep up with the number of deaths.

As we continued to visit each of the feeding centers, we encountered the same conditions. There was too little food and medicine to reach the overwhelming number of people. Everywhere we traveled we were greeted by death and starvation. The odor of decaying flesh permeated the environment, which was filled with flies. They crawled across our skin, in our nostrils, and into our mouths. I could swat them away, but for the people sitting and lying in the scorching sun, they did not have the energy to protect themselves. The flies crawled across unblinking eyes. It was impossible to determine if the people were dead or alive.

Norman spent the next few days meeting with his staff while pulling both the UN and other humanitarian organizations into a coordinated effort to assist with the crisis in Baidoa. The coalition forces could ensure supplies would arrive in Baidoa, but they needed the humanitarian organizations to direct and focus the distributions. Norman's efforts were not just for his own organization, they were for the needs of everyone suffering in Somalia. He was not dramatic or flashy. He simply spoke the truth and conveyed it in such a way that the self-interest and pettiness of institutions and individuals disappeared.

During that time, I attempted to learn how Norman was so proficient at building consensus. The answer was that he entered every discussion with no ego. He was a leader with intellect, compassion, and the courage to take a stand for what is right. People gravitated to him because he found the answers to daunting problems through a quiet sense of character and inclusiveness.

Throughout the ensuing weeks, he was instrumental in leading the effort to reduce the death rate and increase the humanitarian services. His actions were consequential. Word about the quality and care at the Baidoa feeding centers filtered to the people who were still fleeing the famine and fighting. Thus, each day the numbers of people arriving at all the centers throughout Baidoa increased. This caused a significant surge in the demands for food, supplies, and staff. When Norman explained this to me, with a request for more support from the military, he had a brilliant smile on his face. He said, "What a wonderful problem. We are now serving more people and saving more lives."

Throughout the emergency in Somalia, there were three distinct groups of people directly involved in the crisis: the vulnerable population, the international staff of the NGOs and the United Nations, and the Somali national staff. The internationals attended all the meetings, appeared to make all the decisions, and directed the relief efforts. However, it was the national staff who did the operational work, took the more significant risks, and made the efforts successful. At every level, from project management, logistics and proposal development, the Somali staff were essential. It was their country, their culture, and their language. They understood the realities of the crisis in a way no outsider ever could.

Often, though, their advice was disregarded, or they labored under the impression by the internationals that their work was biased in favor of a particular clan or group. Indeed, there may have been such incidences, but it was a tiny fraction when compared to their collective contributions. There was another issue that people from North America and Europe did not understand: the Somalis were risking their lives to assist the international humanitarian efforts. Some warlords decreed all Somalis were forbidden to work with foreigners, except for the security guards, who essentially held the NGOs hostage. Sometimes the warlords condoned the work but levied a tax on the staff to ensure their safe passage in an area.

These threats were not merely directed at the individual who worked for an NGO, but included the staff member's parents and siblings, and even their distant relatives. In many cases, the staff were paying 50 percent of their wages to several intermediaries. It was not uncommon for a Somali who was an essential part of an organization's humanitarian effort to disappear. Their colleagues would remain mute, but eventually the truth would be told. The threats had caused the person and their family to flee.

Norman grasped the scope of the problem. He

could cross cultural divisions and quietly encouraged people to talk with him. There were no easy answers. Any engagement by coalition forces would make the problem worse and was unsustainable. The solutions had to come through negotiation, which required Norman to meet with the two significant warlords in Mogadishu, Mohamed Farrah Aidid, and Osman Ali Atto. This was not a casual endeavor. Both men were bitter enemies, and most of the fighting in Mogadishu and the surrounding area was focused on their desire to destroy one another. The coalition forces and the UN would not be welcomed at their headquarters, so to meet with them Norman had to negotiate the different lines of confrontation. The journey included the risk of being killed, injured, or kidnapped in areas identified as no-man's-land. Each trip included the possibility that one misunderstood word would have catastrophic consequences while in the warlord's compound.

But Norman persevered and returned to each of the warlord's areas on many occasions to continue the dialogue. There were no quick solutions, and much of the discussion depended on an individual's whim or mood on a given day. Occasionally, his arrival at a designated time for a meeting resulted in being ignored. Eventually, things changed for the Somali staff. It was not rapid, but it was tangible. The pressures on them diminished. The value of his efforts was consequential during the presence of the international military forces, but it became essential when the UN and the coalition departed.

I witnessed one man starting a plan to place national staff in their rightful roles as leaders of the humanitarian efforts throughout their country. Norman's actions began a lifelong commitment throughout the humanitarian community to foster and facilitate the development of national staff.

As Norman's reputation began to broaden so did his influence. At any humanitarian emergency on the planet, one would find Norman quietly assisting and ensuring national staff take the lead, with international workers supporting the response rather than controlling it.

This arrangement would appear to be a logical response to a crisis. The national staff understands the culture, language, and subtleties of their own society. However, the norm was that foreigners arrived with crisis response teams to provide direct assistance. They were earnest, but most had never been in the region before the disaster. Many NGOs hired locals to assist and controlled their assistance. Nationals were appointed to advise, but often they were relegated to drivers, translators, or leaders of minor distribution efforts.

Norman reversed the formula. He had locals represent him at meetings and oversee the assistance, along with other strategic planning and coordination efforts. Norman assumed the role of advisor and coordinator with his headquarters. Although he was not able to direct other organizations to follow his actions, the results of his approach were notable. How his agency delivered assistance was timely, direct, focused, and professional. While other organizations spent a great deal of time trying to assess the needs before delivering results, Norman's organization was supplying aid. It did not take long to recognize why his efforts were working. National staff leadership in a humanitarian crisis is now standard.

Norman made a pledge to humanity, and his obligation was not swayed by race, gender, country, religion, or creed. His efforts were not promoted by ceremonies, with stirring strains of music, flags, or symbols of institutional obligation. His commitment was purely personal. He made a quiet decision to do something about the human misery he saw around him. His actions did not entail personal desire, God, or country. Rather, he believed in himself and had the courage to sacrifice the little things in life to engage in actions that supported the well-being of humanity. In doing so, his leadership and commitment pushed all our engagements to a higher standard. We stopped wasting time on routine problems and discovered how to move our boundaries forward.

CHAPTER 5
IT IS NOT OUR WAY TO LET YOU STAY

"Life shrinks or expands in proportion to one's courage."
—Anais Nin

I MET DR. HAWA ABDI DIBLAAWE ON A rainy afternoon in Somalia. It is hard to believe it rains in Somalia, but when it does, the rain is torrential. Mike McDonagh and Norman Sheehan had talked to me about Hawa's hospital and camp for internally displaced people (IDPs), which was approximately fourteen miles northwest of Mogadishu in the village of Lafoole. She was not affiliated with any international humanitarian organizations, but was doing extraordinary work assisting her countrymen, women, and children. Both Concern and GOAL provided some supplies to her, but she was overrun by the number of people fleeing Mogadishu and seeking shelter in her camp. They asked me to visit the center to see what assistance the US military could provide.

The route to Lafoole was dangerous, crowded with many barricades that forced a vehicle to stop. They were manned by local gunmen who demanded money, equipment, or anything of value. The Marines ran convoys with armored Humvees throughout the day and night to ensure these checkpoints were dismantled. When the warlords lost the ability to construct them, they resorted to ambushes. They let military vehicles pass, but shot at NGO vehicles, killing the drivers, and looting the survivors. A trip to Lafoole was not simple.

Hawa's camp was far different from those built by the UN. There were no blue tarps, which was what the UN provided for makeshift shelters. The compound was developed and maintained by Somalis helping one another. As far as I could see, there were small igloo-type shelters constructed from thin scrub brush branches. There were two to four shelters in an area, and the space was protected by an interlocking wall of Somali thorn bushes as sharp as standard concertina wire.

The Somalis used the thorn bush for centuries to protect their homes and encampments from lions, as well as to demarcate private property. They are so adept at handling and working with the bush that they could weave an impenetrable barrier and not get hurt.

The compound was anchored by a large block structure in the center. It was the hospital. Several surrounding buildings served as storage for food, and a residence for Dr. Hawa and some of her staff. As I stood in the middle of her compound, people and shelters stretched in every direction. There were no cooking fires, because there was no individual food or firewood. The landscape was stripped of everything that could be burned or used.

When I greeted Hawa, I was struck by her size. She was tiny—maybe four feet six inches. She had amazingly kind eyes and was not intimidated by my uniform. She spoke excellent English and, after a traditional greeting, looked at me and said, "I am happy you have come to Somalia. We need America."

During the Cold War, and before the collapse of the Soviet Union, Somalia was part of the Soviet's sphere of influence. Hawa received a scholarship from the Union of Soviet Socialist Republics (USSR) to attend a medical school in Ukraine. She became the first female gynecologist in Somalia.

After returning, she earned a law degree at the Somali National University in Mogadishu and remained at the university as an associate professor of medicine. When the warring and fighting began to intensify in 1991, she moved to her family's ancestral lands in Lafoole and sold some of her property to use the money to assist people who were fleeing the fighting in Mogadishu, and to open a small clinic.

Next to her hospital was a large tower. It held the only source of water for the encampment. It was ancient, its structure riddled with termite trails, and had an antique pump and generator from the 1930s. The entire system looked like it would collapse at any moment. Fresh water was scarce and valued, and this single borehole was the only source for all these people. Meanwhile, in Mogadishu, the warlords and their lieutenants lived in walled compounds with lush grass, man-made streams, and beautiful gardens.

While in the compound, I had to use the latrine. The facilities were located well away from the living and cooking areas and segregated for males and females. Each bathroom had a small tarp around the entrance for privacy. I gagged when I entered. I was used to outdoor latrines, but this was filthy beyond description. As I retreated, I realized there was not much else the residents could do. All the work was done by hand, and with the number of people in the camp they were digging two or three latrines each day.

Dr. Hawa and her assistants were doing phenomenal work, but the sight of these latrines exemplified the difficulty of what she was attempting with little assistance. At our compound, which housed hundreds of servicewomen and men from many different countries, each set of latrines had accompanying canvas water bags to supply purified drinking water. They hung on a tripod with five water spigots around the bottom.

Next to the bags were numerous bars of soap. Hygiene was essential and we took it for granted. But here I was, standing in a camp of more than 10,000 people in the blistering sun, and the only available water for drinking and sanitizing was limited to two pints per day.

Hawa wanted to show me her camp, and the scope of required assistance. We walked through the compound and eventually reached the far side. Crossing a small hill, I saw hundreds of mounds of dirt, laid out in neat lines of fifty that stretched on for hundreds of meters. In the distance, I saw people standing over new sites. Hawa said most of the dead were very young or old. They did not have the stamina to endure the harshness of the environment without enough food or water. My mind went back to the times I attended memorial services for dead comrades at Arlington cemetery. The row of crosses over acres and acres of manicured lawns was peaceful and calm. Here, in this desert, the burial sites were stark.

Hawa looked at me and said, "My greatest fear is if people keep coming we will run out of land to bury our dead." As we returned to the hospital, I looked at the people. There were no young men and no pregnant women. There was little noise, and the people sat in small groups staring at us, not hostile, but watchful.

Hawa's hospital was a concrete blockhouse, dark inside, with the only light coming from narrow slits at the top of the exterior walls. I learned later this design shielded patients from gunshots and shrapnel. Several rooms had beds, but no mattresses, with only a thin blanket protecting patients from the steel mesh. The rooms were clean, but there was a pervasive smell of urine, feces, and rotting body parts. Attendants spent the majority of time assisting people and disposing of the waste while trying to maintain a hygienic environment.

There were so many people crammed into a

limited space, and regardless of the injury, most of them were emaciated. They had IV tubes for hydration and were being treated for gunshot or shrapnel wounds. The victims were of every age. Hawa said the hospital assisted anyone in need. Consequently, a gunman who might raid the camp for food, money, or women one day would be treated the next for wounds suffered in a gunfight.

I knew our military could assist her and resolved to make it happen.

I returned to our headquarters in Mogadishu, which was on the grounds of the former US Embassy, and sat on more than one hundred acres, all of it surrounded by a high block wall. At one time, it was an impressive building and landscaped beautifully; traces of former gardens and a swimming pool remained. With the departure of the US ambassador and the closing of the embassy in January 1991, after the collapse of the Siad Barre regime, the buildings were attacked and looted. When we arrived in 1992, the area resembled the bombed-out buildings in Berlin at the end of WWII. The main structure no longer had a roof, and the interior was scarred by fire and wanton destruction. However, the compound still had exterior walls, which provided protection. I slept in a large tent with nine other men with a cot and mosquito net. Eventually, wooden floors were added. It was a luxury not to live in the sand.

At the coalition headquarters, which included troops from twenty-six nations, I met with the commanding general and his operation officer explaining what I saw at Lafoole and made a request to allow the military to engage directly with the needs at Hawa's IDP camp. This was a subtle shift in our mission, which excluded direct acts of assistance by the military, but I thought it was desperately needed. At the end of my briefing, Commanding General Robert Johnston simply said, "I think it's a good idea." He told me to ensure the work was coordinated with relevant staff officers. That was the end of the discussion.

The US forces, specifically our medical teams and construction groups, went to work on Hawa's camp. The US Army and Marine Corps Engineer Battalions, and the US Naval Mobile Construction Battalions (Seabees) provided the much-needed physical labor on site.

The US Army and Navy medical staff began visiting the camp regularly to observe and make suggestions. It became apparent that water and sanitation were the priority. This is where the Seabees and construction units became invaluable. The Seabees dug boreholes to find water, and within days they began placing wells throughout the area. This was a delicate process because the water table throughout southern Somalia was so low that too many wells would affect the availability of water for surrounding communities. Oxfam, the preeminent global water and sanitation NGO from Great Britain, had been in Somalia for many years and understood the delicate balance of water supply throughout the region. The military and Oxfam worked together to ensure digging would not create lasting problems.

Digging wells was the easy part of the effort. The more significant problem was pulling the water from the ground and circulating it through the camp. This would require pumps, generators, fuel, and a network of pipes and discharge stations. It was gratifying to see the people and assets come together to make this happen. As I saw the efforts evolve, I realized how many of these soldiers had watched the travesty of Somalia unfold on their TV screens and were now engaging at the most fundamental level of lifesaving. Everything they did counted.

For many of us, the effort at Lafoole symbolized something greater than ourselves. President Bush spoke about a new world order. The Soviet Union was gone, and I believe most of us felt what we were doing was part of a resurgence of "the good" in America. I reflected on the contribution of our nation, which helped to restore the world after WWII through the Marshall Plan. It was a long time since the Vietnam War. It felt good to put faith in the government again.

The camp was a hub of activity. As the sanitation problems were addressed, the construction units worked with Hawa to build several large structures with lumber and masonry as extensions to the hospital and storage buildings. The military categorized these facilities as expeditionary, but in Somalia they were considered long-term additions. Generators arrived to feed the newly-wired buildings with electricity. The US military was building a medical complex that would be in Somalia for a long time.

While the work continued, I was called to the headquarters. General Johnston told me, "The president is coming to visit." President George H. W. Bush was in his lame duck period after his loss to Clinton in November 1992, and Clinton's inauguration in January 1993. The last place I expected him to visit was Somalia, but I admired him for this effort. His presence in Somalia would send a clear message regarding America's involvement to end the slaughter.

Johnston told me the White House requested Bush be shown any efforts of Somalis helping one another. Without hesitation, Dr. Hawa came to mind, but when I departed Johnston's office, I grew concerned with recommending her. I feared we were overwhelming her, and sensed she knew the assistance was needed, but was unsure of its sustainability. At that time, I had no understanding of a humanitarian's concept of sustainability. I thought anything we put our minds to was sustainable, and to link the word "arrogance" to my thinking offended me. We were the good guys doing the right thing. What could be wrong with that?

I drove to see Hawa, and we went into a small sitting room to talk. We had become friends and were comfortable sharing our thoughts. Her English was impeccable. It was I who had to choose my words carefully because she was not accustomed to American slang.

I told her the president of the United States was coming and wanted to visit her. She sat in her chair and stared at me. Like most Americans, I am uncomfortable with long periods of silence. Finally, she spoke, "My concern is that you will go home."

I replied that certainly I would depart, but there

would be others to take my place and do a better job.

She gave me a patient look and said, "No, I mean you will all go home. You do not understand what will happen when you depart."

At that moment, there was a vast gulf of understanding, culture, and life experience between us. I had no idea of the consequences of America's determination to leave Somalia as quickly as possible without helping to build a representative national government. She told me she had to consider the request.

For the rest of the morning, we walked through the camp to inspect the construction. Hawa was genuinely happy and insisted that I see the transformation. I had not been in the hospital and wards for several weeks and the difference astounded me. There were rows of new beds with mattresses and blankets. Each of the beds had proper IV stands. There was a greater sense of efficiency due to its uniformity. Water pipes and outlets were in place. When we entered one of the two operating rooms it was brightly lit, like a North American or European surgical center. The lights had replaced the single forty-watt bulb that had hung from a wire.

I went to one of the sites where a large storage

house was under construction. The engineer told me how he enhanced the protection for the building by making the doors sturdier and replacing the windows. He was not worried about looting from within the camp, but from the gunmen who lingered outside the area.

When I met up again with Hawa later in the afternoon, she told me she had decided a visit from the president of the United States of America would be a good thing. She said she wanted to thank him for the assistance from the American people. She mentioned in passing the visit would have consequences, but it was a casual statement.

We intended to keep the president's visit quiet and contained, but that was impossible. For the next week, as word went out that Bush would visit Hawa's camp, the work increased. Out of necessity, men, and women in camouflage uniforms without designation or rank appeared to survey her land. They were from the CIA, NSA, and FBI, different aviation units who would transport him, and other organizations I had never heard about.

The inhabitants of the camp heard of his visit, and there was a marked increase in spirit. The media and NGO community became regular visitors. Hawa was in the spotlight and overwhelmed. Regardless of the excitement and enthusiasm over the upcoming visit, the needs of the camp continued to surge. The fighting in Mogadishu took a dramatic increase and the city's inhabitants flooded to Hawa's refuge. The displaced did not come by road or by daylight because of the gunmen who lay in wait. They came at night, across miles of fields and desert. Hundreds of people were pouring into the camp while many Americans were preparing for Bush's visit.

The White House fixed the date for Bush's visit as December 31, 1992. He would arrive by helicopter and spend several hours at Hawa's hospital. As the military staff briefed Dr. Hawa, she made a declarative statement that was not conditional: "Colonel Macpherson will be with me during the entire visit." I noted the intensity in her voice. She was always very soft spoken, and I was more curious than concerned. I responded that I appreciated her request, but surely that was not needed. She remained adamant, and so I met the president of the United States of America.

The evening before President Bush arrived, my driver and I traveled to Lafoole. I wanted to be onsite at dawn because of the number of NGOs, media, military personnel, and Somalis I expected to show up at the camp. I had put Hawa in this situation and committed I would not let her face all this on her own. Upon arrival in Lafoole, I joined a group of Marines who were deployed to set up security outside of Hawa's camp to assist with protection for the president. I greeted the lieutenant in charge and requested permission to join them for the evening. I then opened a can of rations, drank some water, rolled out my sleeping mat, positioned my weapon next to me, and fell asleep.

At dawn, Hawa's compound erupted with activity from people arriving in streams of vehicles. I thought every NGO and UN organization in Mogadishu was attending the visit. The military and Bush's security were doing an excellent job of containing the spectators and ensuring they did not get in the way of the most essential aspect of the camp: feeding and aiding thousands of people who were victims of the Somali violence. However, it remained a circus of media, taking pictures and filming desperately impoverished people lining up to get a bowl of food. I was appreciative when the security personnel recognized the intrusions and pushed all the visitors away from the daily routine. It was annoying to see people who had never assisted Hawa clamoring to be part of the event.

At ten thirty in the morning, Hawa and I walked to a large field where the president's helicopters would land. Bush had spent the night on a

US Navy ship anchored well off the coast for safety. In the field, we met Dr. Phil Johnston who oversaw the UN's humanitarian relief efforts in Somalia. He was the president and CEO of CARE and was asked by both President Bush and the United Nations to lead this effort.

At precisely eleven o'clock, I saw a trail of helicopters approaching from the east. I counted sixteen Army, Navy, and Marine Corps aircraft. President Bush arrived in a Black Hawk. I wondered how many other planes were flying off-site and on standby on the ships. I knew there would be at least four F/A-18 Fighter Aircrafts circling above us, which were out of sight and sound, but on station. Hawa and I stood to the side of the group and watched the entourage from the White House move forward to greet the president.

Two things impressed me. The first was how the president's security personnel could surround him but not restrict his movement or ability to engage in a personal conversation. I also noted his height. He was six-foot two but looked shorter on TV. I respected his service during WWII—he was wounded when he was shot down by the Japanese. I took comfort in knowing that because of his military service, when he deployed American forces to combat, he was aware of the personal consequences of such a decision.

When Bush greeted Hawa, he towered over her, but this was her camp and he was the visitor. Years later, when we discussed the visit, I asked her how she remained so calm through it all. She replied, "Allah was with me."

As we toured the camp, the security guards kept the media away and allowed Hawa time to converse with the president. He asked specific questions, and his interest was genuine and sincere. He was not with us for a photo opportunity.

We walked to a small set of buildings the Seabees had just completed. Hawa told Bush that the buildings were used as a school and orphanage for around a dozen orphans in the camp. Surrounding the building and latrines was a large fence of Somali thorn bushes. The entrance to the compound stopped us. It was a two-meter tunnel that served as the passageway, tall enough for an average four-year-old to walk through, but an adult had to crawl.

We stopped, and when I looked at Hawa, there was a hint of amusement on her face. The entrance was explicitly designed to keep adults out of the complex. The president did not hesitate. He turned to his staff and said that only he, Hawa, and me would enter the compound. Hawa led the way and the president got on all fours and followed her. Once we were inside, we walked into the school. Ten children stood and sang the first verse of "God Bless America." Their rendition was flawless, and it was apparent they had rehearsed it many times. Each of them held a small American flag. We were in the middle of an internally displaced persons camp in Somalia with the president of the United States in a school protected by Somali thorn bushes, a group of kids earnestly singing a song to welcome him. The president spent twenty minutes with them as they recited an English lesson and showed him their pictures of the American flag, the Statue of Liberty, and even the face of President Bush. They were happy and their joy reflected in the president's manner and demeanor.

From the school, we walked to the orphanage. There were seven sick children in the building, Hawa said, with illnesses that ranged from dehydration to dysentery. Each was bedridden, and it was heartbreaking. They were dying. The president asked if there was anything he could do, but Hawa said for these children it was too late. All the staff could do was provide comfort. The president sat next to a young girl and used his hand to brush away the flies buzzing around her face. When he stood I saw tears in his eyes. He turned to Hawa and told her how much he admired her and appreciated her efforts. Hawa thanked him. He turned, walked outside, crawled through the tunnel, and greeted the media. He talked with them for about ten minutes. As I watched him walk away, I thought, "There goes a good man."

For a moment, Dr. Hawa's camp was the center of attention for the international media, but their interest quickly ebbed. The military continued to assist, but the daily arrival of engineers and medical teams became an intermittent event. There was still incidental attention given to fixing a pump or repairing a broken structure, but we were shifting our focus. The people of Somalia were turning against the presence of a foreign military in their country, and the coalition force was moving toward open conflict with the different Somali military factions.

In the ensuing weeks, more confrontations with General Aidid took place between his men and the international military. Aidid was determined to use every available means to secure his place as the leader of a united Somalia. After each gun battle, Aidid's radio station declared the United States an invader who was slaughtering innocent civilians.

The Somali people started to believe the propaganda. Although people stood in the streets cheering our arrival when we first came, we were now subject to stone throwing and more sniper fire. The military took on a traditional role of combatant intervention, which meant the use of armed force to establish peace. By opposing Aidid, the coalition force appeared to take sides with the warlords who fought him, and a guerrilla campaign against the international troops began. During the increased violence, Hawa's work continued, but she now had another problem: she was viewed as a pawn of the United States.

In May of 1993, most US forces departed Somalia, and the peacekeeping was turned over to the United Nations military force. I returned to Hawai'i. The leadership of the UN presence was placed under the mandate of a retired US Navy admiral and his deputy, a retired US Marine Corps general. Their policies and actions quickly turned an already violent city into a full-blown war zone. Under the UN's leadership, the UN forces essentially declared war on General Aidid. This conflict ended with a body of a US soldier being dragged through the streets of Mogadishu.

While watching the news reports and films of the fighting in Mogadishu between General

Mohamed Farrah Aidid's militias and the international forces, I was stunned by the military skills of Aidid's soldiers. When I departed Somalia, the fighting capacity of Aidid's army was limited to ambushes, sniper fire, and the occasional use of mortars. They could not challenge a well-trained western military force. Their use of rocket-propelled grenades (RPG) to shoot down two airborne and well-armored US Army Black Hawk helicopters was a skill beyond their capability.

The RPG is a shoulder-fired weapon that uses a rocket with an explosive warhead and can be carried by an individual. It is effective at close range against a tank or truck, but to fire on a moving aircraft required battlefield skill well beyond Aidid's gunmen.

As I reflected on the US withdrawal from Somalia, and the dead US service members in Mogadishu, I looked at the scar that snaked down the inside of my left arm. It was the remnant of the gun battle in the alley in Somalia. Hawa's words repeated in my memory, "No, I mean you will all go home. You do not understand what will happen when you depart. It is not our way to allow you to stay."

CHAPTER 6
AN ALLEY IN MOGADISHU

"I know there's evil in the world, and there always has been. But you don't need to believe in Satan or demons to explain it. Humans are perfectly capable of evil all by themselves."
—Tess Gerritsen

ONE OF THE FIRST PEOPLE I MET IN Somalia was Cedric Pirrella. He was the senior delegate for the International Committee of the Red Cross (ICRC). The ICRC is an impartial, independent organization whose mission is to protect the lives and dignity of victims of war and internal violence and to provide them with assistance. Impartiality is the critical element of their operations during conflict.

When I met Cedric, the coalition force was prepared to provide guards for ICRC convoys, additional vehicles when required, and the use of our helicopters and other aircraft to move their supplies. We had the means to transport humanitarian aid quickly and efficiently during catastrophic need.

Cedric knew our assistance would make an enormous impact on saving lives. Yet, he was caught in the middle of an ICRC mandate balanced against the realities he faced each day. The ICRC would not engage with a military force in any fashion, including the use of protective assistance. Every aspect of this mandate troubled me. ICRC convoys were continually looted and the plunders from these humanitarian goods enriched the warlords, perpetuated the violence, and decreased aid to the innocent. Additionally, every pillaged convoy ended with the needless death and injury of both national and international staff. Cedric knew the ICRC stance on military assistance needed to change and lobbied his secretariat, but they remained rigid.

To accommodate the directive and attend to the resulting risk he and his staff faced, Cedric and I developed a discreet compromise. One of the fundamental principles of the ICRC is transparency.

Forty-eight hours before a movement of their resources, they informed all warring parties of their actions to hopefully ensure safe passage. Unfortunately, the alerts notified gunmen of a vulnerable convoy.

Based on the advisory, the coalition planned mechanized patrols to coincide with their route, and helicopters would standby to assist in the event of an assault. Consequently, the ICRC did not ask us for support, but our assets were in the area to counter an attack. It was a laborious process, but a necessary means to save lives.

On Christmas Cedric approached me with a request for assistance. On December 27, 1992, the head of the ICRC for East Africa was arriving at the international airport in Mogadishu to meet with US Ambassador, Robert Oakley. The aim of the meeting was to shift ICRC's willingness toward cooperation with the military during this humanitarian crisis.

Cedric asked me to meet him at the front gate of the airport and escort his team onto the base. It was critical for him to gain rapid access to the airfield to greet his senior delegate.

Early that morning I went to the base to conduct other business. I had a nineteen-year-old Army soldier as my driver who was a specialist fourth class. This was his first deployment to a combat zone. He was a good man and had to endure endless jokes that he had joined the Army to serve as a Marine.

As we drove along the perimeter of the airfield in our Humvee, I noticed an acquaintance who was an Army Special Forces staff sergeant. I served with him during the 1989 Christmas Coup in the Philippines when a Philippine military force staged a coup to overthrow the legitimate government.[1]

We stopped to give him a ride. He had just arrived from Okinawa and was exhausted. He climbed into the back seat of the Humvee, placed his pack on the seat to make a pillow and reclined. With his rifle along his side, he closed his eyes and was asleep within a minute.

The entrance to the airstrip was a confined space that allowed the soldiers who were part of the multinational military force to maintain control over who was admitted to the base. We parked the Humvee to the side of the gate. There was a tall brick wall to our left. The driver backed the ve-

---

1. Official Gazette, "The Final Report of the Fact-Finding Commission October 3, 1990," Officialgazette.gov.ph, October 3, 1990, accessed https://www.officialgazette.gov.ph/1990/10/03/the-final-report-of-the-fact-finding-commission-october-1990/.

hicle against the partition to watch for the arrival of Cedric and stay out of the way of the normal flow of vehicles into the airport.

A few journalists and cameramen waited outside the gate for an interview with Cedric. It was a chaotic scene, but we were well out of the way. The driver shut off the engine. I thought I would sleep, but the local kids were fascinated by foreigners and quickly surrounded us. There were about nine children, ranging in age from five to ten.

They encircled the Humvee. We had gum and chocolate to share, and the kids were delighted. The moment was pleasant but bittersweet because the children reminded us of our families who were far away this holiday season. I watched their happy chatter and laughter when the driver pulled out his troll doll. He kept it for these moments, using it as a puppet for the kids, who laughed with delight as they munched on their candy. I smiled. The staff sergeant snored in the back seat.

I shut my eyes to snooze. Suddenly, my arm snapped away from my body. A trail of blood gushed from my left forearm. Kalashnikov rifles splayed on full automatic and bullet holes speckled the windshield as rounds came between me and my driver. I thought I was hit in my face because of the blood and gore in my eyes, but it was from the kid closest to my door whose head exploded from a bullet.

My instincts took over. I rolled from the vehicle to find cover. As I fell out of the Humvee, I landed on the girl whose brains were all over my face. I rolled and again hit a hump on the ground. It was another dead child. When I reached a concrete barricade, I looked at my arm. There was a lot of blood, but the wound was not deep.

The assailants' fire continued, and I was stunned by the amount of their ammunition. I could see two gunmen but knew by the volume of shooting there were others hidden in the surrounding buildings. I was armed with a pistol. I saw my driver lying behind a barricade to my left with a rifle, but he was frozen. He had never been in combat. The only return shots I heard were from the staff sergeant's AR-15.

I moved across the short opening between the driver and me and heard a round snap over my head. I asked if he was okay. He nodded, but it was apparent he was not going to use the M-16 rifle he was carrying. I traded weapons with him and began searching for the targets.

Suddenly, a barrage of gunfire started behind me. The Pakistanis had opened fire, and chaos ensued. They had their weapons on full automatic and were spraying the area with rounds. Bullets hit the barrier I was crouching behind. We were being assaulted from the front and rear.

I saw another girl sprawled in the dust in front of me, staring at the sky with dead eyes—a hole in her chest. I remembered her standing by our vehicle because of her bright orange scarf. She was about seven years old.

I noticed five men firing from the front gate of the airport. People still ran for cover, and several gunmen began focusing on specific targets. They did not care if they were military or civilian. They were intent on killing anyone within range and sight.

Two of the assailants broke from a building and sprinted across a small opening about fifty meters in front of me. As they ran, they fired from their hips, looking like characters from a poorly made war movie. I aimed at the last man and had a clear shot. Just as I was about to fire, I saw movement behind him. It was a woman pushing kids through an open door. If I missed, I would hit her or one of the children. I lowered my weapon and simultaneously the staff sergeant fired. The first man stumbled to the dirt. He started to get to his feet as the second shooter grabbed him. They started toward an alley and I fired. The injured man jolted into the air and dropped face forward. He was dead.

The other three gunmen directed their fire toward us, and we sheltered again. I watched the lone shooter enter the alley, then all the firing stopped. I waited for a moment to ensure the fight was over. It was silent, except for children crying. Several media people and Pakistani soldiers raised their heads above the barricades. Journalists began taking photographs and filming the dead.

As I stood, a cameraman pointed to my left at the staff sergeant now jogging across the field toward the alley. I was stunned and yelled, "Stand down!" But he kept going. I turned to find the driver. He looked at me, questioning our next actions with his eyes. I had seen a lot of dumb moves while in harm's way, but the staff sergeant's decision to follow the surviving gunmen had to be top of the list. If we did nothing, there was a good chance he would not walk out of the alley. If we went with him, we were facing a similar fate.

I nodded and mouthed, "Let's go."

The driver shrugged and said, "Okay."

I had two full magazines for the rifle. I handed him the weapon in exchange for the pistol. I asked if he knew how to patrol in a confined area as the last man in the team. He replied, "Eyes and movements to cover our rear."

"Okay, when we get to that passage, take the rear until I get hold of that soldier." As we ran toward the alley, I stopped at the dead Somali and retrieved his AK-47. He still had several rounds in his loaded clip, and a full magazine on his belt.

We started across the field. I counted five dead, and an equal number of men, women, and children crying out or trying to crawl or stand. We entered the alley and it was worse than I feared. The alley was approximately ten feet wide, with twelve to eighteen-foot walls on both sides. Each of the enclosed buildings had windows overlooking the passage. In the event of an ambush, there was no place to find cover.

We were so exposed I strained to control my trepidations to stay focused. When we rounded a small turn, I saw the staff sergeant. We were twenty-five meters behind him. He heard us, turned, and nodded. I pumped my fist up and down in a vertical fashion, the military hand signal to stop. He ignored me and moved another seventy-five meters, with us following to cover his rear. He approached an open space with a community well in the center, an area where three alleyways converged, making it impossible to determine which path the gunman had taken.

As I entered the open area, I detected movement to my right. I could not believe it. It was the shooter. He was coming through a doorway in a wall where he was hiding. I thought, "This guy has to be crazy." He could have stayed behind the wall, but he decided to die by exposing himself. I knew he had to be chewing Khat. His actions were too erratic. I was close enough to look him in the eyes, which were crazed, but intent.

His weapon was on his hip, and he was raising it in my direction. I knew it would be on full automatic. If he squeezed his trigger before I pulled mine, I was going to be cut in half in a Somali alley.

As we aimed toward each other, time slowed like a scene from an old western: two men facing each other on a dusty street, only in this scene a director was not going to call, "Cut." As the Somali raised his rifle, I knew I could get off the first round, but I saw him lifted with the impact of a bullet. The driver had put the round square into his chest.

I kicked the gunman's rifle away from him. The driver and I looked at the Somali lying on his back in the blazing sun in the middle of a nondescript intersection of alleys in Mogadishu. He was still alive and staring at the sky. Then his eyes began clouding. The only noise was rasping air being pulled into his lungs through the hole in his chest. The driver walked to a wall, leaned against it, and vomited. I turned toward the dying Somali. All I could think of were the dead kids lying around me at the airport. This guy was party to killing them. I watched him die, walked away, and never looked back.

When we came out of the alley and across the open ground toward the front gate of the airport, the dead women, men, and children were still lying on the field. The wounded were moaning, screaming, watching, and yelling over dead and wounded children and adults. Military medics and corpsmen were everywhere attending them, and the media was recording. I looked at our Humvee, its windshield shattered, three of the tires flattened, steam or smoke coming from the hood. Dead children were still lying around the vehicle. People were kneeling beside them, and the sight of their grief will never leave me.

We came to Somalia on a humanitarian mission to relieve suffering. So far, my most notable accomplishment was to kill a man lying in a field in front of me. He deserved to die, but I reached the point when I did not want to be the one to do the killing. I was sick of it. At that exact moment, I knew the Marine Corps was over for me. It had nothing to do with the Marines. It had everything to do with me.

I did not have the stomach for it any longer. I had almost thirty years of service in the Marine Corps and could retire when I chose. I decided my time was up.

That night, at her home in Hawai'i, my daughter was watching CNN. In the video, she watched her father walk out of an alley in Mogadishu with blood streaming down his arm, while the cameras panned the field of dead and dying people. On that day, my sixteen-year-old daughter went to combat with her father. She did not mention the video to the rest of my family and waited for me to communicate with her. This was a period before easy access to email in combat zones. We were able to make occasional phone calls to our families, but letter writing was still the primary means of communication. Recounting the events of a battle to family was not a reasonable act. They worried enough without knowing the details. Hearing about a gunfight would only cause them more stress and fear.

It was not until later in the week when I was

able to phone home and talk with her that I learned of the news coverage. She was raised in the environment of the Marine Corps. She comforted friends when their mother or father was killed or wounded in combat or a training accident, and she knew how the system worked. If the Marine was injured and evacuated from battle, a casualty notification officer would visit the family. If a Marine was killed, the casualty officer was accompanied by a chaplain. A family knew the moment they opened the door to their home what was about to happen. In my case, when no one appeared, she knew my injury was superficial.

Five days after the incident, I received a request from a CIA officer assigned to our headquarters to stop by for a discussion and update. I knew they had just suffered a causality in the north when one of their operative's vehicles hit a landmine. I was curious as to why I was needed as that incident had nothing to do with me or the circumstances of my daily routine and work. When I sat down for the meeting, the station chief began briefing me on the events of the twenty-seventh. I already had a debrief with the Marine Corps' Intelligence group and talked to our commanding general.

The CIA officer asked me if I had ever heard of a Saudi by the name of Osama bin Laden. Having recently returned from Operation Desert Storm and spending time in Saudi Arabia, I thought for a moment and answered, "No, the name means nothing to me." He went on to say that Bin Laden was a wealthy Saudi who hated the United States. He started an organization called Al-Qaeda in Sudan. Bin Laden sent a group of terrorists to Somalia to train the fighters of Mohammed Aidid. The men who attacked us at the airport were a group trained by Bin Laden. I never forgot the name.

But the most immediate reason I found this discussion of interest was the CIA's concern over the link between Bin Laden, the Saudi government, and the establishment of madrassas, the Islamic religious school in Somalia. There they teach Wahhabism, a particularly severe and rigid form of Islam, most prominent in Saudi Arabia. Today, many of the Taliban are educated in Saudi-financed madrassas in Pakistan.

The CIA discovered the Saudis were opening orphanages and schools across Somalia. However, there were few orphans in Somalia. When a child was left without parents, he or she was integrated into another family within the clan. There were some orphans, but not to the degree that required the number of orphanages opening throughout the country and in Mogadishu.

As the CIA began investigating this phenomenon, they found the orphans were children of impoverished and starving families throughout southern Somalia. Intermediaries approached the families, offering them a sum of money and a promise that their children would be educated and supported in the schools. Once the bargain was complete, the children were taken to a madrassa. They were segregated by gender, and formal education began with its emphasis on fundamental religion.

There is a direct link between the thirteen years following the establishment of the madrassa's schools, and the emergence of Al-Shabaab. Beginning in 2006, references began appearing in the media regarding the development of a hardline militant youth movement called Al-Shabaab. These young men had a fanatic faith in Allah and remained outside associations with different clans that had traditionally held sway over their armies. The boys who entered the madrassas in 1993 grew into the young men who populated the ranks and leadership of Al-Shabaab and swore allegiance to Al-Qaeda.

Killing the terrorist was justified, but the battle

affected me deeply. I felt nothing for the gunmen, but I knew my time as a Marine was over. When I stood in the field after the fight, I had the blood of children covering my uniform and body. I could smell and feel their death. Looking at the blood pouring from my left arm, I felt dizzy and sat down in the dirt. It took all my concentration not to vomit.

In the blazing sun, my mind returned to the Vietnam War. No matter what movie is seen, or book read, it's impossible to understand that war's violence. Possibly, the ground soldiers in Iraq and Afghanistan experienced similar brutality, but in the jungles and foliage of Vietnam the fighting was often feet and yards apart. It was personal, reduced to the basest animal instincts. Frequently, decided by a knife or how quickly I raised my weapon to fire. In those moments, I was close enough to smell my enemy's sweat and fear. While looking in his eyes, I saw a reflection of my own youth, fear, courage, and determination. As I watched the life drain from his body, his face remains with me in my dreams.

At the time, I had never heard the term post-traumatic stress disorder (PTSD), but mine began at that moment.

Now, nearly a quarter of a century later, sitting

in the dirt in Somalia with a Navy Corpsman bandaging my arm, all I felt was the pain of unrelenting violence and injury. It no longer made any sense. Around me were humanitarian workers demonstrating another way to achieve peace without guns and violence. I wanted to be a part of their world, but did not realize how quickly it would happen. Within eight months, I had resigned from the Marines and begun my career as a humanitarian.

CHAPTER 7
CROSSROADS

"There are moments in our lives when we find ourselves at a crossroad, afraid, confused, without a road map. The choices we make in those moments [will] define the rest of our days...."
—Lucas Scott

WHEN I WENT TO SOMALIA AS A US Marine, we arrived to "set it right." We were the good guys. We were also naïve and woefully unprepared to assume the role of protector and supporter in a humanitarian crisis. What the international military forces accomplished at Hawa's camp was a minor part of the work. We built roads, improved buildings, and aided in setting up camps for people who fled their homes. We rebuilt or established new hospitals and clinics, and repaired and extended the water system throughout Mogadishu. We cared. We witnessed extreme deprivation and had the means to help rectify it. There were no ulterior motives.

America sent us to Somalia to end the suffering, but we had no idea what we were doing.

Humanitarian aid programs transfer food, and provide shelter, water, healthcare, and education, bringing resources into an environment deprived of them because of drought, war, or natural disaster. These resources represent power and wealth and can become part of the conflict. Some people attempt to control and use aid to support their side and weaken another faction. If the organizations with the resources fail to recognize the impact of their programming decisions, their assistance will cause harm.

Consequently, throughout the US military's efforts in Somalia, and because of my own actions in Hawa's camp, we imposed ourselves on a fragile system we did not understand. Our intentions were heartfelt and sincere. We saw problems and rushed to fix them.

What else were we to do?

We had everything at our disposal to improve the issues. Yet, as the level of fighting between the coalition forces and warlords increased, the road from Mogadishu to Hawa's camp became unsafe because of sniper attacks. We wanted to help, but the fighting impacted our ability to assist. I hadn't see Hawa for several weeks and knew I wouldn't have the chance to say goodbye.

I made many friends in Somalia with both national and international humanitarians. I spent several days saying goodbye and thanking them for their support during my tour of duty. On my final night, they held a surprise reception for me to thank me for my efforts. I was appreciative and touched by their kindness.

On my last day in Somalia, I visited Phil Johnston and told him about my decision to retire from the Marine Corps. He knew killing the Al-Qaeda gunman on December twenty-seventh had affected me. It wasn't the act that bothered me, but the experience of continually finding myself in such situations. During our last conversation, he asked me what I would do after retiring. I was reluctant to tell him, as I did not have a clue. I said, "Since I live so close to the water on Oahu, I plan to spend the rest of my life swimming, running, surfing, meditating, reading, and writing." We shook hands. I thanked him for his help and believed I would never see him again.

The return trip took me through Washington, D.C. to brief staff officers at Marine Corps Headquarters about lessons learned concerning working with the UN and humanitarian organizations in a crisis. From there, I flew to Atlanta to catch a direct flight to Honolulu, and finally, to home. On each leg of the journey, I became more apprehensive. Returning home from a long deployment—particularly one in a combat zone—is never comfortable. I wanted to shed the stresses of watchfulness, insomnia, and fatigue as quickly as possible and become the ideal picture of a father and husband I imagined I was.

My multiple deployments created a gulf in my household. We said the right things because, as a military family, we knew the words that needed to be spoken to make us all feel good. But there was a separation. My kids lived with their dad "being away" for extended periods. They learned to keep safe emotional barriers with the man who wouldn't be there for them to rely on and help guide them.

Yet, kids are resilient, and forgetful. I knew in a few days they would follow their own schedules, and we would fall into the same routines of school, ball games, track meets, movies, and friends.

I was most anxious about seeing my wife. She

was a Marine's spouse for more than two decades. She supported the deployments and kept things stable while I was gone, but there was a distance that had opened between us. The detachment seemed to be on my side, not hers, and I was ashamed. Inside I wanted to run from the responsibility of the Marine Corps and family. I grew up in a dysfunctional family and promised myself as a young man I would do better. The Marine Corps gave me a sense of personal pride and stability, and my family loved me.

What in the hell was wrong with me? I had it all, but I couldn't cope.

I told my wife I was going to retire. I was a US Marine for twenty-nine years and it was the only profession I ever had. The Marine Corps had given me a sense of identity. It sent me to college and a graduate-level war university. My wife and I were married on my way to the Vietnam War. My children did not know life outside of the Marine Corps. I was going to walk away from it all and did not have a clue what I was going to do as a civilian. All I could tell her was, "It's done. I can't do it anymore." I could not explain what the "it" was, but inside I knew the answer. "It" was the killing, destruction, and war-fighting, and "it" was over for me. I had not become anti-military, Marines, or government. In fact, I loved the Marine Corps and the Marines who serve this nation, but I couldn't do one more combat tour.

It is difficult to describe the shame that followed my decision to retire. I'm not sure there is a higher bond than that which exists between members of the military. The armed forces were not my fraternity, they were my family, and I was about to abandon them because I could no longer stomach the fighting and killing. As I moved toward publicly announcing my decision, I harbored a secret desire that something or someone would interrupt my judgment. I knew my wife was uneasy, but she supported my choice.

I returned to work and met with General Stackpole. We served together for years, and he was my friend and mentor. We had another bond as well, although we never spoke about it. We were both badly wounded in Vietnam. We had a shared understanding of living with constant pain and issues of mobility. When I saw him limping at the end of a long day, I knew what that throbbing and burning pain was like.

I lost twenty pounds in Somalia, and he was immediately concerned about my health. I told him I was fine and just needed to catch up with some sleep.

I told him I was going to retire.

He sat in silence, looking at me for a long time. Finally, he asked, "Why?"

I tried telling him about my anxiety and fears, and that sense of living outside myself, but my voice cracked, and all the emotions of Somalia poured out. I cried. I was ashamed. Marines don't break. I could see the concern in his eyes and managed to get control of my emotions. I apologized. "It's just the jet lag," I said.

For the next week, we met every day. He did not try talking me out of my decision but wanted to ensure I had thoroughly considered what I was leaving behind.

In December 1993, the final day came. I stood in front of a retirement ceremony with a band and a platoon of US Marines. We were outside the Marine Corps Headquarters in a large field. From where I stood, I could see the Pacific falling gently onto the golden beaches of Hawai'i. My kids were on the mainland in college and my wife had a professional commitment. In her absence, General Stackpole's wife, Vivian, was at my side as her husband presented me with a medal.

But I was in agony. Every fiber of my body wanted to scream, "I made a mistake! I want to take it back. I don't want to do this." I was frightened. The Marines were my life since I was seventeen. They were my family, and I could depend on them. Not in the rigid ways of discipline and regiment as portrayed in movies, but in more profound ways. We were bonded to each other by respect, camaraderie, and trust, and now I was alone.

When the ceremony finished, people came to shake my hand, but eventually disappeared. I walked to my car, closed the door, looked at the little box with a medal, and wept. I was now a civilian, and terrified.

I spent the next few weeks trying to adjust to civilian life and not having a job. I spent time at the beach, tried to meditate, write, and read. But I was restless. I could fill my day with "make work," but I was anxious and volatile. On a trip to the Tripler Army Medical Center for treatment for a bad cold, I passed the Fleet Marine Force Pacific US Navy psychologist. She and I chatted for a moment and she asked how retired life was going. I told her it was great, and then hesitated for a moment and said there was one thing that bothered me. Every night, I dreamed I was putting on my uniform and going back to work. It made me restless and ill at ease.

She told me that after thirty years of service I

would not easily obtain closure from the Marines when the retirement ceremony was over. It would take time to disassociate from a life that lasted for decades. She offered her availability if I ever wanted to talk. I thanked her. As I walked away, I thought, "The last thing I need is a psychologist. I can handle it."

Six weeks from the day I retired, I received a call from Phil Johnston. After several minutes of polite conversation, he asked me, "How's all that reading, running, and meditating going?"

I hesitated for a moment, deciding whether to be honest or not. "It's not going well. I'm miserable."

He laughed. "That's not too hard to understand. You need to be engaged and active. I need an assessment done in Bosnia and want you to do it. It should take two or three weeks, but I want it done right. So, use as much time as you need."

I told him I had no idea how to do a humanitarian needs assessment, but inside I felt excited and nervous, hopeful that I would find a new purpose in life.

Phil had served in the US Army during the Korean War and asked if I had ever done a commander's estimate of the situation while planning a military operation. I replied, "Of course." In an estimate, the commander considers all the conditions affecting the military situation and decides on a course of action to accomplish the mission.

Phil explained that a humanitarian needs assessment used an identical process, except in the end we delivered aid and not war.

I told him I would give him a call after I had a chance to consider it. He said to take my time, but he needed to send someone in the next two weeks.

He had thrown me a lifeline. I liked and respected the aid community, but I believed my lack of humanitarian experience would exclude me from working in the community. He had just offered me that chance.

Ten days later, I walked into the headquarters of CARE in Atlanta, enthused, but anxious. I was going to Bosnia and couldn't wait, but once again I was leaving my wife and two adult children behind. Although they were supportive, their feelings were founded on the acceptance that I was drawn to these environments for reasons they didn't understand. It took two more decades to make sense of my post-traumatic stress disorder.

Worse than my guilt about the separation from my family was a voice in the back of my head telling me my actions were selfish and self-serving. I loved my family and cared intensely for them, but after countless years, and so many wars and disasters, I was increasingly drawn to these environments because within them I could cope and relax. I knew something was wrong that this was my normal, but immersing myself in these emergencies eased my anxieties.

While others saw a dedicated humanitarian worker, I engaged because I found relaxation in the familiarity of disorder. The worst part was knowing this was an addiction; I couldn't help myself.

I spent the next fourteen years with CARE. My job evolved into humanitarian emergency response, protections and human rights issues for refugees and displaced people, and crisis mitigation for national and international staff. Mainly, I responded to humanitarian crises by helping provide life-sustaining supplies, overseeing staff security matters, and ensuring the rights of the people affected by war, conflict, or disaster.

I loved what I did. I had a quiet pride in being able to handle myself in adverse situations, being able to set aside my ego and the comforts of the western world, and assisting others in times of need.

CHAPTER 8
A POWERFUL WOMAN WILL MAKE A DIFFERENCE

"The only thing necessary for the triumph of evil is for good men to do nothing."
—Edmund Burke

IN APRIL 1992, THE REPUBLIC OF BOSNIA-Herzegovina, a majority Muslim socialist republic within the Yugoslav confederation, was a composite of three population groups who identified as either Serbs, Croats, or Muslim, and maintained their respective loyalties. The situation was like the American Revolution when the British colony was divided by people who associated themselves with Great Britain, France, or Spain, as well as rebels who wanted to establish a free nation separate from England.

In May 1992, when Bosnia declared independence from Yugoslavia, both the United States and the European community recognized Bosnia's independence. Within two days of this sanction, Bosnian Serbs, backed by the Yugoslav army, bombed Sarajevo, the capital of Bosnia. They refused to be part of a Muslim nation.

For the next three years, a Bosnian Serb Army, supported by the country of Serbia, conducted a brutal war against the Bosnian Muslims. Because of the fighting, approximately one hundred and forty thousand civilians died. It was the worst act of genocide in Europe since the Nazis killed nearly six million Jews during WWII.

The Serbian forces attacked Muslim towns throughout eastern Bosnia and rapidly gained control of nearly three-quarters of the country. In each city, they drove Muslims from their homes and land. They burned their houses and forced them to flee. This type of expulsion was known as "ethnic cleansing." The findings of a commission of inquiry headed by the UK's Dame Anne Warburton found that Serb forces systematically raped nearly 30,000 women during the first year of fighting.

As the war marked its first anniversary, there were approximately two million Bosnian refugees. Most of them found shelter in Croatia or Germany, but they were considered an unwelcome inconvenience throughout most of Europe.

When I came to Sarajevo in February 1994, the UN passenger reception area was a tented compound next to the helicopter landing zone. It served as the greeting point for humanitarian staff lucky enough to catch a UN or military helicopter to arrive or depart Sarajevo.

The tent had a sign that said, "Arrivals" in several languages. I was grateful for the rush of warmth from the space heaters. In front of me was a large sign stating, "Absolutely No Smoking or Guns." I had trouble seeing it through the haze of cigarette smoke.

I was told my colleague Brenda Cupper would be waiting for me. I had never met her, but she was a legend throughout CARE and the humanitarian aid circle in Bosnia. Clichés like "legendary," and "larger than life" are used so often they become trite. However, in Brenda's case, the words are accurate. Some people engage in humanitarian assistance as a job or profession. Brenda was born to it. I scanned the tent and saw a woman with a jacket that had a small CARE logo on it. I introduced myself to Brenda, and we left the airport.

As we drove, Brenda asked why I had come to Bosnia. In a time before cell phones and in a place with infrequent access to communication, she had simply received a message that said a CARE USA staff member would be arriving at an approximate time and requested pick-up and lodging. I replied although CARE USA did not have a presence in Bosnia, they wanted to provide financial support for Brenda's work and wanted me to prioritize projects to fund. With my answer, my visit was no longer an encumbrance to her.

At that time, CARE was a loose confederation of a group of nine separate CAREs. There were three in operation: the USA, Canada, and Australia. There were also smaller, supporting organizations in Austria, Germany, Japan, Norway, to name a few. In Bosnia, Australia and Canada operated together in partnership.

Brenda, part of CARE Canada, had worked in Bosnia for more than a year and lived in Sarajevo. She knew every nuance of the city, and the safest routes to move around the snipers and violence. As I sat in the rear of her Land Rover, I was struck by the destruction of the city. Modern Sarajevo was endless blocks of large, gray, monolithic apartment buildings, most devoid of color or the architectural style of the Eastern Bloc countries of the era. Depressing in the best of times, but now, during the devastation, these buildings testified to the ceaseless violence. Every structure seemed to have wounds where artillery and tank shells tore away massive chunks of concrete and steel. The damage was shocking, but made worse because these were residential dwellings, the homes of families who were gathered together when a shell ripped their existence to pieces. Every building, road, shop, sign, fence, tree, post, and wall was evidence of a systematic campaign of directed violence against the city and its inhabitants.

Before the war, Sarajevo was a town of engineers, poets, writers, and businesspeople. Its opera house and symphony were world-renowned. The level of their education system was one of the highest in Europe. Now, people were subjected to unrelenting violence, enduring a constant barrage of mortars and artillery day and night. The bombardment would ebb, but it never ceased. It became part of the environment, only noticeable when it stopped.

The worst were the snipers. "No man's land" became known as "sniper alley." The formal name for the passage was the *Ulica Zmaja od Bosne* (Dragon of Bosnia Street). It was the main section connecting the old part of the city with the airport and industrial areas surrounding the town. The fighting was so close that Serb snipers used the rolling hills that surrounded Sarajevo as their vantage points to indiscriminately kill anyone who crossed through the sights on their weapons. Victims were murdered solely because they became targets of opportunity. Nearly 14,000 people were killed because of direct violence during the siege.

Yet, what I witnessed were people who refused to be diminished. They maintained every element of their individual and collective dignity. As they moved about the streets, they were watchful, but not intimidated. They were aware of the dangers but walked with a purposeful pride. One of my lasting memories was the way the women presented themselves. They were always well-dressed. Their hair, dress, and makeup gave an image of people who had not cowed to the relentless pressures of the war.

Without exception, nearly every family in the city suffered through the death or injury of a relative or friend. These fatalities happened within hours, days, or weeks of one another. Each death was fresh until another was heaped on top of it.

The burial intensified the grief. The cemetery in Sarajevo was in the northeast quadrant of the city and close to the Serb lines. The act of burying the dead became an opportunity for Serb shooters to kill even more. Occasionally, the firing became so intense that the burials had to be done at night. However, when the snipers began using night vision scopes, burying the dead became a heroic act.

Throughout this nightmare, men from twelve to seventy-five helped defend the city. They were poorly trained and were learning how to fight in the middle of the conflict. Their primary duty was to guard the city's defensive lines. The image of a citizen army without uniforms, flags, unit designations, and the assortments of modern warfare was new to me. This was an army that lived at home and reported to their assigned station at a specific time. There was no fanfare, motivating speeches, or parading formations. The men and boys quietly assembled and held the line against a well-armed and trained aggressor.

Yet, even on my first sight of Sarajevo from the vehicle, I saw it was the women who maintained the sanity of the city. As they collected the food, gathered any available firewood and charcoal, and tended the wounded, they carried themselves with a special strength of wives and mothers. Not only did they care for their families and frequently other households, but they also held Sarajevo together with the force of their quiet dignity and resolve. While the men fought, the women gave strength through reason and conviction.

Amid this carnage was Brenda Cupper, a pillar of self-control. She refused to allow her work to be undermined by the hardships and would not let adversity dictate what she wanted to achieve.

Every morning, she began her work by assessing with her thirty-five-member staff who may have been killed or wounded overnight. Even if all of her staff were safe, there was seldom a time when one of their family members was not killed or injured. In Sarajevo, a severe wound was a death sentence because there was little medicine in the hospitals, the clinics, or on the black market of the city. Aspirin was a luxury; anesthesia and antibiotics did not exist. Almost every day Brenda excused a staff member to attend a funeral or let them leave early if the burial was going to take place at night.

Her programming included many traditional humanitarian activities, such as distributing food and fuel. However, the Serb blockades limited the number of humanitarian supplies allowed into the city, particularly restricting blue tarps used to cover destroyed windows, walls, and roofs that were blown off by the shelling. The tarps helped insulate and protect the living areas from the rain and snow. Brenda's most remarkable achievement was an initiative she began during the worst part of the siege.

She created an outreach program for the elderly, injured, and housebound. On each floor of the city's apartment buildings were as many as eight families. The apartments were divided into sections based on the size of each group. The hallways were poorly lit, with no windows or ventilation. In the winter of 1994, Sarajevo had become a city without electricity and only occasional water supplies. The constant shelling destroyed the electric and plumbing systems, and the sewage plant was a continuous target.

Everyone suffered, but particularly the elderly, infirm, injured, and others who were vulnerable. They huddled in damaged structures unable to care for themselves. The lack of electricity had a devastating effect. Although there were stairways in the buildings, many were damaged or destroyed, and the lack of power made elevators impossible to use.

Consequently, throughout the city, many people lived by themselves with insufficient food and no heat, electricity, or water. They were trapped on the upper floors of the buildings. Often, they lived in an apartment with a gaping hole in the wall. Neighbors and families tried to help, but the city was under siege. People lived day to day in a constant search for the means to survive. The few rations went to the men and boys who defended the city. Every day began with clearing the dead from the streets and shelled structures.

Brenda began the outreach program to determine the location and number of the most isolated individuals in the city. Her staff, in constant danger of Serbian snipers, went from building to building, speaking with neighbors or anyone who could help them identify the most helpless. In the end, they identified 15,000 people trapped in buildings and unable to find assistance.

Another extraordinary project Brenda initiated involved the children of Sarajevo. Frequently, they were sent to the water points because they were the fastest. But many of the wells were in open areas and targeted by the snipers. Many times the children were killed or wounded during the trip. In response, Brenda created a project to dig water points in protected areas. The wells were powered by solar panels to run the pumps in place of hand taps. One little girl thanked Brenda, saying she had been afraid to go for water every day, but had to. "Now, I won't be afraid anymore."

For the next year, Brenda's staff made routine visits across the city. Several times each week, they would call on the trapped residents with whatever food and assistance they could bring. Years later, as Brenda reflected on the outreach program, she felt the most significant support might have been human contact. The trips were not just a quick delivery of supplies; each visit required time when staff would sit to talk and listen. It was the greatest comfort they provided.

Brenda had a tough exterior. She had to stay and work in Sarajevo as long as she was needed. There were other international humanitarians who spent as much time in the city as Brenda, but they were few. Most of us came and went as quickly as possible. She stayed. She possessed the compassion to create the outreach program. No one came to her and said, "What about the aged, infirm, and wounded populations?" She sensed the need amid the bloodshed.

During my work with Brenda to determine which of her projects I would recommend that CARE USA support with additional finances, she made me aware of another horrific human rights violation: rape camps. This was 1994, and WWII had ended nearly half a century ago, yet the vestiges of Nazi-era atrocities were continuing all around me. The Army of the Republika Srpska, the same army that surrounded Sarajevo, determined to exterminate the Bosnian population. They carried out a systematic process of rape and impregnation of captured Bosnian women. This atrocity was called "genocidal rape." The various estimates as to the number of women who experienced this violence range between twelve to fifty thousand.

The purpose of the camp was to rape a woman repeatedly until she became pregnant. Once she was with child, she would be released to give birth to a Serbian baby. It was not uncommon for the woman to be gang raped or subjected to public rape in front of her village or family, including her children. The rapists would tell their victims, "You are going to have our children. You are going to have our little Chetniks and the reason for [your rape is] to plant the seed of Serbia in Bosnia."[1] In 1992, a UN commission of experts reported, "It was apparent rape was being used by Serb forces systematically and had the support of commanders and local authorities.... Pregnant women were detained until it was too late to have the fetus aborted. Victims were told they would be hunted

---

1. Patricia A. Weitsman, "The Politics of Identity and Sexual Violence: A Review of Bosnia and Rwanda," *Human Rights Quarterly* 30, no. 3 (2008): 561-578, doi:10.1353/hrq.0.0024.

down and killed should they report what had transpired."[2]

While continuing to work with Brenda and seeing the war through her eyes and activities, the brutality invaded every corner of my psyche and I started to have a recurring dream. Lying on the bed of a stream, I saw the sun and clouds through the water. Suddenly, it was dark, and I watched blackness overcome the light. I choked as the water filled my lungs, and a sense of corruption and evil entered my body. It filled me with fear and dread; I could not move or run. An evil force captured me.

Yet, there was Brenda. What I learned from her helped me mitigate the shock of this war. She gave me an understanding of a universal longing that runs through humankind, even, if not more so, in dangerous and violent places. As this was my first experience as a humanitarian worker, Brenda exposed me to the necessity of taking time to listen to people. She showed me the value of not only listening but hearing. I began to understand the compassion and understanding in a light touch to the shoulder of a desperate person. People needed to connect with me. They never asked for money or supplies, but instead wanted me to listen to their

---

2. Ibid., 561-578.

story. They wanted me to be an outside witness to their fear and trauma. I would sit for half an hour with a mug of black coffee and a cigarette and allow them to start talking, and when they did, it became a flood of emotion. Seldom was it anger; most often it was pain and loss.

Sitting in an apartment on a gray afternoon with snow and rain falling outside, plastic sheeting covering a hole in the wall from a tank shell, I listened to a woman in her early thirties. I accompanied Brenda to assess the damage to the building and a resident invited us into her rooms for coffee. She began to tell us her story.

She and her husband lived in an apartment with high ceilings and a row of tall windows that opened onto a balcony overlooking the city. On the day the war started, and the Serb aircraft bombed Sarajevo, her mother was visiting. When they heard the explosions, they each grabbed one of her two children and darted to the wide staircase to reach the basement. As they ran, a bomb struck the building. She watched her mother and youngest child disappear in front of her.

As I listened, I could see her hands shaking, but there was little emotion in her voice. I realized my role was to accompany her through her pain and trauma silently; nothing more was expected of me other than bearing witness.

I understood my role was not merely delivering food, medicine, or other supplies in a crisis. Brenda expected me to bring my compassion to people. She did not care about burnout or psychological protection. Those words were anathema to her.

I learned to spend time with groups of struggling people. An outsider was a safe ear. They wanted me to listen to their stories and to try to understand their grief.

I came to Bosnia intending to stay for several weeks, and instead I remained for six months. The requirements were overwhelming. There was never enough food, medicine, water, fuel, or shelter. While the world's governments and leaders talked and dithered, the body counts piled up, and the graves in the cemeteries got closer together. In Sarajevo and other cities blockaded by the Serbs, people were running out of space to bury their dead.

The winters were harsh with penetrating and unrelenting cold. Bosnia was also the first place I experienced chronic hunger. I was not starving, but there was never enough food and I was always hungry. As a humanitarian worker, we lived with no additional access to food, water, medicine, or fuel than any others in the city or town.

Amid this, I felt that everything I did counted. If we could get a supply of food into Sarajevo or other parts of the country, more people stayed alive. When we managed to transport medicine into an area, people did not die from wounds and infections. Every success had an immediate consequence. I made friends, and people relied on me for help. I felt a commitment to do the right thing. As the world ignored the slaughter, I couldn't walk away.

My body finally told me I'd had enough. I was in the town of Zenica and started coughing, sweating, and running a fever. A Bosnian colleague took me to the local clinic. As I waited, sitting on a wooden bench in the hallway, all around me people were coughing and looked as bad as I felt.

My doctor was a Bosnian woman who spoke English. She told me I had pneumonia but wanted to confirm it with an x-ray. She led me to an old machine and took the picture, which confirmed her diagnosis. When she finished, she apologized because she had no medicine and told me there were no drugs in the city, not even on the black market.

I had no choice but to leave the country and

return to Split, Croatia, where I could get the required medicines.

Climbing into a UN helicopter for the trip to Croatia, my pneumonia had worsened, and I felt increasing pain with every breath. We lifted from the ground and followed the safe route that was negotiated with the Serbs. If we stayed in this flight path, they wouldn't shoot us out of the sky.

Watching the country from two thousand feet, the landscape was beautiful, but I knew the pain and suffering beneath the trees and in the houses that passed so quickly below us. I shut my eyes and consoled myself with the thought that I would heal swiftly and soon return.

Landing in Split, a colleague from CARE's administrative office met me at the small airfield used by the UN and took me directly to the local hospital.

During the Bosnian War, humanitarian organizations couldn't maintain their administrative headquarters in the country. In addition to the dangers of open conflict, the ability to communicate by phone and fax in the war zone was nearly impossible. The UN's headquarters was in Split, as the requirement for daily coordination with the United Nations was essential. Humanitarian relief supplies from international donors were delivered to the warehouses in the city, then loaded on trucks for transport into the war zone.

My visit to the hospital, another x-ray, and several other tests confirmed I had viral pneumonia. Antibiotics wouldn't help. I was given aspirin and cough medicine, and told to rest and return in a week.

My colleague drove me to one of three apartments CARE maintained in Split. One was large, with several bedrooms for people transiting to and from the war zone, while the other two were private and not shared with others.

My apartment was in an old stone building overlooking the Adriatic Sea. The foundation also served as a sea wall. The bedroom and living room had large French doors opening to a balcony where I could watch the quiet and gentle swell of the water. At night, I opened both doors to hear the soft splash of waves against the stone. From my bed, I could see the stars and an occasional trail of a meteor streaking across the sky.

Although I was sick, it was peaceful. The woman who owned the building brought me breakfast, lunch, and supper each day. When I had a coughing spasm, she appeared with a shot glass of home-brewed Rakija—a very potent brandy made from plums. I'm not sure if the brew abated the coughing or its alcoholic content put me to sleep. Regardless, it worked.

After a week, I was well enough to visit the CARE headquarters in Split. I saw a fax for me from CARE Deutschland headquarters in Bonn, Germany. The message outlined their desire to begin a humanitarian response in the refugee camps surrounding Goma, in the Democratic Republic of the Congo (DRC). They wanted to assist refugees who fled the genocide in Rwanda and asked if I would do an on-site assessment to determine the viability of the initiative.

I knew Rwanda was composed of two ethnic groups, the Tutsi and the Hutu. Although the Tutsi were the minority, they gained power when the country achieved independence from Belgium in 1961.

Between that time and 1994, there was an insurgency between the ethnic groups, and the hatred exploded on April 7, 1994. The presidential jet, which was transporting the Rwandan president, Juvénal Habyarimana, and the Burundian president, Cyprien Ntaryamira, was shot down as it approached the Kigali airport. Witnesses reported two surface-to-air missiles hitting the plane. All on board died. The Hutu blamed the Tutsi for the assassination and started killing them.

They erected checkpoints and used national identity cards to execute Tutsi citizens methodically. Influential Hutus began recruiting and broadcasting orders over the radio for all Hutus to rise and kill any Tutsi they could find. They were encouraged to murder, rape, and maim without any consideration of repercussion. The more horrific the act, the more the violence was applauded. The radio messages singled out Hutu who had not joined the slaughter and threatened them by name.

After one hundred days of massacre, French forces intervened and drove approximately 800,000 Hutu into the DRC. The current Rwandan government estimates the number of victims of the genocide to be 1,174,000. Over one hundred days, 10,000 people were slaughtered every day. This is 400 every hour, or seven people killed each minute—all this death in a country the size of Maryland.

I finished reading the fax, greeted a few people, and returned to my Split apartment. It was noon. I was shocked that the short trip took so much out of me. I fell into bed and slept until the next morning. After breakfast, I unfolded the fax and reread the request. The personal logistics of moving myself from Split through Europe into central Africa and finding my way to the DRC seemed overwhelming.

For several days, I ignored the request while I wrestled with knowing I did not want to return to Bosnia. I had witnessed the brutality and misery and lived under the constant exposure and threat of mortar and artillery and the continual sound of sniper fire for six months. Every trip to a refugee center or town blockaded by Serb forces was dangerous and difficult. Yet, while sitting in a comfortable chair, on my small balcony overlooking the brilliant green and blue water of the Adriatic, guilt weighed my thoughts because I was not in Sarajevo with Brenda.

The following week, I made a trip to the hospital for an x-ray to confirm the pneumonia was gone. Meanwhile, I was following the humanitarian events in the refugee camps in the DRC on the BBC news. Regardless of the reports about the destitute situation, I didn't believe anything could be as bad as the war in Bosnia.

I called my wife in Hawai'i.

I had committed to being gone for weeks, now it was months, and I would extend by going to Zaire. She watched the tragedy unfold in Rwanda and was sympathetic to the refugees' needs, and didn't try to dissuade me. Still, I knew these trips were different from my deployments as a Marine. In the armed service, extended separations are part of the profession. Now, it was a personal decision at the expense of my family. I could rationalize this was a necessary humanitarian endeavor, but that was not true. I was more comfortable in a crisis environment than away from it. Years later, I began to understand the symptoms of post-traumatic stress disorder but at the time. I was ashamed because I was growing distant from my wife, not for someone else, but for something I didn't understand.

I got in touch with CARE Deutschland and confirmed I would do the assessment in Goma and asked them to make the flight arrangements. Three days later, I received their fax outlining my flight from Split to Frankfurt, Germany, and onward to Nairobi. I would stay in Nairobi for several days awaiting local authorization from the UN to allow me to fly on their aircraft and gain access to the refugee camps.

On July 19, 1994, I began my first humanitarian trip to Africa.

CHAPTER 9
MISERY GROWS, LIKE DEBT

"Hell is empty, and all the devils are here."
—William Shakespeare

I RESTED FOR TWO DAYS IN NAIROBI before receiving a fax from CARE detailing the UN authorization. The endorsement identified me as an implementing partner, allowing me access to a flight to the city of Goma in Zaire.[1]

The following day, as I debarked the UN flight in Goma, the heat and humidity struck me. It had to be 95 degrees and 90 percent humidity. In Bosnia, day temperatures in July were in the

---

1. Renamed the Democratic Republic of the Congo (DRC) in 1997

seventies, at night dipping into the forties and fifties. I collected my bag and made my way to the small immigration center.

By the time I finished the short walk, my T-shirt was soaked with sweat. I walked into a large UN tent. Although a Zaire official reviewed my documents, it was apparent this was a UN controlled entry and exit point. I was grateful for their intervention, as I did not have the energy to negotiate the routine requirements for bribes in humanitarian emergencies. I learned about the bribery in Bosnia, where at every checkpoint some kind of goods, such as coffee, sugar, or cigarettes, ensured your passage. I was thankful I had no checked luggage. In my pack, I had an extra set of jeans, one long-sleeved shirt, two T-shirts and several changes of underwear and socks.

With a stamp on my passport, I walked outside to a small patch of cleared land surrounded by a broken fence. There was a single tree in the yard. I saw a man standing in the shade wearing a CARE T-shirt. He walked over and asked if I was "Mr. Robert." I told him I was, and he took my backpack and gestured toward a white Land Rover Discovery with a CARE emblem on the side. As we departed the airport, he asked if I wanted him to turn on the air conditioner. I declined, even though the air reeked of decaying jungle foliage and the acrid smell of the burning charcoal from cooking stoves. "Welcome to Goma. I'd better get used to this," I thought.

It is impossible for the pictures and videos in the media to capture the real sense of a humanitarian emergency. The images focus on the destitute and misery of the setting. Yet, in most cases, camps are established around towns to facilitate the enormous logistical requirements of assisting so many people. We drove through Goma on an asphalt road. The city had several hotels, large homes, and bustling markets. I saw banks, grocery stores, churches, and a number of small apartment buildings. This was not a suburb in Europe or North America, but it was not the destitute area I saw on television. I noticed men in uniform, but most of them were guarding the larger buildings and banks.

When we passed through the town and approached the camp, the scene changed. The asphalt road turned to dirt, and foliage disappeared into fields of volcanic ash that had solidified over centuries into fragments of rock and glass. The terrain was like a coral reef with razor-sharp barbs that would cut through skin, clothes, or tennis shoes as quickly as a steak knife.

In the camps, regardless of UN presence, the Hutu militia oversaw control, including leaders who had perpetrated the genocide against the Rwandan Tutsi population. In the main compounds around Goma, the camps were home to approximately thirty to forty thousand soldiers of the former Armed Forces of Rwanda, also known as the ex-FAR—the acronym adopted from the French pronunciation of *Forces Armées Rwandaises*. Ex-FAR soldiers were a fully equipped and trained army that retained a complete system of command and control with the officers and leadership still intact. They had departed Rwanda with a full complement of military transportation, which allowed them to move throughout eastern Zaire easily.

While the ex-FAR focused on fighting the Rwandan forces, the Hutu leadership in the camps depended on the *Interahamwe* to maintain control of the refugee population. The *Interahamwe* was a Hutu militia responsible for some of the most notorious atrocities in Rwanda during the genocide. The militia had the unconditional support of both the Hutu government and army. Today, they are considered a terrorist organization and still operate throughout the eastern DRC.

The swift exodus of refugees from Rwanda into the surrounding countries left little time to prepare for the settlement of such a large population. In the first week of July deaths among the refugee community were occurring at 600 per week, increasing to 2,000 in the following weeks as the refugee population increased and the health situation worsened. By late July mortality rates from cholera, diarrhea and other diseases reached 7,000 per week.

The sanitation problems were catastrophic, as digging latrines in the volcanic terrain was impossible. The vast population quickly filled the few existing facilities. While walking through the camps, the smell of decomposing bodies and feces filled the air. This combination was intensified by the extremes of heat and humidity. When it rained, the wetness trapped the smell and increased its sordid concentration. It is difficult to recount the scene of 100,000 people living on volcanic ash in lean-tos made from blue tarps provided by the UN, herded into the squalor of unrelenting humidity, rotting bodies, and feces.

Once the camps were established, the former Rwandan government made the decisions, not the UN. Their first objective was taking control of the food supply. They enacted this goal by creating a symbolic system of elected leaders in the camp. These leaders were supposedly chosen by popular vote to act on behalf of the camp inhabitants for the distribution of humanitarian aid. In reality, the former Hutu government officials appointed these managers.

By controlling the food and other items of assistance, the camp leadership maintained control. By engaging in this system, the UN and NGOs were blocked from the day-to-day accounting for relief supplies. Consequently, the leaders inflated the number of inhabitants at random to obtain more food, then sold the excess on the black market, or in the shops in Goma. Seeing 50 kilogram bags of rice and flour emblazoned with a picture of the American flag and a statement reading "A Gift from the People of the United States of America" was a common sight in the marketplaces. The camp leadership sold the excess humanitarian aid to support the military units of the ex-FAR.

The Hutu militants held so much power in the camps the UN was simply a de facto supplier of food and other resources. The sites around Goma grew to a point of becoming small cities. They established "a certain permanence, eventually containing 2,323 bars, 450 restaurants, 589 shops, 62 hairdressers, 51 pharmacies, 30 tailors, 25 butchers, five ironsmiths and mechanics, four photo studios, three movie theaters, two hotels, and one slaughterhouse."[2]

To demilitarize the camps, the UN debated moving the sites farther from the Rwandan border. The UN began employing young boys who had formed a Boy Scout Troop in each of the camps to assist with providing income to some of the families. The young men were asked to make a daily check of the tents in their area to determine if anyone had died. Although obtaining the full uniform was impossible, each of them had a distinctive Troop scarf. In the event of a death, they alerted camp management to ensure the body was retrieved as soon as possible to mitigate the spread of disease. However, throughout the camp, the Hutu militia routinely murdered individuals who irked them. The victims' bodies were left in the tracks around the sites as a warning to others. As the Scouts made their daily checks and reported the bodies, their efforts challenged the desires of the militia, who decided *when* the bodies of their victims would be removed. Their reaction was to murder several Scouts, leaving them to be found.

---

2. Gerard Prunier, *Africa's World War: Congo, the Rwandan Genocide, and the Making of a Continental Catastrophe* (Oxford: Oxford University Press, 2008), 4–28.

Upon arriving at the refugee camp, the entrance was clogged with trucks and vehicles of every type from modern SUVs to old Nissan and Toyota taxis. The road was not designed for this amount of use and had deteriorated to potholes and yawning crevices. At the checkpoint, I anticipated seeing a contingent of soldiers from Zaire but was surprised to see a random group of men armed with Kalashnikov rifles. They did not inspect the vehicles. Their sole intent seemed to be intimidation and control.

Inside the camp, we stopped in front of a small cluster of tents with a UN flag limply hanging from a makeshift pole. It began to rain. It was a routine event in the afternoon at this time of year. It rained in torrents and instantly turned to steam. It seemed to boil into the atmosphere over the volcanic fields. In the distance were rolling hills with vegetation, but around me was a vast desert of volcanic ash. The fields were not flat but rolled like the waves in the Pacific Ocean that surrounded my home in Hawai'i.

Regardless of the severity of the landscape, an endless number of lean-tos stretched for miles in every direction. There was a sense of organization to the small structures. Passageways between the huts became small streets that fed into the main corridors. Standing by the UN headquarters tent in the drenching rain, watching rivulets run through the shelters as humans huddled inside, I was miserable. The sky was dark and malevolent. The combination of humidity and smell from the decaying bodies and feces overwhelmed me. If this wasn't Hell, it was close enough.

When I introduced myself to the UN staff, they were polite, but distant. They were working very hard to cope with the refugees and the militarization of the camps. I was just another NGO arriving for an assessment. I was a distraction.

I was passed to a young Canadian who would be my point of contact. She was from Quebec and English was a distant second language, but she was eager to help, and familiar with CARE as she had interned with them while in university. She had a master's degree in public health and was concerned about the spread of dysentery and diarrhea at the camp. As we toured the camp, I saw she had every right to be worried: there was raw sewage everywhere.

All the humanitarian and UN staff I met had one common characteristic: they were exhausted. In Bosnia, the relief work was hard, and the constant dangers of the war zone were debilitating. In this setting, the sheer number of refugees and the environmental misery made these workers hollow. Everyone was worn, both the refugees and the humanitarian workers. International governments condemned the UN for offering a safe haven to people who perpetrated the genocide in Rwanda. Yet, the UN and NGO staff were following the dictates of impartiality and trying to save lives, including those who had committed unspeakable acts of savagery.

The humanitarian staff had themselves become refugees, sharing in the wretched conditions of the camps. All the analysis, accusations, and deductions taking place in New York and other national capitals had no place here. Those discussions existed in a world of black and white, sustained by the comforts of convenience and affluence.

This was the monarchy of gray, a domain of shades, and even those were unnatural. The ex-FAR soldier who continued the killing raids in Rwanda, the Hutu family that did nothing during the genocide and huddled in their tent to escape the rain, and the demands of the Hutu militia—the UN and NGO staff were charged with sustaining all life, not determining who was the victim or the perpetrator.

As I traveled through the other four camps surrounding Goma, they were the same, isolated in the middle of fields of volcanic ash. Every site was a blend of humanitarian necessity and guerrilla warfare. In Bosnia, I thought I had seen it all: the snipers, constant shelling, and rape camps. Then, I was dropped into a different genocidal mania. I began evaluating my mental stamina.

I believe humans have an incredible ability to reach a place that allows them to deal with the present, based on this assumption: "I will deal with all this stuff, later." But how many times can you do this before something breaks?

And yet, the Congo was not the place to address my own problems. I felt a great deal of responsibility. CARE would undoubtedly make its own decisions, but my recommendation would influence that choice. I could read about a genocide that exterminated nearly 800,000 people, walk among those who were part of that atrocity, and see refugee camps become the shelter and logistic centers for a rebel army. However, most of the camp occupants were victims of the genocide. They may not have been the Tutsi population who had suffered at the hands of the Hutu militias and supporters, but they were forced to leave their homes because of the atrocities.

The dilemma was the enormous necessity for humanitarian aid without the international community answering the requirement. Thus, the camps themselves were becoming another type of extermination center. They were filled with malaria, diarrhea, and dysentery. When a measles epidemic started in combination with diarrhea, both adults and children perished by the thousands.

Drafting my recommendations, I found myself trying to balance my realization of the tremendous need for humanitarian assistance with the reality of the situation. The camps in Goma were going to follow one of two paths: They would implode because of disease, corruption, and brutality, and the residents would simply die or move further into central Zaire, or the entire situation would explode. Rwanda could not allow the situation to continue and other observer states were not going to intervene.

As I wrote my summary, it struck me that a humanitarian worker does not take an oath to "support and defend a constitution or country." I worried that what I wrote and recommended would cause my colleagues to place themselves in the middle of unimaginable violence and suffering. The men who had caused the genocide would not hesitate to recreate that violence if the members of the humanitarian community were no longer useful to them.

From a makeshift desk of an old board spanning several empty boxes, I looked across the lava fields and recommended CARE begin operations.

Once that memo was completed, I departed Zaire and returned to Hawai'i. I thought my association with this mess was over.

CHAPTER 10
THE UNFINISHED JOURNEY OF CAREY GRANT

*"The world is always going to be dangerous,
and people get badly banged up,
but how can there be more meaning than helping one
another stand up in a wind and stay warm?"*
—Anne Lamott

For most of 1995, I stayed with my family in Hawai'i, working with CARE on short-term contracts in Haiti, Sudan, Kenya, and Cambodia, and staying away from Bosnia. Although there was much humanitarian deprivation and injustice present in the four countries where I was working, there was not the war or genocidal mania I found in the Balkans.

After the Dayton Peace Agreement was signed

in November 1995, which ended the three-and-a-half-year Bosnian War, CARE asked me to travel to Croatia for a short-term assignment moving the organization's assistance from emergency programming, designed to keep people alive during the violence, to the support required to help rebuild Bosnia.

I spent two weeks in Zagreb, Croatia, a beautiful city that looked and felt like Vienna. Its imperial architecture characterized in the monumental public buildings and quiet cobblestone streets made me feel like I had returned to a gentler time.

After we developed a plan, I returned to Hawai'i. I wanted to understand why I was subjecting myself to all this work. All around me, friends, neighbors, and acquaintances were able to hold "traditional jobs," which allowed them to stay at home, earn a decent living, develop relationships, and live seemingly peaceful lives.

Early on a Sunday morning, I was sitting in an open-air church on the slopes of Diamond Head where the sides of the old volcano gently fell into the blue brilliance of the Pacific. It was peaceful, and the gentleness of the Aloha spirit nurtured the surroundings. I could hear the soft surge of the ocean waves join the melody of nearby birds.

I casually looked at the church's weekly

bulletin and saw the word Bosnia. My muscles contracted and my eyes tightened. The place I was trying to escape had invaded the serenity of this quiet morning. When I read the insert, my emotions constricted. A local architect had decided, in the spirit of Aloha, to gather several thousand teddy bears and send them to the children of Bosnia. My moral superiority took over, and I harshly judged the action. Teddy bears? Not, food, safety, education, clothing, but toys? I threw the bulletin on the pew and tried focusing on the rest of the service.

When I left the church, I put the bulletin in my pocket. I was indignant. I tried to imagine the naivety of the organizer. He had never been to Bosnia, and his efforts were pretentious. After all, I had suffered through it and knew what was right for the children of the country. Why did he have to remind me of the misery and reinforce my guilt over not being there?

I had come to loathe Bosnia but was lost without it. Everything about the humanitarian work overwhelmed me. My emotions were shot, and thoughts of suicide occasionally drifted through my mind. I was not too worried about it and rationalized that if I ever got serious two things would stop me: I did not have the courage, and I would never burden my wife and children with such an act.

As the days passed, I thought about Carey.

Every war has unsung heroes. During the Bosnian conflict, there was a small group of men and women who came to the country as members of the UN, or separate humanitarian organizations, and worked as truck drivers. Their job was to move the tons of humanitarian aid from the ports in Croatia to the distribution points throughout the war zone in Bosnia. Because the journey required passage between the combat zones of Serbs, Croats, and Bosnians, the drivers had to be international. One of the largest groups was from the CARE Australia trucking fleet. The drivers were a diverse and tough group of German, Danish, French, Scottish, English, Irish, and American individuals. Many were soldiers with service in wars from Vietnam to the French Foreign Legion. They lived and worked hard and spent eight to ten days on the road with only four days of downtime between trips.

It was harsh and relentless work.

Back when I worked in Bosnia, I used the CARE trucking fleet to carry our relief supplies, and the drivers assisted with the distributions. The journeys were stressful, dangerous, and never went as planned because of the fighting, road closures, or sniper fire. Along the way, I tried to split my rides between different drivers. For the most part, they enjoyed someone to chat with as the hours passed.

It was on one of these trips that I met Carey Grant. He was a natural leader, well-read, and thoughtful, with opinions about everything—most of which were counter to my own. I enjoyed the banter and his quick intellect. Over time, we became close friends. When I departed Bosnia in late 1994, Carey remained and continued delivering aid throughout the war zone.

I recalled listening to the intensity of his discussions about the plight of the children he encountered on his trips. Although email was new, I would get an occasional message from him via a UN computer system. He was still engaged with an international NGO, but his communications were filled with damning reflections on their ineptitude and incompetence. My patience for his rants was thin.

But I could not get the "Bears for Bosnia" out of my mind. I was ashamed that I had come home. I should have stayed in Bosnia and done more. The architect collecting teddy bears was doing something of consequence. He was trying to harness the power of the most gentle and peaceful place in the United States and use it to encourage the children in a ravished land.

After several more days of denial and self-pity, I realized my problem was not with an architect who was simply trying to do something decent for the children of a war-torn nation. My discomfort was the recurring nightmares about the day the gunmen attacked me at the Mogadishu airport in Somalia. The dreams are vivid, and images of what the bullets did to the children are too graphic to recount in any form. I was afraid to engage with the children of Bosnia. In their eyes, I saw fear and the loss of their innocence while baffled by the violence and hatred. But it was for those reasons I contacted the organizer. Children need to be allowed to be children, to have something personal and special to love, even in the face of war and horror.

I phoned the architect and explained my association with humanitarian work in Bosnia and my military background. I offered to help. He told me his most significant dilemma was to find a way to transport the bears to Bosnia. I said I would be happy to contact the US Air Force Command in Hawai'i to see if we could move the bears as an opportune lift under the parameters of the US

Department of State, Denton Humanitarian Assistance Program, which authorizes the US Air Force to fly humanitarian cargo to areas in need.

When I visited the Pacific Air Force Headquarters to make the request, I was amazed by their response. They were enthusiastic about the idea and forwarded the request to the Pentagon with a recommendation to assist. Within several days, I received a call from an Air Force public affairs officer. She told me the request was approved and there was a hand-written note from the chief of staff of the USAF, "If there were any extra bears would we consider sharing them with the different US Military peacekeeping units to give to the children in their areas of tactical responsibility."

I replied there would be several thousand bears, and we would be happy to share. The Air Force said they would store the bears in an empty warehouse at the Rhein-Main AFB near Frankfurt, but we would have to move them from Germany.

Within several days of trying to find a means to move the bears, I received a call from the International Rescue Committee (IRC) Chief Operating Officer, Roy Williams. He was a soft-spoken man with immeasurable impact on humanitarian assistance throughout the world. He explained a problem his staff were experiencing in the Balkans and asked if I would consider returning for several months to assist. Since I was still on a consultancy contract with CARE, I appreciated the opportunity to gain experience working with another NGO. I agreed to a short-term contract. The work in Bosnia was a means to help IRC and oversee the delivery of the bears.

I contacted my friend, Gordon Bacon, who headed the charity organization Children's Aid Direct in Bosnia and maintained their own fleet of trucks. I explained the Hawai'ian initiative and my dilemma regarding transportation from Germany. He asked how many vehicles I needed. I was confident I would only require one. He offered to let me use a truck, but I would have to find my own driver and pay for the fuel—about one hundred dollars. He would happily store the bears and asked if he could use some of them on occasion. He thought the inclusion of teddy bears with official papers could soften the driver's passages through the conflict areas. It was a great idea. Providing a toy for kids was much better than a demand for cigarettes, coffee, or sugar. It appeared all the pieces were falling into place, except for a driver. It was not a great leap to think about Carey.

I tried to reach Carey at his place of employment and was told he was no longer with them.

That made me nervous. I contacted several acquaintances in Split and found out Carey had moved to Zenica in Bosnia. After several attempts, I finally found a contact number. He was made redundant by his former employer and decided to remain in Zenica. Although Carey still manifested the familiar anger toward the management of the aid agency, I also noted a sense of optimism. He was trying to put together a deal to open an Australian-style pub in the town. The Dayton Peace Agreement included the provision for more international military forces to maintain the peace. Bosnia would soon host an increased number of British, American, Canadian, Australian, and New Zealand peacekeepers. Zenica would become a logistics hub and headquarters center for many of them. An Australian pub made sense. We chatted for a while, and he was filled with enthusiasm. He had always been a "pub landlord" at heart. I worried about how much of the stock he would consume, but he was a natural entrepreneur and an engaging speaker. I hoped this new venture would work. He told me he had made a deal with the owner of a building to lease the space for a share of the profits.

I asked how he felt about volunteering to pick up a truck from my friend, Gordon Bacon, driving to Frankfurt, finding the Rhein-Main US Air Force Base, and picking up a load of teddy bears. He hesitated for a moment, laughed, and said, "Sounds like a great idea, mate!" I knew I could count on him. We had all the pieces in place. Teddy bear collections had begun across all the islands of Hawai'i. Every bear had to be new, and people were encouraged to put a personal note on each of them. The first reports were encouraging, but modest. In the first week of December we gathered about 300 bears. I was hoping for a thousand. As we approached Christmas, the initiative exploded, and by New Year's, we had to end the collection. The people of Hawai'i had donated more than 22,000 new teddy bears to the children of Bosnia, each with a hopeful and nurturing message attached. Churches, schools, clubs, universities, YMCAs, and individuals came together to send a message of Aloha to the Balkans. I was humbled by the gesture and embarrassed by my earlier cynicism.

As I prepared to return to Bosnia, I received a call from the headquarters of the US Marine Forces, Pacific, at Camp Smith on Oah'u. The captain asked if I would be available to meet with the commanding general concerning the Bears for Bosnia initiative. I had served with him several times since the Vietnam War and respected him. Entering the main gate at the headquarters the next day both comforted me and made me uneasy.

The disquieted feeling that began when I retired from the Marines never left me. While others embrace organizations associated with the Marines after retirement, I had isolated myself. I was not bitter. Instead, I had lost the one real sense of grounding and purpose in my life. Working in Bosnia was a quest to find something to replace the feeling of principled attachment I had as a Marine.

It was odd and uncomfortable to walk into the headquarters as a civilian. Everything was familiar, but I was an outsider. Many of my former coworkers greeted me warmly, but they had to excuse themselves to hurry to their next task. I smiled. I had done the same when I worked there.

After some small talk with the commanding general, he began outlining a problem in another part of the world that was becoming a threat to national security. I knew the area and the problem well. I had studied and worked with the dilemma for several years. He asked how I felt about being recalled to active duty to assist. I was startled. Recall to active duty made sense to quickly reinstate the level of security clearance I needed to review the problem. Nearly two years since I retired, I wanted to know, "Why me?" Other active-duty women and men possessed more knowledge about the current condition. As we talked, the real reason for the request became clear: we were friends, we trusted one another, and we were comfortable in our working relationship.

I was intrigued and honored to be sought by someone I deeply respected. As I sat in the office, I thought about the teddy bears. The delivery of the bears was not enough reason to say no, but what struck me was what the bears signified in my life. I had begun to understand the Marines had been my profession, but my work with humanitarian assistance was my calling.

I declined the offer. The commanding general was disappointed but gracious. He did not force the issue or press for my reason.

Finally, the day arrived. We brought the bears to the Hickam Air Force Base on Oah'u and watched as they were stored in the warehouse, pending transport. The entire lift took approximately two weeks.

With the bears in Frankfurt and my plane ticket booked to the former Yugoslavia, I contacted Carey and Gordon about moving the bears from Germany to Split. Gordon calculated we needed two large lorries and another driver. Carey knew a certified and licensed Australian who remained in Bosnia after the peace agreement. I was confident with Carey's assessment but knew Gordon would check his qualifications and abilities before he allowed him to use a Children's Aid Direct vehicle.

When I arrived, my esteem and appreciation for Gordon, which was always high, increased by quantum leaps. Our teddy bears were neatly stacked in his facility, and I was surprised by how much space they occupied. Gordon never complained nor urged me to disperse them quickly. I was now responsible for moving 22,000 bears sitting in a warehouse in Split, Croatia, into the hands of children in a war zone. My feeling while looking at the bears on a cold winter day in a dark warehouse was considerably different from the enthusiasm I experienced in the warmth and Aloha of Oah'u.

I thanked Gordon and checked into the IRC office in Split where I met the country director. We discussed his desire for my consulting role. It would be difficult to work and extensively travel throughout the region. Although the direct fighting had ceased, the armed hostility between neighbors and adjacent communities had not. Grudges here were carried for hundreds of years, and Bosnia was still a dangerous place. My assignment was developing a plan for conflict resolution for the International Rescue Committee to use throughout the country.

During my discussions with the country director, I mentioned the bears. I offered some to his staff for their visits to different towns, hamlets, and camps for the refugees and internally displaced people. He loved the idea, and we agreed to move several thousand bears to his warehouse.

My next trip took me to the local headquarters of the newly formed NATO Implementation Force (IFOR), created after the signing of the Dayton Peace Accord. As part of the agreement, NATO committed to providing 60,000 peacekeepers for the region. The public affairs officer was expecting me. We decided to move 10,000 bears to the NATO storage facilities, which freed up a substantial portion of Gordon's warehouse.

After several days, I loaded the Jeep Cherokee provided by the IRC and set off for Zenica. The city is in the center of Bosnia and from there I could access most of the country. IRC maintained several small apartments in the town for visiting staff and consultants. I was grateful for the accommodation and the removed hassle of finding my own lodging.

I put my backpack and laptop into the Jeep and

then crammed it with as many bears as possible. When I was finished, all the side and rear windows had the smiling face of a teddy bear beaming into the sunlight. I loved it.

In the past, the journey from IRC's base in Split, Croatia, took four days. Fortunately, they had several guest houses along the way where I could stay with a local family overnight. The first couple had a comfortable room in the attic for me. They had three young children, and I immediately became a hit when I gave each of them a teddy bear from Hawai'i. If my trip had ended there, the look in their eyes would have made the whole project worthwhile.

When I arrived in Zenica, I went to the IRC sub office and met the manager. Nancy Hofmann was from Canada. We knew each other from my time in Bosnia with CARE. She was very competent and engaged and wished me luck on my assignment. We both knew it would be a complicated contract.

The US government wanted to provide money to humanitarian organizations to implement reconciliation projects, which would engage the different Bosnian ethnic groups in a joint effort to rebuild infrastructure for the common good of all the people. The projects would require various groups to work together positively and productively. It was a great idea, and worth a try, but five hundred years of ethnic, religious, and cultural hatred overshadowed the endeavor. "Changing mindsets must begin somewhere," I thought, "and why not here?"

I mentioned the bears to Nancy, and she beamed. I asked if she could store them in her warehouse while I found a way to transport them to Zenica. I planned to center them in central Bosnia and then announce their presence to my colleagues in the humanitarian community. At that point, they could take as many as they needed to assist with their own distribution efforts. Nancy was happy to assist.

I took my backpack to my temporary apartment. It was on a quiet street that overlooked the Bosna River. The residence had a bedroom, kitchen, and private bath. It was small, but comfortable. It also had a parking place for the Jeep off the street behind a fence. Car theft and breaking into parked vehicles had become ordinary. Local vehicles were generally exempt, but any auto or truck associated with the international community was fair game.

After a long and deep sleep, I woke to a peacefulness I had not experienced in some time. I laid in bed before getting up, watching the river flow by my window. Why did I feel so comfortable in the middle of Bosnia? I barely spoke the language. I had no close friends or family. I was an outsider, but when I started my journey from Croatia into the country of Bosnia, I felt at home and could feel my stress shedding from me like a second skin.

When I went to the main floor of the apartment home, I saw the property owner had prepared me a breakfast of eggs, potatoes, thick homemade bread, honey, and tea. This was a good sign that commodities were beginning to flow into Bosnia and people were making enough money to buy them.

I found the address Carey had given me for his pub and drove through town toward Zenica Steelworks. The plant, which employed 22,000 people, had shut down during the war. There was some talk it would open again soon, but there was no evidence to back it up. I stopped in front of a dark and dilapidated building. Opening the door, I found a work in progress. It was obvious it had been a bar, but Carey had his work cut out for him. I went outside and walked to the rear of the structure. I climbed a set of stairs to a doorway on the second floor and knocked. A middle-aged woman answered, dressed in a worn housecoat and with a cigarette dangling from her mouth. She turned and shouted, "Carey," and walked away. I waited for a moment, and Carey appeared. He looked good. It was ten in the morning and he invited me into the apartment. We sat at the kitchen table and he introduced me to his landlady. She tried being gracious, but indicated she had to leave.

I asked about the pub, and he said he was having trouble with the owner. He continued to tell me that he was not working and was desperate for cash. He was trying to find a logisticians position with an NGO, but they were beginning to only hire locals. This made sense. During the war, there were too many lines of confrontation between Serbs, Croats, and Bosnians. It was impossible for a local to find any work that required travel.

I had funding for an assistant in my budget for the conflict resolution grant from the US government. I wanted Carey to join me in this position, but I was hesitant. He knew how to engage people, speak the language, and be a peacemaker, but I needed to examine my motives. I liked Carey. Although I would never admit feeling sorry for him, this lingered in the back of my mind. I knew this project was a gift. It had been a long time since any endeavor put fire in my belly. The previous peace building I did in Somalia, I had a weapon at my side. This was different. This was a means to build trust and help heal wounds. I told Carey I had to drive into Sarajevo and meet with several members from the UN Human Rights Commission and would be back in Zenica in three days. I asked if we could meet for dinner. He agreed, but I still had not decided if I wanted to work with him.

During the drive to Sarajevo, there were few vehicles on the road so I relaxed and let my mind process. I was amazed the road held up as well as it did through the war. I passed farms, houses, fields, and barns, all of them damaged, but people were repairing the destruction and painting over the war slogans and ethnic insults splattered on the houses and barns. It was healing to see people rebuilding and emerging from the darkness of war, but the still visible ethnic slurs and insults served as a reminder of how much hatred existed throughout Bosnia.

As I thought about Carey, I was not worried about his competence or leadership, I was concerned about his penchant for cutting corners, but I decided to look at his inclination as an asset rather than a detriment. It was not a difficult switch. Carey came from a tough background. He had wrecked many things in his life, but he had one consistency: he embodied Teddy Roosevelt's speech, "The Man in the Arena":

It is not the critic who counts; not the man who

points out how the strong man stumbles, or where the doer of deeds could have done them better. The credit belongs to the man who is actually in the arena, whose face is marred by dust and sweat and blood.

Carey spent his entire life in the arena and related to strong men who had stumbled. Was he opinionated and direct? Yes. And those traits came from a sense of justice. He was never afraid to crawl back into the fight. He brought another asset to the reconciliation initiative. I was not going to engage in anything illegal, immoral, or unethical, but Carey's ideas would force me to think creatively. With his creativity, he could help uncover alternative ways to accomplish the task.

The next evening, Carey and I met at a newly-opened restaurant in Zenica, and I was fascinated by how many people he knew and embraced. There were several young men and women in hospital scrubs. They spent a good deal of time talking and conversed in Serbo-Croatian. I was impressed with how well he spoke the language. After a short period, they realized I did not understand and switched to English. They were attendants at the paraplegic ward in the local hospital. Carey volunteered to help at the clinic and knew a number of the men who had become paraplegic or quadriplegic during the war. Learning of this moved me. Suffering this type of injury anywhere was traumatic. Sustaining it in Bosnia must have been beyond extreme. Carey spent a large portion of each week assisting them.

Sitting with a beer in front of me, in a city with a damaged soul, in the aftermath of a horrific war, I watched a man who had lost everything in life. Yet, he was still engaged with love and compassion for the victims of violence. He was rough, loud, and at times quick-tempered, but this guy cared about people. During his own struggles, he had stopped running and was building a new life in Bosnia.

The following morning, I visited Carey in his apartment to outline my scope of work and voice my feelings about the viability of the initiative. I believed we could find one thing that would help move the peace process forward. I laid out the conditions of the agreement and my personal requirements. He was happy with the offer, we signed the document, and I gave him an advance of a thousand dollars.

Armed with our Aloha bears, we set off to build peace and reconciliation. We had seen too much during the war and knew the word "peace" for a Bosnian simply meant a temporary stop to the fighting. As far as reconciliation, I was not sure there was such a word in the Serbo-Croatian language. However, as Carey and I talked about different initiatives, we were excited. For one of the few times in our lives, we had a blank slate in front of us.

We embraced the opportunity, one Australian, and a guy from Hawai'i who was at a crossroad in his life. Being able to focus on words like "peace" and "reconciliation" was an answer to many shattered ideals. We stuffed the Jeep full of bears and set off in hopes of doing something valuable in a desperate place.

I had seldom been as happy or at peace. Carey came alive. We spent hours talking about living life rather than observing it. Neither of us would admit it, but we were inspired. Carey stopped drinking. He became quiet and thoughtful. No matter where we stayed, I started to sleep through the night. My terror dreams of the gunfight in the alley in Somalia began to diminish.

For several weeks, our routine was to arrive in a village, find the mayor, elder, or informal leader and talk to him or her about the bears and our project. We learned some hard lessons in the beginning. On one occasion, as we drove into a village unannounced, we almost started a riot as the women rushed the vehicle to snatch as many of the stuffed animals as possible. I was pushed to the ground as they pulled open the Jeep doors and looted the vehicle.

Developing a peace and reconciliation initiative was going to be a tough sell after a climate of war and deprivation.

Yet, that incident forced us to discipline our thinking. Bosnia was not Africa. In Africa, the people would have quickly worked out their own means to ensure equal distribution. This incident showed me how much trauma and lack these people had suffered. The women were going to ensure they got whatever they could for their own, and I could not blame them.

After looking through some potential projects, we found one that seemed to be a perfect fit. The water supply for the city of Zenica started at four springs, approximately forty kilometers from the city. The source provided significant hydrological pressure as it rushed from the streams and melting snow in the mountains. There was a small pumping station at the site powered by four generators, but they had long ago been looted. Three of the pipelines were damaged or destroyed by the fighting, and the remaining line was entirely gravity fed as it forced water along the route to Zenica. At the end of the source, a population of

300,000 people had an intermittent water flow of approximately two hours per day.

Carey and I drafted a proposal for the IRC, which included rebuilding the pump station and repairing the four pipelines that carried the water to Zenica through all the villages along the route. IRC liked the concept and presented it to the US government. They liked the idea and were willing to provide 2.3 million US dollars for the project. It was a win-win for everyone.

The only caveat was that Carey and I had to obtain a consensus of support from every town and village along the pipeline. This appeared to be an easy task. It would take time, but the advantage of having clean and fresh water continuously must be a desired outcome for everyone. We thought the toughest part would be the logistics of arranging a meeting with the mayor of each town as it was winter and the roads were always bad.

Our colleagues forewarned us of the difficulty of obtaining these agreements. Yet, with a sense of optimism, we began the task of visiting each village along the 40-kilometer route. Carey was a gifted negotiator, and his grasp of the Serbo-Croatian language grew with each trip.

We aimed to have the mayor or village give consent to having the pipeline repaired in their area and guaranteed the labor involved would be offered to the people throughout the region. However, the ethnic divides that fueled the recent violence separated the mentalities of each town as well. Their hatred for one another was visceral. People in one hamlet would refuse to sign an agreement based on atrocities and grudges from another village only three kilometers away. The grievances were two hundred years old. In the beginning, we thought that ensuring a steady water supply to their own area would be enough to overcome their hostility, but that line of reasoning did not work. The villagers would rather choose to go without water over cooperating with another town of Bosnian-Croats, Bosnian-Serbs or Bosniaks.

In the Bosnian villages, our meetings degenerated into protracted discussions about the Srebrenica massacre. The atrocity was etched in their minds and would be retold three hundred years from now. They told us the stories of the slaughter in detail.

Srebrenica was a Muslim enclave in eastern Bosnia close to the border of Serbia. In 1993, the Serb Army surrounded the region. To protect the Muslim population, the UN demanded that "all parties and others concerned treat Srebrenica and its surroundings as a safe area, which should be free from any armed attack or any other hostile act."[1] The area was to be protected by the United Nations Protection Force (UNPROFOR), which was the first United Nations peacekeeping force in Bosnia during the war. The UNPROFOR forces assigned to safeguard the people of Srebrenica were from the Dutch Army.

As signs of a peace settlement began to develop, Serbia wanted to eliminate the Muslim enclave in Srebrenica before they agreed to a treaty. To cleanse the area, the Serb Army advanced on the Muslim region, and 25,000 Bosnian Muslims pressed into a UN designated protected area to seek shelter from the Serb forces.

Only several thousand could enter the Dutch Army compound, and the rest stayed in the fields surrounding the Dutch camp.

The Serbs threatened the Dutch peacekeepers, and they immediately surrendered. Without the protection of UNPROFOR, the Serbs surrounded the Bosnians, separated the men and boys from the women, and began executing them. The killing continued into the night as giant lights lit up a

---

1. United Nations Security Council, Resolution 819, "1993," April 16, 1993, https://digitallibrary.un.org/record/164939?ln=en.

field where bulldozers dug mass graves. Witnesses reported the bulldozers pushed both the living and dead into the excavations. Throughout the entire area, the rape of Bosnian women became a common occurrence.

The mass executions followed an established pattern. The men were housed in empty schools or warehouses, then loaded on buses or trucks and taken to a site for execution. Usually the killing fields were in isolated locations. The prisoners were unarmed, bound, and blindfolded with their shoes removed. In the kill zones, they were lined up and shot. During these atrocities, at Serb insistence, the Dutch expelled the remaining 5,000 Bosnians from their compound. They were collected by the Serbs, who killed all the men and boys. In the end, the Serb forces massacred more than 7,000 Bosnians in four days.

While the Dutch may have been on the front line of witnessing the genocide, the entire UNPROFOR was aware of the slaughter and did nothing to stop it. The senior military and civilian leadership within the UN watched it unfold without intervention as they debated a response. Later, UN Secretary General, Kofi Annan, investigated UN action during the Srebrenica atrocity. The critical report stated:

Through error, misjudgment and the inability to recognize the scope of evil confronting us, we failed to do our part to save the people of Srebrenica from the Serb campaign of mass murder.... These failings were in part rooted in a philosophy of neutrality and nonviolence wholly unsuited to the conflict in Bosnia.[2]

Every Bosnian village along the proposed route for a new water supply line was courteous and grateful for the presence of the Aloha bears, but none of them would sign a joint document of cooperation with any Serb town along the water route. In fact, not one village, whether they were Croat, Serb, or Bosnian would consider signing any agreement. I reported to IRC that the water supply initiative was impossible to accomplish.

Carey and I were dejected, not from a sense of failure, but from such immersion in hate. When the media began reporting the atrocity at Srebrenica, I thought of an adage I learned in the Marines: "Nothing is ever as good or bad as first reported." Because of this, I was skeptical when I

---

2. Wikipedia, "Bosnian Genocide," Wikipedia, The Free Encyclopedia, February 24, 2019, accessed March 5, 2019, https://en.wikipedia.org/w/index.php?title=Bosnian_genocide&oldid=884892354

first learned the initial estimates of the massacre. I thought, "If this occurred, how do the Bosnian Serbs expect to get away with it?" In retrospect, I am amazed at my naivety. After all I had witnessed in Somalia, I still could not accept the existence of absolute evil.

I debated my next step. I still had time on the contract, but the magnitude of the problems overwhelmed me. The humanitarian workers I worked with during the war had gone home. There was a new set of development staff. Their role was long-term engagement and assistance with communities in rebuilding a nation or region.

After two and a half months, I told Carey I was going to pass the search to find reconciliation projects to the IRC development team. I was not a development worker, and it was time for me to move aside. He was disappointed. I knew he needed the money, and told him he could continue with the development team, but he declined. Unlike me, Carey loved Bosnia. He wanted the opportunity to stay and work with the reconstruction but knew continuing with another set of people on the reconciliation project was not the right thing for him.

My decision saddened me. I knew it was the right choice, but I witnessed Carey come alive during our time together. I saw the real Carey Grant emerge and observed what I always suspected: he burned like a bright flame. This was a man of conviction who loved justice and had abiding compassion for people in need. His past made him pragmatic. He understood what it was like to be an outsider looking at life through the eyes of a "have not." Carey connected with the Bosnian people because he knew how it felt to lose everything.

We talked about him returning to Australia, and I began to understand that if he went back he would find no peace. Even if he managed to overcome the psychological and emotional difficulties of returning to a place where he had lost his wife, family, business, and reputation, Australia would remind him of failure. Bosnia offered him the opportunity to participate in the rebirth of a home and people.

I still worried about him, though. He was a man with grand ideas, but little patience. When he saw an opportunity, he seized it with little care for consequence. In the middle of humanitarian deprivation, this could be an asset. When he recognized a need, he cut every corner to resolve the deprivation. This trait had merit on occasion, but it could not be the norm. I was not sure why, but I did not want to leave him on his own in Bosnia. I had a deep unease he could easily get mixed up in something quick, easy, and illegal. Each day, I saw black Mercedes-Benz cars with Albanian license plates driving the roads of the area. It seemed every form of European corruption was flooding into the country the moment the hostilities ended.

Yet, there was something I missed. I did not understand how deeply Srebrenica affected him. He couldn't leave Bosnia. He wanted justice for the massacre. CARE asked me if I knew of a senior logistician who could work with the United Nations at a small border town between Bosnia and Montenegro. Because of the number of trucks coming into Bosnia with reconstruction materials, the traditional access points were overwhelmed, and the UN wanted to open other routes. I recommended Carey, and he was selected. He was happy, filled with hope, and excited about his salary because it was a senior position, so his pay was far higher than what he earned in his previous humanitarian jobs.

With his first paycheck, he bought a computer and subscribed to a local internet provider. We stayed in contact and exchanged emails several times a week. He was doing well and enjoying his work, but then suddenly he went silent. I sent several messages with no response and tried his UN cell phone without result. After several weeks, I received a message. He had returned to Zenica. The organization was incompetent, and the staff were corrupt, he said. I had heard it all before. I called a colleague and found out he was terminated after three months.

I was angry—I had invested in him, and he betrayed me. All my irritation was about what Carey had done to me. I judged him and found him guilty. I stopped corresponding.

Five months later, I received a call from him. He had returned to Australia and was driving a bus. Each call he raged about the genocide in Srebrenica. For the next several years, he went back and forth to Bosnia. He would stay for several months and then return to Melbourne. Eventually, he started his own home remodeling business. He hired several men and emailed me pictures of different projects. He sounded good, but I kept my distance. I would not engage as a friend. He told me how well things were going for him. He was getting out of debt and had just started a new relationship. He sounded steady and happy. I was skeptical.

Three months later, my phone rang at three in the morning. After a polite inquiry to identify the caller, the voice came back that it was Carey's son. Carey had died by suicide the previous night. His son had found my number in Carey's personal effects. He said his father always respected me, calling me one of his closest friends.

As I lay in the dark trying to process, I remembered Carey telling me his father was a Japanese prisoner of war during WWII. He had died by suicide.

I did not know what to do. I wanted to reach out to several people who knew him, but I had a strange thought. The few friends we had in common were all going through some type of crisis, ranging from divorce to psychological issues associated with Bosnia.

So I did nothing.

I buried it.

I grieved for Carey, but I was ashamed of myself. I could have done more to help him, and I didn't.

That's on me.

CHAPTER 11
RWANDA

"I once spoke to someone who had survived the genocide in Rwanda, and she said to me that there was now nobody left on the face of the earth, either friend or relative, who knew who she was. No one who remembered her girlhood and her early mischief and family lore; no sibling or boon companion who could tease her about that first romance; no lover or pal with whom to reminisce. All her birthdays, exam results, illnesses, friendships, kinships—gone."
—Christopher Hitchens

LEAVING BOSNIA IN LATE SPRING 1996, I went to Cambodia for a short period to help set up a landmine demining program along the border of Thailand but contracted typhoid fever. After several days in a Cambodian clinic in Phnom Penh, I was medevaced to my home in Hawai'i. During my recovery, I followed the crisis in Burundi, Zaire, Tanzania, and Rwanda. It appeared the Rwandan government was stable. However, the intensity of the raids and terrorist activities by the ex-FAR increased, commencing raids into Burundi, Tanzania, and Uganda.

In my comfortable surroundings in Hawai'i, I considered the ethical and moral implications of the UN supporting the militarized refugee camps, and the lack of dedicated humanitarian assistance, but a broader quandary concerned me: Rwanda was a traumatized state emerging from genocide, and Uganda remained an impoverished third world nation, which had survived Idi Amin. Yet, both seemed to have the money and resources to build armies and support rebel groups in Zaire.

In November 1996, CARE asked me to journey to Rwanda. I felt well enough to handle another assignment and accepted their offer. They wanted me to evaluate the safety of their staff while operating in the region and suggest recommendations to help mitigate the growing insecurity. A confluence of events were leading to a flashpoint. The UN was predicting the refugees inside Zaire were going to be pushed further west into the jungles. The government of Zaire was uncomfortable with the ex-FAR control over the eastern part of their country. Rwanda was seeking to displace the Hutu from the camps. Both Rwanda and Uganda were secretly arming, training, and supporting a rebel group inside Zaire to overthrow Mobutu, the military dictator, and president.[1] All of this was occurring in an area the size of West Virginia.

Inside Rwanda, poverty and disease reached epidemic levels. While the bones of those slaughtered still rotted in the sun and tropical climate, a group called the Alliance of Democratic Forces for the Liberation of Congo-Zaire (AFDL) moved against the ex-FAR in Zaire. The AFDL had precise knowledge of its enemy that could only come from sophisticated intelligence.

Although the governments in the US and European Union had ignored the Hutu-led genocide in Rwanda, they were now using their resources to support Rwanda and Uganda to eliminate two problems at the same time—destroying the ex-FAR and overthrowing Mobutu.

With the support of international money and

---

1. John Pomfret, "Rwandans Led Revolt in Congo," *Washington Post*, July 9, 1997. https://www.washingtonpost.com/wp-srv/inatl/longterm/congo/stories/070997.htm (accessed October 16, 2012).

weapons, the first goal was to clear rebel camps along the Rwandan border. As the AFDL captured several perimeter towns beginning in September 1996, with lightning precision, the Hutu militants forced nearly 500,000 refugees into the single camp of Mugungu. By doing so, they sent a message to the world. They had created a hostage situation with half a million people. As the militias gathered their captives in Mugungu, tens of thousands of others fled further into Zaire. Some of these were former Hutu government officials and members of the military who were instrumental in causing and executing the genocide. However, most of the individuals were merely trying to flee the continued violence. The AFDL and Rwandan military forces pursued the militants, and tens of thousands of refugees died from crossfire, exposure to the elements, and starvation.

Throughout the first two weeks of November the ex-FAR and former Rwanda Hutu government officials fled in more significant numbers into the central jungles of Zaire. By November 15, those of us in Kigali, the capital of Rwanda, were receiving messages from NGO staff in Mugungu camps that the refugee population was preparing for a mass exodus. The Tutsi NGO staff members in Rwanda reported plans that the ex-FAR was going to relocate hundreds of thousands of people. The information was chaotic, and no one quite knew what was going to happen.

At approximately the same time, the Tanzanian government announced it was considering the forcible return of 550,000 refugees. As we shuttled from meeting to meeting, we gathered that most of the information was conjecture. If the UN in New York City had useful information they were keeping it to themselves.

As we discussed options, few had journeyed to the border to see the situation for themselves. My patience ended. I obtained a decrepit Nissan pickup truck to drive to the border of Zaire in the town of Gisenyi. I had no idea what I would find but knew the advantage of seeing the situation from Gisenyi firsthand.

After loading my backpack, I had one intent: to get away from the office. Kigali was overrun by government and NGO consultants earning paychecks by talking. Gisenyi seemed to be the right place to go. That was the extent of my planning. I checked the oil in preparation, and as I replaced the dipstick, a voice behind me asked, "Where are you going with that truck?"

When I turned, I recognized a permanent CARE Rwanda staff member named Joan Sullivan.

I barely knew her. The permanent staff was reluctant to embrace me, and I couldn't blame them. My most significant activity to date was drinking beer with a blond journalist from Zimbabwe in a local bar. More consultants appeared daily with no clear mission. The office resources were stretched to capacity and my use of this truck might not have been considered wise.

I replied with my plans, fully expecting Joan to launch into why I shouldn't take the trip, and the truck needed to stay in Kigali. She looked at me and said, "That old thing will never make it. Why don't you take my truck? I'll use the Nissan until you get back?" She had a 1994 Land Rover Defender, a perfect vehicle for central Africa. I appreciated her kindness in the moment, but in the next few weeks, I came to believe it was an act of divine intervention.

The trip from Kigali to Gisenyi took approximately three and a half hours. I was impressed with the two-lane blacktop road. There were few automobiles except UN or NGO vehicles, and a good number of mini-buses crammed with people speeding between the towns and villages. There were few petrol stations and, with fuel supplies short, the prices were exceptionally high.

I had no idea where I would stay in Gisenyi.

Most of the NGOs were in Kigali, but a few lived on the border with Zaire. However, I heard that my friend Mike McDonagh was in the town, and I knew I could sleep at his office. If that was impossible, I had a sleeping bag and would rest in the Land Rover. I intended to spend the afternoon getting a sense of what was going on in the area and return to Kigali the following day.

For much of the trip, I traveled through the highlands of Rwanda full of coffee plantations. The horrific events of genocide and the delicate beauty of the region were impossible to reconcile. Gisenyi itself had a soft splendor. The roads were lined with tall trees and palatial homes with vast lawns and unobstructed views of Lake Kivu. The former German and Belgium administrators of the colony built these idyllic mansions.

I was surprised to find the town teeming with NGO and UN staff. I expected to see a few aid workers, but not in the numbers present.

I stopped in front of the UN administrator's office and asked to see the NGO coordinator. After ensuring I was from CARE and not a journalist, I was escorted into a small office with a Frenchman who was very busy and had little time for me. I had one question before being dismissed. I asked where the Concern office was located. He looked at me with disdain and relief that I was both wasting his time and that I would be gone in a moment. He mumbled that his assistant could give me the information.

I followed the assistant's directions to a tiny building crammed with people, with a Concern logo in the window. Status and project updates covered every inch of the wall. Concern was well into programming in this area, and particularly across the border in Zaire. I noted Mike was following his template from Somalia. Several health-related initiatives provided direct service to the refugees in the camps. Much of it was maternal health care—valuable work in the first world, but lifesaving in refugee camps throughout Africa, where even a minor infection is a death sentence.

Mike had just departed to one of the border crossings to check with the guards and get a sense of what others were reporting. He was told there was some movement on the other side of the boundary.

A Concern staff member called him on his Codan radio. He was at the southern crossing and would wait for me at the checkpoint. It was a ten-minute drive.

Before leaving the CARE office, I made a withdrawal of $5,000 from the office emergency response fund. I didn't know what I would find in Gisenyi, but in the event of aiding in a humanitarian emergency five thousand dollars would be a good start. Traveling with that amount of money in an African nation in 1996, though, made me a vulnerable target. I had the cash wrapped around my waist with saran wrap. I was anxious to get the dollars into Concern's safe.

I asked the administrative officer if I could put $4,900 in her safe to ensure its security. She agreed, and we verified the count of the money, put it in an envelope, and into the safe. She gave me a scribbled receipt on a small scrap of paper. One of the first things a westerner learns in an emerging nation is how we take so much for granted in our affluence. Objects like pens, pencils, paper, and notebooks, which we discard like empty cans of soda, are a precious and guarded possession, protected and never squandered. Using an entire sheet of paper to write a receipt would be an unforgivable waste. I left the office and drove off to find Mike.

As I drove to the rendezvous, I was comforted. I respected Mike's experience and knew any association with him would be a good partnership. When I approached the border, I saw him standing in the distance talking on his radio. The checkpoint was quiet, and the guards were lounging under a tree. The sky was overcast as the clouds piled up with the permanent threat of rain. Thankfully, it was November so the temperatures were moderate. It was the ideal time to be in Rwanda.

I parked my Land Rover and walked toward Mike as he finished his radio call. He gave me a short greeting. This was the first time I had seen him since leaving the Marine Corps. He stepped backed and gave me a long look. Then he ruffled my long hair, and with a broad Irish smile said, "Well, Boyo, you've got the look of a tree hugger. It suits you." It was a good compliment. Then, switching subjects, he said, "They're entering at the northern crossing," which was three miles from us.

I drove to the northern crossing. When I crested a small hill, I stopped and stared in amazement. The northern checkpoint separated the open plains of the volcanic desert in Zaire from the foothills and ridgelines of Rwanda. I could understand why it evolved into a border between nations. It was a clear geographic separation between natural topographic elements. An open area stretched for miles, and as far as I could see, people moved along a road toward Rwanda. There was no vehicular traffic, only masses of people. I later heard this exodus accurately described as a "movement of Biblical proportion." I looked to my right, and just inside the Rwanda border I saw a small building with two flags on it, one from Médecins Sans Frontières/Doctors without Borders (MSF), and the other from Trōcaire, an Irish NGO. Refugees were sitting or lying on the ground nearby. I drove into a small patch of land, which served as a parking lot, and saw Mike's vehicle.

The refugees who surrounded the structure were of two categories. They were either the sick and aged who struggled to the border and collapsed, or women with newborns. When I found Mike, he recounted the stories he heard from the NGO staff at the clinic. In the early hours of the morning, well before dawn, ADFL soldiers who had surrounded and isolated the refugee camps for nearly a week entered the sites and told the people to pack their belongings and start walking toward the border of Rwanda. They were not brutal, but there was no mistake the camps would be cleared. No one was exempt from the orders. If someone was too infirm to walk, they would be carried or left to die. MSF and Trōcaire were already overwhelmed by those seeking help. Mike called his office in Gisenyi and directed all staff to stop what they were doing and come to the border to assist.

Mike and I joined the movement and walked down the middle of the trek in the opposite direction. The only sound was the rhythmic tramp of feet, pots and pans clanging together while being carried by the returnees, and the occasional cry of a child. Our presence seemed to reassure the people that, at least for this portion of their passage, they would be safe. It was not difficult to imagine their fear, as months earlier these Hutu people fled Rwanda because of the genocide. Now they were being herded back to a country controlled by people who survived the slaughter. Even if they were able to cross the border safely, they expected to be rounded up and murdered.

We walked for several miles into the crowd. No one made eye contact. I did not see any emotion other than strained determination. This was a group of people whose spirits were crushed and still they marched, forced into the possibility of another horror.

I realized this is what Jewish people may have felt as they were marched into the Nazi death camps. Each step took them deeper into the final consequences of someone else's madness. I was ashamed of being a spectator. I had the privilege to climb onto an airplane and return to the world of Big Macs and the Simpsons.

When Mike and I returned to the border, the crowds were dispersing and starting the evening cooking fires. There was little talk. It did not take long to realize the wood along the route would quickly disappear. In the twilight, I stood on top of my Land Rover to take in the sight. As far as I could see, people were beginning to bed down for the night. Looking at the vastness of this humanity beneath the Milky Way, I realized my insignificance and the transitory nature of my life.

The next morning, I met Mike in Gisenyi. He knew I was sleeping in the Land Rover and invited me to stay with him. We pulled an old mat into his room, and I put my pack and sleeping bag on the floor. I had a satellite phone, which in 1996 was a rare commodity. The design made it look like a laptop computer. I had to disconnect the "screen" portion and find the right angle to access the satellite. There were not many civilian communication satellites circling the Earth.

Consequently, there were limited periods to communicate with the phone. I managed to determine the proper settings and called the CARE office in Kigali. After reporting, they acknowledged they knew about the movement, but I sensed they were skeptical of the numbers I was quoting. I was not offended as I still had trouble comprehending the size of this movement myself. I had conversed with the MSF facility on the border, and they were reporting 10,000 people crossing per hour.

When I arrived in Rwanda, I met a young Rwandan program officer, Michel Simbikang. He was in his late twenties with a degree in civil engineering from a university in France and returned to Rwanda to assist with reconstruction. His family had fled to Uganda when he was a boy. He had limited memories of the country, and many of his relatives had disappeared. He was visiting the central CARE office from the town of Ruhengeri, which was approximately thirty-six miles from Gisenyi. As he described his rural development program, I was impressed with his pride and enthusiasm. He told me his project involved building a gravel road from a local village to a water site. He had a dump truck to haul gravel and two small container trucks to transport the day workers to and from the job site.

The mass movement of so many people in such a short period had overwhelmed the capacities of the Rwandan government, the UN, and the humanitarian organizations. There were not enough vehicles or trained staff. I wanted to assist with the crisis, but I did not have workers or equipment.

I asked the CARE office to arrange for the

project manager and his crew, along with their trucks and tools, to meet me at the UN office, located along the road halfway between Gisenyi and Ruhengeri. I said I would wait for them between noon and four, two days hence.

Over the next days, the different humanitarian organizations solidified their roles into a coordinated effort, and our plans became a blend of expertise and resources. The first decision was building thirteen medical clinics along the road to Ruhengeri. The Government of Rwanda was providing trucks and buses in Ruhengeri to transport the returnees to their home villages, but getting to these pickup stations had to be on foot. Moving trucks along the road was impossible. Any vehicular trip through this mass of people could only be accomplished at less than two miles per hour.

The clinics were placed every two to three miles, depending on the terrain. Médecins Sans Frontières had the resources to build and maintain ten stations, and Mike McDonough's organization, Concern, could handle the final three. Each station consisted of three or four tents in a small compound. Each tent had a floor, which helped to keep out the rats, vermin, and insects. They were covered with plastic sheeting and replaced several times a day. There were no beds or mats, and the sick and dying quietly awaited assistance. Each clinic had one nurse. The physicians traveled between each facility throughout the day and night.

Diarrhea and vomiting were common. The MSF and Concern staff worked to keep the areas as sanitary as possible, but it was a constant battle. I recall watching an unaccompanied person lying on the floor, quietly dying while a nurse held her hand. In another tent, I heard a newborn baby. The sight of a death replaced by a new and vocal birth seemed a symbol of renewal.

The only way to accommodate new arrivals was the hourly task of removing the dead. Off to the side of each compound, a makeshift fence woven from banana leaves denoted a mortuary. Despite the continual bustle, each of these areas had a sense of quiet dignity. Those who lost a loved one quietly grieved as the migration moved around them.

Only the unaccompanied bodies were left behind. The others were absorbed into the movement like a leaf carried by a river. There were clinical and pragmatic reasons for families not to carry the dead within the movement, but the magnitude of this event did not allow for those nuances. The water and sanitation requirements exceeded the scope and capacity of every agency, organization, and governmental institution. The fledgling Rwandan government had to allow the UN and NGOs to handle the event. I saw some food delivered from USAID and the European community, and I do not want to denigrate that assistance. However, these institutions and governments maintained the same detachment from Rwanda that had allowed the massacre of 800,000 people. This was Rwanda's problem—that was their mindset.

At best, the dead were laid to the side, at worst they remained on the road and the movement walked around them. The numbers of dead were impossible to count, but there were hundreds. Many elderly and women died, but the worst sights were the children and babies.

The sanitation problems were priority. There were less than 150 humanitarian workers in the area, and double that number of media people. Although the world knew about the movement, the sky was not filled with NATO helicopters bringing supplies. I am still amazed at the reluctance of any government to assist. The only way provisions reached the area was through UN trucks moving at one to three miles per hour through the crowds. The distribution sites were sparse, and the numbers of trucks were few.

On November 19, I went to the rendezvous point to await the arrival of the CARE trucks and staff. It was a cloudy day, interspersed with rain showers that dumped torrents in the countryside. I sat on top of the Land Rover and wrote some notes in a small notebook. At approximately three in the afternoon, I heard a strange sound coming closer to me. It sounded like cheering, but I dismissed that as fanciful thinking because the returnees barely made a sound as they trekked toward Ruhengeri. But it was cheering. I saw the first of the three CARE trucks moving toward me. It was the dump truck and two cargo vehicles. The CARE staff was sitting on the hood and on top of the trucks as they helped guide the vehicles safely through the crowd. As they crawled along the road, the returnees knew CARE and were cheering their arrival.

At that moment, I had never been prouder of being part of an organization. I looked at the progression and understood what it felt like to be part of something that counted. The arrival of the CARE vehicles was as pragmatic as it was symbolic. These terrified individuals saw the presence of CARE, which gave them a sense of support from an international entity concerned about what happened to them.

Mike directed his small convoy into the UN compound. At the five o'clock meeting that evening to update the staff on the next day's activities, we announced the presence of our trucks and tools. We decided to focus on water and sanitation.

Our colleague from Oxfam offered us a six-thousand-liter water bladder to mount on our dump truck and fill it with potable water. We planned to drive continuously through the day and night along the road between Gisenyi and Ruhengeri. The truck would move at one mile per hour so people could walk to the rear of the vehicle and fill their water containers with fresh water.

As a group, we moved the bladder onto our dump truck and filled it with water. We were elated. It worked! The next morning, our driver pulled onto the road and started toward Ruhengeri. The drivers would rotate on a schedule to ensure constant coverage. Our little truck never faltered. Today, if I could find it, I would put it in a museum. The UN station had a petrol tank and allowed us to refuel as required. This initiative, with its simplicity and resourcefulness, remains one of my most valued memories.

Encouraged by the success of our water re-supply activity, we decided to replicate it with the distribution of high protein biscuits. The biscuits are distributed during humanitarian emergencies because they are easy to transport and can sustain life and energy until more substantial types of food arrive. They can be crushed and mixed with water to feed small children and infants. We loaded the supplies and joined the water distribution movement. Occasionally, I joined our staff as they passed the provisions to the people who came to the rear of the biscuit vehicle. The returnees accepted what was handed to them and made no requests for additional rations. There was a sense of cooperation among the travelers.

As good as we felt about the water and biscuit distribution, the problems surrounding sanitation were critical. At every point on the road, under a cloud of thick and stifling humidity, was the pungent smell of tons of human feces decaying in the heat.

The quickest way to mitigate the sanitation problems is the most obvious: dig latrines. We had a truck and tools, but I needed more money. The US Department of State's Office of Foreign Disaster Assistance (OFDA) in Gisenyi were offering direct grants for assistance projects. I found the OFDA staff in a small room in the UN compound and outlined my plan to build latrines. They agreed and gave me $25,000 with a written agreement on one sheet of paper. With the additional cash added to my $5,000 from CARE, we were ready to make a difference. Our greatest resource was labor. The men who were part of the trek were more than willing to earn five dollars a day to dig the necessary holes. As we built the facilities, we put up blue tarps to provide privacy, and separated the areas for men and women. It was rudimentary, but effective.

Our most significant problem was digging the appropriate six feet into the solidified volcanic magnum. Consequently, the pits filled up each day, attracting disease-bearing animals and insects. Every day, we spent as much time closing latrines as we did digging new ones. Our efforts earned us a nickname throughout the UN and humanitarian community: the "Shit Kings of Rwanda." We were proud of the title. In approximately two weeks, we dug more than a thousand latrines.

As the days passed, the dead bodies became a significant problem. I had the financial means to hire a group of remarkable men. In the evening, with a closed truck, they made their way along the route to collect the dead and take them to a temporary mortuary established by the government in Ruhengeri. Although the vehicle had no distinctive markings, everyone seemed to know its purpose and directed the men to a corpse. On most occasions, the people who identified the remains would load the man, woman, child, or baby onto the truck. What a grim process that became—an action devoid of emotion. Even the international media did not document the process.

By the fourth day, Michel from the UN and I had a routine. We traveled late in the day from site to site inspecting the work and paying the laborers. I routinely carried $1,000, but never feared being robbed or assaulted. I was not naive, but the collective fear of the returnees forced them to keep a low profile. The last thing any of them wanted was to draw attention.

After Michel and I had inspected a set of new latrines by an MSF clinic, I talked to several of the workers, paid their daily wage, turned to walk to the Land Rover, and collapsed. The next thing I recall is lying on the floor of the MSF tent with an IV in my arm and a nurse asking me my name. I was exhausted, dehydrated, and starving. For days, I was catching quick naps in the rear of the Land Rover, eating high protein biscuits, and drinking as much coffee as I could find in the clinics or different UN stations. I was unshaven and filthy. The French nurse told me in broken English I needed to rest and drink as much water as I could find.

Then she said she needed my space on the floor, and I should go back to Gisenyi. I could see Michel nodding in agreement.

We made our way to Gisenyi and found Mike McDonagh in his office. He told me I looked like "shite." He picked up my gear and took it to his room. He wanted me to take his bed, but I found my sleeping mat. Over the previous days, several of our friends and acquaintances from other NGOs had arrived, and while searching for their own accommodation, Mike gave up his rooms to house them.

My satellite phone battery had been dead for days, and I had not contacted the office in Kigali or the CARE Headquarters in Atlanta. While in the field, CNN and the BBC interviewed me several times. I knew CARE had a sense of what I was doing, but I needed to check in with them directly. I saw Mike had a satellite phone on the rooftop. I found a plug and crawled onto the roof, setting my phone in the same general direction as Mike's. It would take several hours for the battery to charge, and I was famished.

I walked downstairs and toward Mike's office. From the hallway, I heard a soft, west Cork lilt, "Well, this is another fine mess, me brother has gotten me into..." It was probably the result of fatigue, dehydration, and stress, but I felt my throat clutch and eyes swell with tears in recognizing the voice. My close friend, Norman Sheehan, was standing in the doorway. His next words were, "You look like dog shite—what you need is a beer." The last thing on this planet I needed was alcohol, but it was Norman.

Next to the Concern office was a small but booming cafe. When we sat down, Norman joked Michael was probably part owner. Sheehan and his team of two had just arrived that morning. They were using Michael's accommodations until they could find their own place. As we talked, the afternoon showers began, and for the next hour there was a constant deluge of rain and thunder. I was grateful to be in the cafe.

After talking with Norman, I made my way to Mike's room. I knew I should call the Kigali CARE office and give them an update, but I was exhausted. I did not have the energy to answer any questions, so I took the luxury of stripping to my shorts and T-shirt and crawled into the sleeping bag. When I woke the next day it was past noon, and I had slept for fifteen hours. I have always been a light sleeper but had no recollection of being disturbed when the others came and went from the room.

Walking downstairs, I had a detached, floating feeling. I had missed the morning UN meeting, and made my way to the Concern office to receive an update from one of the staff who attended. This was day six of the repatriation, and the exodus was not slowing. I felt guilty. My team was hard at work, and I had just enjoyed approximately twenty-four hours away from the movement.

Both Michael and Norman were at different way stations. I filled my water jugs and the vehicle's petrol tank and started down the road to find Michael and the rest of my crew. I needed to take better care of myself. I started this emergency at a sprint, thinking all we had to do was put our heads down, power through it, and it would be over soon. But this was not the case. The people kept coming.

Driving along the shoreline overlooking Lake Kivu, I pulled into a roadside stop to look at the water. The sun cast a dazzling array of colors across its quiet swells. I noticed a beautiful white building with a well-maintained lawn overlooking the lake. I had passed it several times and assumed it was the home of a local official or expatriate. For the first time I saw a sign, which identified it as the Stipp Hotel. It looked like a peaceful place to stay but was probably fully occupied. Passing its entrance, a saying my mother used came into my head, "If you never ask the question, the answer is always, no." I turned into the parking lot.

The hotel's foyer had beautiful wood paneling, high ceilings, and tile floors. I anticipated damage from the genocide, but it appeared the extremes of the violence had passed this site. There were many foreigners in the lobby, and I assumed most were journalists and UN staff. When I reached the attendant, I made my request for a room. She hesitated for a moment and asked what organization I was with. I replied, "It is the international humanitarian organization, CARE." She said she had two vacant rooms, one reserved, but the other I could look at before making a decision.

"No," I said. "I'm sure it will be fine." As I registered, she told me of their strict rules about noise and additional guests. Any other occupants had to be approved by the hotel.

When I entered the room, I opened the curtains to a panorama of the lake. A giant magnolia tree grew at one side of the lawn. The entire setting was peaceful. The scene evoked a conflict between conscience and consciousness. It was possible that on the lawn in front of me people were butchered with machetes, but I had to step away from those thoughts.

In the early afternoon, after arranging my room, a light lunch, and waiting for the proper time of day for the satellite to be in place to use my phone. I went through the triangulation process to find it. I was always grateful when it worked and dialed my boss, Marge Tsitouris, in Atlanta. She answered on the second ring. We talked about my health, the status of the repatriation, and what I was doing in association with other humanitarian organizations. She mentioned she saw me on TV broadcasts and counseled me to wear a CARE T-shirt or cap during a TV interview. I agreed and looked down at my T-shirt, which was now the only one I owned. It read "Irish Concern."

Marge said that the interview I gave to the Associated Press Radio Network was excellent and appreciated the detail I provided regarding CARE's engagement in the repatriation effort, and then laughed at how I described the sanitation efforts. She received accolades and appreciation from CARE's external communications department. Marge told me to stay for as long as necessary, but to check in more often. As I placed the satellite phone handset into its cradle, I realized I had no idea what interview she was talking about. I never had a call with AP Radio News.

I found Michel and went over the work

accomplished in the past twenty-four hours. The water and sanitation trucks were operating non-stop, and the latrine building and filling efforts continued expanding. We now had subgroups and divided the route into specific areas of responsibility. Some of the men who began the trek from Goma would remain within a specified area to earn a daily wage. The amount of work was easily verifiable, but it took an entire day to make the rounds to inspect the labor and pay the workers. It was not a sustainable system, but it worked for a short period.

That evening, I returned to the café. I found Michael and asked about Norman. He said he was settling into a small lodging for himself and his team and gave me directions to a nearby building on a side street. He mentioned I had to walk around the structure and enter through the back gate.

I set off and found the building. It was an old factory that had been burned and looted over the past several years. Walking around both sides, I finally found a gap where a gate used to be. I was convinced I had not found the correct building but continued walking to the rear of the structure. As I turned the corner, I gagged. In front of me was a cesspool approximately forty square feet across.

Old boards formed a walkway around the pit. On the other side of this pool was a building with a curtain hanging over the doorway. I could see the light from the inside. I walked to the door and hollered, "Norman are you in there?" He opened the cloth and said, "Welcome to our wee home." He introduced me to the two new arrivals, and explained that after two days of searching, this was the only facility he could find in the city. There was a single light bulb dangling from the ceiling, and their beds were pads on several boards supported by concrete blocks. The returnees were probably sleeping in a better environment.

I told Norman about my good luck at the Stipp Hotel and its policy that each additional person cost thirty-five dollars. After a short discussion, we loaded their gear into my Land Rover, and I had three roommates. On the way to the hotel, I mentioned my conversation with my boss about the AP Radio News interview. "Not only do I not remember it," I said, "but I was also accused of adopting an Irish accent while in a state of sleepwalking." Norman chuckled and relayed what happened.

During the night, as I was sleeping on Michael's bedroom floor, my satellite phone rang. Michael thought it was his, but realized it was the

CARE handset. He answered, intending to field a CARE office call so I could continue sleeping. The caller identified herself as a member of AP Radio News and wanted to do a phone interview with Bob Macpherson, and Michael decided he knew enough about what I was doing to field the questions, and if he didn't, he could make a reasonable guess. So, he identified himself as me and handled the interview. Anyone who ever met Mike knows his gift for the gab is legendary. On a moment's notice, he could deliver the State of the Union address before the US Congress and receive a standing ovation.

Over the next week, we continued our work, but the number of people returning each day diminished quickly. By the fourteenth day, only ten to twenty people were crossing the border. The road from Gisenyi to Ruhengeri became an easy drive. On my trip to meet colleagues from CARE in Ruhengeri, I was shocked by the land's devastation. Over the centuries, the hillsides of Rwanda were stripped to allow for the growth of tea and coffee. The terrain was green, but it was covered with horticulture, not trees. Now, a blanket of brown covered the land. Everything was gone except the vestiges of human passage. There were empty boxes, old pots, broken carts, and discarded plastic tarps. I knew I had caused some of this spoilage by cutting any tree we could find to support the latrines; it was a case of sacrificing the environment for the greater good of humans. Not an easy reconciliation, but it worked.

After a meeting with the CARE staff who would be engaged in long-term assistance with the returnees, I returned to Gisenyi. I spent several days ensuring the men who assisted us were paid and coordinating with the Office of Foreign Disaster Assistance to properly account for the $25,000 they provided during the emergency. Most of that coordination took place at the cafe over increasing numbers of bottles of beer.

The emergency had ended. I was hanging on because of the brief moments when there was no posturing, hypothesizing, or dissecting. All the work and decisions were on me. People can read about a crisis, watch it in a movie, or listen to an account, but until you are in a crisis, no one fully understands. You cannot rationalize it. You either act or you don't. If you engage, you cannot go back. It is a moment of purity. I crossed the threshold from ego and self-importance to understanding the tenets of humanism.

The real world was catching up with us, though. My colleagues were getting messages from their headquarters saying, "It's all over. Where are you?" I loaded my Land Rover, said my goodbyes, and started the drive to Kigali. As usual, it was cloudy with intermittent rain. The roads were empty except for an occasional convoy of UN trucks or a passing NGO vehicle headed to Ruhengeri. I stopped in the little town of Tare, purchased several cans of Coke, and drove on. After several minutes, I pulled to the side of the road and started to cry. In fact, it was deeper than crying. I was sobbing.

It was an out-of-body experience, as if I was watching myself in a movie. I was curious: What's wrong with him? He is not injured. No one close to him was killed or injured. It was a very safe event. But here he is, sitting alone in a vehicle, sobbing.

Oh, I see, he feels guilty.

Why?

I don't know.

I still wonder.

I did my part.

Was I afraid of returning to my normal life?

I knew my constant immersion into humanitarian disasters was neither healthy nor sustainable. Why was I doing it? What was wrong with me?

Was Rwanda my refuge? A place where I could hide?

I returned to the CARE Headquarters in Kigali. Many of the same people I met two weeks earlier were still there and many new staff had arrived. They were pitching tents in the courtyard of the office compound, preparing to begin their work in shelter, health, water, sanitation, and advocacy.

It was their turn, and I was grateful for their presence.

I searched for Joan to return her Land Rover and was told she was at her office in the town of Gitarama. I was not in the frame of mind to stay in Kigali or sleep in a tent, so I called Joan and asked to come to Gitarama.

The drive was pleasant. A few returnees walked along the roadside. On the surface, all looked calm, but it was impossible to believe there would not be wholesale retribution against the Hutu when the world's attention shifted from Rwanda.

I found Joan in her office and took a quick tour of the facility. Her primary focus was on HIV/AIDS prevention. As she detailed her work, she mentioned the infection rate in her area was approximately 33 percent. I was stunned. In 1996, HIV/AIDS was a death sentence. It was hard to imagine one out of three people with whom I interacted were HIV positive.

In addition to her work with HIV/AIDS prevention, Joan collaborated with the World Food Program (WFP) to establish and administer food distribution centers for the returnees. She asked me to assist, and I was excited to be engaged with something so essential, and grateful to remain in Rwanda as there was more I wanted to contribute to the emergency response. I was not ready to return to the world of Monday night football in America.

What I witnessed was beyond description. Nearly a million people full of fear, without resources, and returning to a country where they are a marked people, all fleeing down a narrow two-lane blacktop road. I knew I had to use Joan's offer to regain my own balance after so much drama and intensity.

We spent several days coordinating with the WFP. The primary products for distribution were cooking oil, peas, maize, and lentils. Each day, the amount of food readied for delivery amazed me. Finally, aid seemed to be arriving.

On the first day of distribution, we arrived at the site at five in the morning. The WFP trucks were already in place. We assumed the distribution would be well attended but were unprepared for the number of people already queued. There were six separate lines, and each was approximately 200 meters, or more than two US football fields long. The morning was already hot and humid. Joan realized the impossibility of managing such a crowd. She sent for assistance from all her staff and asked them to bring others.

As I watched her staff arrive and engage with the returnees, most of whom were women, I remembered the UN report that estimated nearly a quarter million women were raped during the six months of genocide.

Yet, at this moment, the men and women who experienced the brutality were assisting the Hutu. There was no idle chatter or people greeting old neighbors and friends. It was safe to assume many of them recognized one another, but they were not calling out indictments and recrimination. They handled the distribution with efficiency and respect. I watched amid a pile of peas, in the burning sun, amazed.

For the next several weeks while working throughout the central part of the country, I saw no open hostility. However, the leadership of Rwanda had to address the atrocities and hold people accountable for what happened, while trying not to rip the nation apart. I listened to my international colleagues discuss the requirements and outline the difficulties of asserting law over such an experience. I came to believe it was an impossible task.

But my thoughts were naïve and simplistic. In my own bubble of white, American privilege, I was judging a culture far older and more knowledgeable than my own. My experience taught me the only way justice could be served was to find a legal way to balance the scales. I had no idea how justice could be achieved without legal retribution.

The resolution came from the custom of village courts known as *Gacaca*. The name means, "Resting and relaxing on a green lawn in the Rwandan homestead." It is a time when family members or neighbors meet to discuss issues directly affecting them. The Gacaca trials were held in public, which gave the survivors the opportunity to confront the offenders in full view of their families and neighbors. The defendants faced many penalties. The worst was a life sentence of hard labor in prison. However, most of the convicted men and women were given shorter punishments in exchange for making a full confession and seeking forgiveness from those they brutalized.

The Gacaca court system lasted for

approximately a decade, with locally elected judges hearing approximately 1.9 million cases. Phil Clark captures the essence of how this worked in his book, *The Gacaca Courts, Post-Genocide Justice and Reconciliation in Rwanda*. He describes the Gacaca courts as:

A way of doing intimate justice for what was a very intimate crime. It was incredibly successful at coming to terms with the very specific crimes committed in communities.... The courts closed in 2012. The process of reconciliation continues today, but informally. Nearly all the perpetrators convicted through Gacaca now live alongside survivors.[2]

How Rwanda found peace during chaos is remarkable. Its healing process has been gentle. The world does not know about it because it lost interest and moved on to the next crisis. On every other continent, the combination of evil circumstances would cripple the state for decades. Indeed, there may be exceptions, but most cultures would seek rapid and extreme justice.

The scope of that understanding came to me on

---

2. Phil Clark, *The Gacaca Courts, Post-Genocide Jusice and Reconciliation in Rwanda: Justice without Lawyers* (Cambridge: Cambridge University Press, 2010).

a dreary, rainy afternoon, as I parked my vehicle at the bottom of a hill and walked up a dirt track, which had turned to mud. I was at the Murambi Technical School, now known as the Murambi Genocide Memorial Centre. In late 1994, it was little more than a deserted building with a grim history. It is the site of a massacre beyond the scope of what the human mind can comprehend.

When the killings started, the Tutsis in the region tried hiding in and around a local church, but the bishop and mayor lured them to the Technical School. They promised them the French troops would protect them. With that assurance, more people rushed to the area until 65,000 Tutsis had gathered. Once there, all water was cut off, and the area was blocked to ensure no food came to the people. When the men, women, and children became too feeble to fight, they were attacked by the Hutu Interahamwe militia on April 21, 1994. The French soldiers who were in the area and witnessed the preparation for the assault on the school had disappeared.

Approximately 45,000 Tutsi were murdered at the school in a single day. Nearly all of those who escaped were killed the next day as they tried to hide in a nearby church. According to a man I met at the site, the French brought heavy equipment after the massacre to dig pits and bury thousands of bodies.

Walking around the school, I saw the survivors stacking skulls as a reminder to the Rwandan people of what occurred. But I am an American. I can flee to my couch to watch the next episode of Seinfeld. This was Africa.

I had my own reckoning. I claimed to be a humanitarian worker and journeyed to these places to do good, but I was separate from it. I cared, I listened, I wrote stories to convey an emotion and solicit attention to the crisis, but it had not happened to me. I was removed from it, and in the end I knew I would get on an airplane and leave it behind. Rwanda was not my home.

No matter how hard I tried, I remained a bystander to injustice. Here, I witnessed total evil facilitated by the refusal of governments with the power and strength to stop it. I believed if I came to Murambi to this museum it might open a door in me, allowing me to walk away from Rwanda psychologically. But I knew the genocide was embedded in me. No one can be exposed to the massacre of nearly one million people and not have that evil invade your mind like a virus. I read and listened to the history and accounts of the political and tribal feuds, rivalries, and foreign interventions that caused the hatred. I understood the words, but I could not grasp how human beings could slaughter nearly a million people in six months.

If the people of Rwanda could build a memorial to the genocide as part of their healing, maybe I could find my own way home from this site. But what I found unsettled me. There were too many stacks of human skulls to count. People quietly and lovingly cleaned the skulls and placed them on the small pyramids. I watched from a distance, but I might as well have been ten thousand miles away. By culture and nationality, I could not relate. The hatred that generated the genocide and the forgiveness that resulted in peace were both outside my comprehension.

If we are forged by what we see and experience, we are ruined by what we ignore. There are times these exposures become too much. Humans are glorious animals, but we are limited. We can perceive, analyze, and create, but also ignore and destroy. Our curse and blessing is our free will. If we carry events too deeply, they will destroy us. I look for light, and on occasion, find it, but too often it is clouded by the skulls of Murambi.

Although all is not lost, I am reminded by those I've met. Even in the fog of wicked brutality, humans emanate brilliant and cosmic bursts of decency, caring, and kindness. I know this because I continue to meet the women and men who are the keepers of this light.

CHAPTER 12
SOMALIA II

*"Fear...
has no decency,
respects no law or convention,
shows no mercy."*
—Yann Martel

IN APRIL 1997, I LANDED AT A DIRT airfield known as K 50, fifty kilometers from Mogadishu. The Mogadishu airport was closed due to fighting and significant damage to the runways. CARE had a programming office in the capital, and its administrative office was in Nairobi, Kenya, because it was too dangerous for internationals to locate to Somalia permanently.

The fighting between clans throughout

southern Somalia and Mogadishu had become so intense that CARE had to decide whether to continue programming or suspend operations. They wanted me to visit the area and make a recommendation about the continuance of CARE's activities. Without a doubt, Somalia was the last place on earth I wanted to see.

I was apprehensive. The last time I was in Mogadishu, I had the strength of the US Marines surrounding me. Now I had to depend on the good reputation of CARE and the respect our staff had from all parties associated with the violence.

Kidnappings of international staff were becoming prevalent. CARE had a no ransom policy. While most aid agencies had a public policy of "no payments," they would quietly negotiate a settlement. CARE's stated position was, in fact, their operational policy: they would not make any type of compensation. If I were taken, it would be a long process of intermediaries petitioning for my release.

On disembarking the plane, I walked to a small wooden building that served as an immigration site. It was primarily a means for the local warlord to collect twenty dollars from each arrival. As I waited for the clerk to return my documents, he looked at a piece of paper lying on his desk, and said, "Colonel Macpherson, General Aidid sends his personal welcome on your return to our country."

After General Mohamed Aidid died because of a gunshot wound in August 1996, his son Hussein Farrah Aidid returned from the United States to take his place as the leader of the clan. Within days of his arrival, he declared himself president of Somalia with the promotion to the rank of general.

Hussein Aidid was the second son of one of his father's four wives. When his mother divorced the warlord, he emigrated with her and five siblings to southern California in 1978 and graduated from high school three years later. He enlisted in the United States Marine Corps and deployed to Somalia during Operation Restore Hope. At the time, he was the only U.S. Marine who spoke Somali.[1] Additionally, the U.S. State Department hoped his presence would help smooth America's relations with his father. After three weeks, their association soured when Aidid realized his son's loyalties were to the United States and not to a Somali clan.

I was shocked. There were no protocols to hide

---

1. E. A. Cohen, and T. E. Ricks, "Making the Corps," *Foreign Affairs* 77, no. 2 (1998): 148, doi:10.2307/20048815.

my identity, and no formal visa applications to arrive in Somalia. You flew to K 50 on an International Red Cross or UN flight and ensured someone was there to meet you. Hussein Aidid's reach into the CARE office in Mogadishu was deep. Using my military rank and title to welcome me indicated that Hussein knew I was in Somalia.

A CARE driver met me at the airstrip and loaded my pack into the old Toyota. As we began the long drive to Mogadishu, I tried chatting with him, but my greeting from Aidid made him uncomfortable. He made it clear he would drop me at the Green Line, where I would walk across no-man's-land and be met by another CARE driver on Aidid's side of the zone.

When I left Mogadishu in 1993, the city was devastated. Now, four years later, it was destroyed. Every building had significant damage. Through the large shell holes in the side of the structures, I saw people living in open spaces. Each room housed a family. There were endless numbers of naked children playing in the streets and the old courtyards.

Arriving at the Green Line, there were two groups of armed militias lounging in the shade of destroyed buildings, glaring at one another across an old strip of road. They were separated by twenty meters of open space punctuated by open cavities from exploded mortar and artillery shells. Both sides had four Toyota pickup trucks with fifty-caliber machine guns mounted in the beds. The fifty-caliber shell can shoot down aircraft and cut a building or human into pieces in seconds.

The Green Line divided two of Somalia's warring clans. It was a physical border between the territory controlled by Aidid and his principal rival, Ali Mahdi Mohamed, who had recently been recognized by the international community as the president of Somalia in place of Aidid. However, Ali Mahdi was unable to exert his authority beyond parts of the capital. He had no army, there was no police force or legislative body. His title was in name only. He commanded a militia, which was used against Aidid.

For me to cross this boundary required a request from CARE to both sides for an agreed transit. Thus, my fate depended on a "safe-passage" promise between two notorious warlords.

I wished someone had mentioned this process to me in Nairobi.

Crossing the Green Line was precarious. Vehicles were not allowed to traverse the zone. Arriving at the makeshift barricades, the driver stopped, unloaded my backpack, and indicated I should walk across the open road between the warring sides, then he was back in the vehicle and gone. I couldn't blame him. I turned to look at the scene and saw people glowering at me from all sides. I was a white westerner. Regardless of clan affiliation, everyone around me believed I represented the foreign interventions responsible for most of the misery in Somalia.

As much as the Somalis despised rival clans, they all agreed the state of their nation was a result of western and European pillage. In the past, northern Somalia, called Somaliland, was a protectorate of Great Britain, and the southern part of the country was a colony of Italy. Neither of the European countries invested in Somalia, but rather used their power to extract its natural resources. When Somalia gained independence, it fell under the influence of the Soviet Union and later the US and NATO. That transition was the fuel that started much of the fighting that still exists in the country.

As I pulled on my pack, an old Somali man approached me and indicated it was "safe" for me to cross. Two things went through my mind. The first was, "What in the hell am I doing here?" and the second, "Am I really going to do this?"

Starting my walk, the guns on both sides

followed me. These were not well-trained soldiers—they were ill-disciplined gunmen, mostly young, around sixteen years old. Bandanas wrapped their heads and sunglasses covered their eyes. They wore T-shirts with logos from Virginia Beach, the YMCA, and the US Marine Corps. I was nothing more than an ant that could be casually stomped on by a group of children playing on a hot summer day.

While crossing, I silently repeated, "Hail Mary, full of Grace…" I thought about a quote by Albert Einstein, "Insanity [is] doing the same thing over and over again and expecting different results." Undoubtedly, building a world order based on the size and power of weapons seemed to meet Einstein's equation.

When I reached the other side, a boy armed with a Kalashnikov rifle jabbed me in the stomach with its muzzle and demanded to examine my passport. Even in the middle of a passage bordering on a scene from Dante's Inferno, someone is still interested in the administrative side of a government process. The boy examined my passport, noted the entry stamp from K 50, but surprised me when he asked, "Why did you visit Israel?" My first thought was, "Oh shit." I had made a trip to West Bank and Gaza for CARE earlier in the year and had an Israeli entry and exit visa stamp. I said I had visited Palestine where CARE works. I pointed to the entry and exit stamps from Gaza. He seemed satisfied and allowed me to pass. I turned to find two CARE colleagues waiting for me.

On our way to the CARE compound, I saw nothing untouched by bombs and gunfire. The streets were full of shooters ranging from twelve to fifty years old. Toyota pickups with a 50-caliber anti-aircraft machine gun mounted in the truck's bed, called "Technicals" raced up and down the streets. The spots where I remembered rows of snacks, cigarettes, Khat, and fruit kiosks were gone.

The CARE compound was on a side street with high walls surrounding it. The structure served as both an office and residence for visiting staff. There were no guards because CARE rented the compound from Hussein Aidid, whose headquarters were on the same street. The resident staff made a single request of me: do not appear on the balcony outside my room on the second floor. My presence might incite a militiaman high on khat to use me for target practice.

Somalia remained a perilous place for international aid workers, resulting in a debate in the humanitarian community and UN. Many organizations felt it required too many accommodations with the warlords and withdrew. CARE did not, and with the assistance of local NGOs, began programs in education, health clinics, and feeding centers. The desperate need in Somalia remained, and CARE's continued engagement saved lives.

Every time our vehicle departed the compound, one or two of Aidid's technicals followed us. Hussein Aidid was uncomfortable having me on his turf. My security and freedom rested on his whim. However, the most significant impact was on the CARE staff and the people we were attempting to aid. The presence of Aidid's gunmen trailing CARE vehicles scared people into not attending a food distribution or other assistance efforts. The most telling sign of this fear was at the schools. Children who would typically pour out of their classroom to sing and play did not venture outside of their buildings.

Aidid made his point. He wanted me out of Mogadishu. I had been a ranking US Marine officer who interacted with his rival, Ali Mahdi Mohamed, and other warlords when I attempted to ensure the safe passage of aid through their territories. Although Hussein Aidid understood the workings of the Marine Corps, it was difficult for him to accept that a former US Marine infantry colonel would return to Somalia as a humanitarian worker. He made the CARE staff aware he believed I was a CIA spy using humanitarian work as my cover to undermine his authority and work with his enemies.

The longer I remained, the more dangerous my presence would be for the CARE staff. Although I wanted to see Dr. Hawa, I felt it was too dangerous for her to be associated with me. I asked a colleague to contact her and explain my situation with Aidid and let her know I would not see her. Her reply was quick and direct. She insisted on seeing me and would be glad to send her own vehicle to fetch me. The CARE staff assured her they were happy to take me to her camp.

The following morning, we set off for Hawa's compound. For the first time since I was in Mogadishu, an Aidid vehicle did not accompany us. The road to Hawa's compound was in the opposite direction of the Green Line. The drive to Lafoole reflected the same destruction I witnessed in Mogadishu. The countryside had always been sparsely populated, but now all the structures were abandoned or destroyed. The asphalt road was churned to rubble, pocketed by an infinite number of craters from mortar and artillery rounds.

The continuing proliferation of sophisticated weapons in Somalia amazed me. Arms are expensive, but the real cost of a weapons system is the ammunition. Both artillery and mortar rounds cost hundreds of dollars. Throughout Somalia, they seemed to be used without concern. These weapons came from stockpiles of armaments provided by the US and the Soviet Union, both of whom were key arms suppliers at different times during the Cold War. Other munitions were provided by Libya, Ethiopia, Italy, some Gulf states, and Kenya, who all backed different clans in the fighting.

Lafoole, the small town surrounding Hawa's compound, was gone. It was looted and destroyed so many times it ceased to exist. There were no buildings left, not even a remnant. Most of the buildings the international forces built inside Hawa's camp were destroyed or had collapsed. Several water towers lay on their side, and the water tanks and pumps we constructed had disappeared. However, the most startling sight was the size of the camp. There were over 40,000 people in residence. When I last visited Hawa in 1993, there were approximately 10,000 inhabitants. The field where President Bush's helicopter landed four years earlier was now covered with small thatched huts.

When my vehicle stopped, Hawa greeted me. Her eyes showed someone who knows the purpose and meaning of her life. Her face conveyed the sense that nothing could break her or her spirit. She greeted me in the manner of a conservative Muslim woman by putting her right hand on her heart and nodding her head toward me. It was several years since I last saw her, but it seemed like ages. In her small sitting room, one of her assistants poured sweet tea with camel's milk. After she left the room, Hawa relayed the story of her work since my departure.

In March 1995, after the United Nations peacekeeping force departed Somalia, she expected trouble from the warlords. She was aware she was labeled a CIA spy and a pawn of the United States. However, the warlords' revenge did not come with the directness she expected. The gunmen did not make her life easy, but there was not a wholesale attempt to close her camp. Her refuge continued to grow as more people deserted Mogadishu to find a place where they could escape the violence.

She speculated there were several reasons for the warlords' restraint. The clinic treated the wounds of their gunmen, and they needed her site to assist with keeping a balance in Mogadishu and the surrounding countryside. There was no other place for people to go when they no longer served a purpose for looting and extortion and deserted the city.

When Mohamed Aidid died in August 1996, clans and subclan alliances broke, and there was no control over the bandits. Her camp frequently suffered incursions from different groups. She spent many hours standing in front of armed intruders and ordering them off the site. They promised retaliation because they claimed she was a CIA spy and a puppet of the Americans. She believed she would be assassinated, but this was her home and she refused to be intimidated by bandits and thugs.

She continued in a soft voice, telling me their revenge was far worse than her own death. A group of men kidnapped and killed her only son, claiming he was a spy and agent of the US government.

I turned ashen, and Hawa asked what was wrong. I broke down and said I was the catalyst who started her public association with the United States. As I spoke, I forgot my ego, fear, and the shields I hid behind. My answer was beyond an apology; I had to accept accountability. It was me. I brought the Americans to Lafoole.

She looked at me and said, "Robert, you only tried to help. You had nothing to do with this. *Inshallah*. It is God's will."

I tried to accept her absolution, but the guilt is always with me. There are things in life you cannot rectify, no matter how hard you try.

Inside myself, I knew this trip to Somalia was like a Vietnam veteran returning to the former battlefields of southeast Asia to reconcile the past. I still struggled with killing the man in the field outside the Mogadishu airport. He was not the first person I killed in battle, but that death troubled me.

I thought by going back, I could somehow resolve the gunfights, the senseless killings of their own countrymen by the warring militias, and the use of starvation as a weapon. I wanted to see Hawa. She was my friend, and her selfless actions symbolized the humanitarian dedication I wanted to achieve.

What I found was the worsened disintegration of the country and my culpability in the death of her son. Adding to my confusion was the responsibility of deciding whether CARE should continue to risk the well-being of its staff to assist the people caught in the middle of this chaos.

I tried separating my emotions from this

decision. In the end, CARE staff who were programming daily throughout the country reminded me that CARE existed for precisely the situation we faced in this turmoil: assisting people in crisis.

I recommended CARE remain. To this day they are still working in the country.

CHAPTER 13
THROUGH THE LOOKING GLASS, AGAIN

*"Justice, like beauty, is in the eye of the beholder.
Some see an innocent victim.
Others will see evil incarnate getting exactly what's deserved."*
—Emily Thorne

AFTER SOMALIA, I RETURNED TO HAWAI'I and worked remotely for the next year. I made trips to monitor ongoing CARE humanitarian efforts in Afghanistan, in the West Bank, and in Palestine. However, we did not mobilize a rapid response to any significant refugee movements of people, such as we did during the repatriation efforts in Rwanda.

The most significant humanitarian emergency

on the horizon was in Kosovo, a region in the former country of Yugoslavia. After the Dayton Peace Agreement in December 1995, which ended the Bosnian War, the Serbian leader, Slobodan Milošević, who caused that conflict remained in power. The peace accords failed to mention the rising ethnic tensions in the Kosovo region. Few people knew about the problems in the area, and fewer cared.

For years, the territory of Kosovo was a self-directed region within Yugoslavia. It was home to a majority Albanian Muslim population. When Yugoslavia dissolved, Serbia gained control. CARE had its headquarters for the region in Belgrade, and a smaller office in Pristina, the capital of Kosovo. At the end of the Bosnian War, a lightly-armed militia called the Kosovo Liberation Army (KLA) started an insurgency against Serbia, and the conflict worsened as the insurgent group became better trained and armed.

The CARE Country Office in Belgrade asked me to assess the situation and review the scope and effectiveness of their programming activities. In early December 1998, I arrived in Belgrade. After what I had seen and experienced in Bosnia and Sarajevo during the Bosnian War, I was both cautious and curious about entering the Serbian homeland and capital.

This was my first trip to a conflict area since moving from Hawai'i to Atlanta. In August after my wife and I agreed to separate and divorce, I moved to Georgia to physically work from the CARE Headquarters. For the first time, since I was twenty-one, I was on my own. My daughter was in Law School in San Diego, and my son elected to stay in Hawai'i. December in the Balkans fit my emotional state, bleak and dark: I was not angry. It was the opposite. I made a wedding vow in 1968, "through the good times and bad," and blew it. This woman nursed me through war wounds, raised a family while I was continually deployed as a Marine, and kept faith that eventually, things would settle down. Things never did because I couldn't.

Upon arriving at the airport, I encountered numerous men and women in Soviet-style uniforms that seemed to spend most of their time glaring at newcomers. Because the United States had forced the Bosnian Peace Agreement on Serbia, my American passport caused a cluster of people to examine it and me. I was not a welcome visitor.

I was directed to a small room with my luggage, which was completely disassembled. I had anticipated a less than friendly arrival, but this was worse than expected. After an hour of questioning, I was free to leave.

Eventually, I found the man assigned to meet me. He was not a CARE team member but a taxi driver contracted to greet me and transport me to the office. He did not speak English. Although I spoke little Serbo-Croatian, he was not inclined to converse with an American. We arrived at the office building, and the elevator was broken. After four flights of stairs, I entered the CARE office and waded into a cloud of cigarette smoke, which began in the morning and hovered until the end of the day.

I met with the Country Director, Steve Pratt. He was from Australia and had been a career military officer. We met on occasion over the years, and I admired him. He had followed a path from the military like my own and spent time in several complex humanitarian emergencies in Rwanda, Cambodia, the Democratic Republic of the Congo, and Yemen.

After a cursory greeting and an introduction to his team, he suggested we go for a walk to escape the cigarette smoke. He laughed and said he considered making the office a "smoke-free environment," but faced two problems: an open revolt, and all his staff spending their whole day gossiping in the smoking area.

We followed a pleasant path along the Danube River. Despite the jet lag, I found the setting beautiful.

Belgrade was a city of grand buildings and architecture, but also a place that had endured a communist regime for centuries. Much of its beauty was overshadowed by monolithic concrete structures that housed apartments and government offices: squat monuments to a fallen experiment in politics. Any sense of individuality was sublimated to function. Yet, the stately buildings of an era of art and free expression remained. The weather was grim and the city gray.

As we strolled, Steve outlined several cautions about staying in Belgrade, the foremost being that anything I said in the office would be reported to the government. He was convinced his office had implanted listening devices and that several of his staff were government informants.

In a humanitarian situation involving hostilities, NGOs assume one or several local staff also provide information to the government or forces that control the area. All available paperwork gets reviewed in the evening by cleaning staff or security guards. Whether right or wrong, it is a fact.

It is a "damned if you do and damned if you don't" situation. If office staff lock all their documents in a safe at night, suspicion arises. Thus, most work is left exposed, and only sensitive organizational details such as performance reports and budgets are safeguarded. The first operating instruction is to never write anything that cannot be handed to the presiding government or armed faction.

Although CARE is an international organization, most of the world sees it as an American entity. Steve cautioned I should assume that my room at the InterContinental Hotel was bugged as well, my phone line monitored, and my room searched daily.

Later, at the hotel, I took in its shabbiness. At check in, an overzealous desk clerk greeted me with another interrogation. I bit my tongue. He had all the power, and this was an inconvenience, not an assault.

I also knew, despite my self-moralizing about human rights and justice, I lived in Sarajevo during the worst of the siege and held a grudge against the Serbs. For a moment, the desk clerk symbolized that bitterness but did me a favor by helping me realize my prejudice. I had characterized an entire nation as bad, but Serbia, like all places, was a collection of diverse people with the same individuality and moral attributes as any other country.

This awareness became more critical in the coming days as I waded through the death and destruction in Kosovo. I struggled to separate my emotions from the realities of the moment. I was here to assist, not condemn.

For the next two days, Steve and I reviewed his humanitarian and development projects taking place throughout the former Republic of Yugoslavia, including Kosovo. His portfolio impressed me as his projects spanned the entire country.

In the evenings, I returned to the hotel, making my way through the prostitutes gathered in the lounge. The hotel served as a gathering place for working girls, black market enterprises, and thugs who were in some way associated with the government. I had a feeling everyone knew I was an American, and their response was less than enthusiastic.

After two days, I traveled to Pristina, three hours away. The driver chain smoked and spoke no English. The route was lightly traveled, but we passed several military encampments with numerous armored vehicles and tanks. I was shocked by the strength of the army deployment around

Kosovo. It was not difficult to foresee this situation ending badly.

However, I was pleasantly surprised when most checkpoints waved us through. Occasionally, when a guard requested my passport, it was simply met with a quick glance and a nod to move on. What a difference from the Bosnian War, where an attempt to pass through Serb lines to enter Sarajevo could take eight hours. These soldiers were in their own country, confident, and an occasional American was assumed to be a journalist.

The countryside was mostly farmland until we reached the city of Mitrovica. Entering the town from the north, we passed several miles of derelict factories. The city consisted of large concrete apartments. There was no foliage, only a landscape of concrete turning black from poor construction and no upkeep.

The Mitrovica Bridge, which spanned the Ibar River, marked the cultural border between Serbia and Kosovo. The north side of the river housed the majority Serbs who identified with Serbia, and the Kosovar Albanians lived south of the river. Even at the time of writing this book, the bridge remained guarded by international peacekeeping forces because of the tensions between the two ethnic groups. However, on this day in 1999, it was a peaceful passage, and those troubles were still ahead of us.

Continuing toward Pristina, the Serb enforcement changed. Before Mitrovica, the soldiers were professional and well disciplined. Their uniforms and equipment were clean and maintained. Inside Kosovo, the character changed to police officers assisted by groups of men wearing a variety of uniforms.

During the Bosnian War, I'd met these types of soldiers with a .45 caliber pistol pressed against my forehead, and the barrel of a Kalashnikov rifle in my back. They were members of various irregular forces known as the Serb Militias, the White Eagles, the Avengers, or Chetniks. They were brutal. These were the militias responsible for rape camps and torture centers throughout Bosnia during the war.

Their name referred to Serbia's national symbol of a double-headed white eagle under a crown. The International Criminal Tribunal for the former Yugoslavia indicted the group in 2003, but no trial followed.

Although the distance from Mitrovica to Pristina was approximately an hour's drive, it was delayed by multiple informal checkpoints. In some places, they were located less than a mile apart.

Both men and women secured them, and my American passport did not win me new friends.

We arrived at the CARE office in Pristina late in the afternoon. No one had arranged for my lodging, a usual courtesy for a CARE international visitor. I asked the receptionist if she would direct us to a hotel. After a seemingly hostile discussion between her and the driver, he indicated I follow him to the taxi.

In the vehicle, I laboriously asked the driver what happened in the office. He said she knew he was a Serb. Consequently, she would only speak to him in the Albanian language to ensure he did not understand her. Fortunately, his mother was from Kosovo, and he spoke Albanian.

The only lodging still operating in Pristina was the Grand Hotel. It was now dark and starting to snow. The hotel was another massive concrete structure dotted with dark windows.

In the lobby, a lone man stood behind the reception desk. He made himself busy moving papers around the counter and ignoring me. After enough time to demonstrate his authority as the desk clerk, he demanded to know what I wanted. "An interesting approach to customer relations," I thought, and replied, "I need a room for a week." It was evident from the lobby that the hotel was deserted, but he went through a cursory examination of his records. He said he had a room, but I could not pay with a credit card. I asked if US dollars were acceptable. He indicated they were. I asked how much per night. "For you, one hundred dollars." It was a ridiculous cost, as the standard rate was twenty-five dollars. I said I would stay for two nights and gave him two hundred dollars. He handed me a key and gave me no receipt, then pointed to a set of dark steps, one hundred and fifty dollars richer from our transaction. I shouldered my pack and made my way up the unlit stairwell thinking, "Welcome to the Balkans."

The next day I moved to a small apartment my driver found in the rear of a home near the CARE office. It was comfortable and included breakfast.

I spent the next ten days with the CARE programming team, traveling throughout the area. Kosovo is about the size of Connecticut and bordered by Macedonia, Albania, Montenegro, and Serbia. CARE work across the country ranged from health and hospital projects to assisting with construction and agriculture. There were other NGOs in the area, but CARE had the most significant presence.

Although the Serbs controlled the major towns, the KLA dominated the countryside. An unspoken non-aggression agreement existed between the KLA and the Serbs, and I witnessed a well-organized militia, consisting of polite and professional young men. There was an occasional attack by the KLA on a remote Serb police station, but in December 1998, most of the activities on both sides involved manning a series of checkpoints. Some of these barriers were within shouting distance of one another. As we approached the city of Peja in the west, we went through a KLA checkpoint at the entry to the town and then a Serb station ten meters away.

The area possessed the standard components of a national uprising and insurgency. In every village, hamlet, and town, there was a similar characteristic: numerous young men between the ages of eighteen and thirty were gathered on the sidewalks or cafes. Many of these young men were well educated with university degrees, but there was no work. In 1999, the United Nations Development Programme (UNDP) estimated nearly seventy percent of men between the age of sixteen and twenty-four were unemployed.

In the opinion of my Kosovo colleagues, the Serbs blocked their industrial or technological growth to force them to stay on the land at a subsistence level of agriculture. Additionally, young men and women were restricted to travel and work in the major towns of Serbia. My companions felt that Kosovo was an enslaved nation.

It was mid-December and the weather was miserable. I had spent too many holiday seasons outside of the United States, and many of them in places like Vietnam, Iraq, and Somalia. Kosovo celebrated Christmas despite being a Muslim region, but it was not the same. I wanted to return to the US. I said goodbye to my colleagues and went to the CARE office in Belgrade to give Steve my impressions and recommendations.

I believed CARE was in a tenuous position being present in a fragile state embroiled in a civil war, but Serbia was being shunned by the international community.

The Clinton administration and other European nations had ignored both the Bosnian War and the Genocide in Rwanda, and the UN, although engaged in both events, made itself ineffective by nonsensical bureaucratic regulations and a serpentine penchant for centralized control from New York and Geneva. Clinton was attempting to redeem his place in history by asserting America would not stand for another Bosnian-type conflict, and his allies announced similar views. However, in the United States, the Monica Lewinsky scandal had become a significant distraction to the presidency, and the entire US government seemed to be on autopilot.

It was not hard to imagine another conflict where UN forces tried in vain to maintain safe humanitarian routes through Kosovo while Pristina descended into conditions like Sarajevo. Ideally, these corridors could be a demilitarized zone allowing the safe transit of humanitarian aid in, or refugees transit out of a crisis region.[1] In reality, these agreements are not enforceable without a commitment to directly engage in armed conflict with forces that violate the agreements.

Kosovo was 20 percent the size of Bosnia. Thus, the Serbs could exercise greater control over the region. Although the KLA was strengthening, it remained a lightly-armed militia facing the Serbian Army, which was well prepared and supported by tanks, jet fighters, and helicopters. The conflict would be slaughter, and I was amazed that NATO would allow Milošević to attempt trampling another Baltic state into enslavement.

---

1. Wikipedia, "Humanitarian Corridor," Wikipedia, The Free Encyclopedia, February 21, 2019, accessed March 27, 2019, https://en.wikipedia.org/w/index.php?title=Humanitarian_corridor&oldid=884454387

I told Steve I was recommending CARE continue its operation in Serbia and Kosovo but must remain under very watchful conditions. The situation was deteriorating and could descend into a significant armed conflict within days. Steve was discerning and could gauge when the status became too dangerous for the CARE team to engage with humanitarian assistance. I trusted Steve and his judgment. He had been in several emergencies and knew how quickly a situation could disintegrate into chaos.

I returned to Atlanta and the CARE headquarters but felt uncomfortable. I had a connection with Steve and thought I had abandoned him. The bond may have been due to our similar age or background. He was competent and able to handle the complexities of Kosovo, but after Bosnia and Rwanda I was not optimistic about the future of Kosovo or CARE's place in the region amid such a volatile and explosive situation.

I was happy to be home, but troubled as I tried to join in the spirit and joy of the holiday season.

I didn't know this then, despite my bad feeling, but within five months, everything in my life and the lives of three of my CARE colleagues would change unimaginably.

CHAPTER 14
INTO THE VOID

> *"We live in a world in which we need to share responsibility. It's easy to say, 'it's not my child, not my community, not my problem.' [Yet], there are those who see the need and respond. I consider those people my heroes."*
> —Fred Rogers

AFTER I DEPARTED KOSOVO IN DECEMBER 1998, the situation became more volatile. As the Kosovo Liberation Army increased its attacks on Serbian forces, President Slobodan Milošević directed his troops to execute an ethnic cleansing of the region. He intended to drive nearly a million Kosovar-Albanians across the border into Albania and Macedonia and resettle the region with a Serbian population.

Although warned by the Clinton administration his actions were unacceptable, Milošević proceeded, encouraged by what happened during the Bosnian War. Between 1992 and 1995, the United States and the European Union threatened him over his actions against the Bosnians. However, except for the presence of a weak UN peacekeeping force, he was able to attack the region at will for three and a half years. The international community complained and condemned but never initiated military actions against him. He had no reason to believe Kosovo would be any different.

To expedite the ethnic cleansing, Milošević expanded the use of Serb paramilitaries in January 1999.

They were turned loose on the Kosovar-Albanian population and given license to kill, rape, burn, and destroy with impunity. Both Clinton and the European Union had to decide what to do. The international community had allowed the Bosnian War and the Rwanda Genocide to unfold with the slaughter of more than a million human beings without an intervention. The political debacle of the Somalia operation in 1992 had paralyzed their response. Now, for the third time in the 1990s, another humanitarian holocaust began.

The international community finally decided to set aside political considerations and act.

As the dialogue and search for a peaceful solution between Serbia and the US and European Union broke down, many aid organizations evacuated Belgrade. They were concerned for the safety of their staff and the response of Serb authorities toward the international team of western charities whose governments were members of the NATO alliance. They had tolerated the humanitarians because of the resources and assistance they provided but also believed many of them were spies.

Steve decided to remain and continue programming. CARE had been in the region for more than five years aiding both the Kosovars and Serbs who were displaced from Bosnia during the war. Steve's decision was not merely an emotional response to the deprivation of much of the population. He had received assurances from the government ministers and directors responsible for humanitarian affairs that CARE's work was valued and appreciated —war or no war. Based on the government's declarations, he began to plan with the UN for the aid needed to assist the 50,000 Serbs forced to flee Kosovo by the threat of war and the KLA.

On Wednesday, March 24, 1999, NATO began bombing Belgrade, Montenegro, and Serb military forces in Kosovo. By Saturday, Steve moved from his apartment to the Intercontinental Hotel accompanied by his suboffice manager, Peter Wallace, who had left Pristina to join him in Belgrade. He believed the hotel was safer from the bombing because it housed civilians and was considered a "restricted target."

When the bombing started, I was in a hospital bed in Bonn, Germany recuperating from the car accident off the cliff in Albania. I was using a lot of pain medication and sleep aids and knew they were affecting my memory because I had trouble remembering how I got to Bonn from Albania. Nightmares about the fire in the vehicle as I struggled to pull the driver from the wreckage plagued me. The nurses woke me from these vivid dreams when I shouted. I had a television set in my room and could watch CNN International, but the drugs and pain made it impossible to concentrate on the NATO intervention.

While I tried following the news about Kosovo from Bonn, 900 miles away in Pristina, Steve was packing office materials for transport to the hotel when a plainclothes police officer appeared. The man was pleasant, but his mission was to search the office for signs of bombing guidance devised to direct NATO airplanes to specific target sites. Soon after the policeman departed, Steve was informed that all the CARE vehicles in a car park approximately 500 meters from the office were confiscated.

He had two other vehicles, an old Opel station wagon, locked in his apartment building garage, and a Land Rover, which was moved from the parking deck earlier in the day for a work assignment. He retrieved the station wagon and drove to the Intercontinental Hotel, where a gruff, unshaven man greeted him. He identified himself as a police official and demanded to see Steve's identification documents. While reviewing the paperwork, he displayed a great deal of knowledge about Steve and CARE, and their activities throughout Serbia and Kosovo.

Steve explained he was merely moving to a safer place to continue CARE's work in the country. As he described his motive, the police officer tore his official residency card into pieces, stating that by leaving his apartment, Steve was no longer entitled to the status of official residency.

For the next several days, Steve, Peter, and the CARE national staff continued assisting the 50,000 displaced people, most of them old, young, or sick, stranded in a cold, dirty abandoned factory with inadequate resources. Some had fled across international borders or more distant and safer parts of the country, but the remainder were unable to escape.

By March the situation had deteriorated. Intensified bombing and increased hostilities from the government and frightened civilians made it no longer feasible for CARE to continue operating. CARE was no longer considered a humanitarian organization by the agitated and demoralized population. Regardless of CARE's proclamations of impartiality and neutrality, it was considered an instrument of NATO.

As dawn broke on March 31, Peter and Steve had packed the Opel and Land Rover with their personal items and essential files. Regardless of the hostilities, donors would still want an account of their funds, and an explanation of the circumstances that led to the closure of the country office. As evident as the action seemed, Steve was an experienced country director and knew the bureaucratic rigmarole that would follow. He needed to be able to account for the money and confiscated resources and explain his rationale for stopping operations.

The route the UN and NGOs used to evacuate

Belgrade was north to Budapest in Hungary, approximately 230 miles away. While preparing to depart, Steve waited for another CARE staff member, Eduardo, who had a UN passport. When he arrived, he had a woman with him, a Serb staff member of the UN, who wanted to evacuate with him. Steve was not happy but was anxious to leave and wasted no time on a lengthy discussion about a stranger joining them. He told her to get in the station wagon, and they left for Budapest. After ten miles, a police officer stopped them to say the road was bombed overnight and impassable.

The dilemma was whether or not to return to Belgrade and wait for another opportunity to leave or turn west and head to the border with Croatia. Eduardo said he could not cross the Croat border with the woman, because she was a Serb and would not be allowed into Croatia. Additionally, Steve was under pressure from his manager in CARE Australia who was adamant that he and Peter depart Serbia that day.

With the Opel and Land Rover, Peter and Steve turned west and headed to Croatia. The road was a four-lane highway, and the trip would take approximately one hour. The border appeared a nondescript crossing with a single building and barrier booth. To accommodate the pending search, Steve pulled the suitcases, briefcases, and boxes from the vehicle and lined them along a single bench. It was a cold and gray morning with occasional snow showers. He reasoned the Serb border guards had no more desire than he to prolong the search.

The situation deteriorated as the police officer opened the first suitcase. It contained an Iridium handheld satellite phone I had sent him several weeks earlier. Because of the increasing prospect of a NATO intervention, I reasoned the international forces would cut the cellular telephone capabilities and interrupt landline use. It was imperative to monitor the safety of CARE staff, and a satellite phone would become our only link.

To ensure the phone was an accepted item under Serbian government regulations, I purposely sent it via a commercial carrier through the national customs and border authority. If it were a restricted item, it would be confiscated, but the phone was delivered the previous week without incident. Although Steve now had possession of the satellite device, he was unable to use it because NATO blocked all civilian satellite transmissions originating from Serbia and Montenegro.

The border control officer was unfamiliar with the equipment, and after Steve explained it was a satellite phone, he became excited and took it into the administration building. He returned with another official, and the search became laborious.

The officials opened a bag with a Koran and prayer rug and pressed for the reason he had Islamic religious items. Steve's wife, who was pregnant, left several weeks earlier. She was from Egypt and a follower of Islam, and the bag was one of several she left behind. It was not difficult to understand that agents at a remote Serb border station would question the motives of two westerners with boxes of reports and files, a satellite phone, and a Koran.

The search continued for two hours. A third officer joined the inspection, dressed in a blue camouflage uniform with the symbol of the Ministry of Interior Police. In one of the boxes he found Steve's résumé.

In addition to the years Steve spent as a humanitarian worker, he served for twenty-three years as a military service officer in the Australian Defense Force. The officials directed him into the administration building and told him to strip. They thoroughly searched his clothes and body. As he dressed, two men attacked him, wrapped his head in his jacket and pushed him into the backseat of a waiting car.

When the car stopped, Steve was dragged from

the vehicle and up a series of steps. In a stone room, the jacket was pulled from his head, and he was shoved face forward against a stone wall.

After another invasive search of his person, he was slammed into a chair. He received a blow from behind, and the interrogation began with the accusation he was a British spy. His résumé and satellite telephone served as evidence. The questioning intensified with as many as eight interrogators screaming at him.

He continued denying the accusation and, in exasperation, one of the men beat him across his head, face, and upper torso. He was dragged from the chair, pushed to the floor and kicked by several men. The questioning and beatings continued through the night.

The next day the interrogators focused on CARE's activities in Kosovo, with questions about his national staff and the activities of Peter Wallace. They examined copies of Steve's situation reports that he sent to the CARE headquarters. Although much of the reporting described humanitarian assistance activities, they also detailed "no go areas" due to the threat from the fighting and identified them on a map. The police accused him of identifying targets for NATO. As Steve proclaimed his innocence, he inquired about the status of his companion, Peter. With another blow, he was told it was none of his business.

After twenty-four hours, the demeanor of the police changed. They said they accepted his account of CARE's activities and assured him things would probably be okay, and he would see his family soon. He would most likely be detained for three more days. Throughout the remainder of the day, he was left in peace in a small room with a view of the village where he was being held and hoped his captivity would soon end.

It did not.

That evening a group of men rushed into his room, put a paper bag over his head and dragged him to another waiting vehicle.

After a long drive, he was pushed into a room with several men and a woman. His interrogation went on for hours, and he began to realize the objective of his capture. His captors were building a scenario where CARE had sent him to Serbia to establish an espionage network and provide NATO with information to prepare for their eventual attack. They insisted he was a British citizen serving as an intelligence officer under the guise of CARE.

After four days of little sleep, food, water, and brutal interrogation, Steve was given some rest and food. On the fourth evening, he was escorted to the office of the man Steve assumed head of the interrogation team. In his book, *Duty of Care*, Steve describes the moment:

The man looked at him and said, "We are both majors in our armed forces, and we know how to be sensible. You are an infantry major with intelligence links, we know this. And of course, that means that you are ready to die for your country, we know this. And maybe, Major [Pratt], it will come to this, he [said] chillingly.... You must play by the rules. The rules of the game are that you will tell us all about your espionage activity and that of your espionage colleagues and your organization's espionage activities." He began a demonstration with his hands... one horizontal, he places the other on top and vertical. "This represents your life, Major. You are finely balanced and could fall to death in an instant. Do you understand?" He nods over his shoulder, indicating another man in the room] and says, He will take you downstairs and kill you quietly in a few minutes; he will then use that plastic bag, and drop your body into the boot of that car down there. A black bag [sat] on the floor next to [the other man]... we will not wake the neighbors."[1]

The police continued to build a case of espionage against him. They started focusing on the forty-odd situation reports he was carrying when he was detained, the reports sent each week to the CARE Australia headquarters in Canberra.

Steve included me in his weekly reports, which provided an overview of the humanitarian situation in the country, the progress of his current programming activities, a review of other possible humanitarian requirements and interventions, and specific administration, financial, and logistic conditions that affected his office. Due to the conflict, he included observations about issues of safety that affected his team and their ability to provide aid due to the fighting.

The humanitarian community used a military format for its situation reports (SITREPs). There was nothing "military" about the communications, but the form was efficient, and its flow precise and easy to follow. Unless an aid worker served in a military associated with the NATO alliance, they would not recognize the similarities in the reports.

---

1. Steve Pratt, *Duty of Care* (East Roseville, N.S.W.: Simon & Schuster, 2000).

Steve was a good writer, and his dispatches were concise and informative. Because of my own military association, I paid attention to his style, use of acronyms, and the type of references he made to the fighting. I knew the documents could make him vulnerable to misinterpretation by governments or resistance groups although he went to extremes to keep his communications as neutral as possible. He never detailed military movements or locations and only referenced fighting by addressing "no go" hostile areas for his staff. He did an excellent job of providing factual updates without compromising his humanitarian neutrality.

Of the forty communiques he had in his possession, the last four referenced a good deal of security concerns for his staff, as well as measures he had taken to mitigate operations in the conflict zone of Kosovo. To augment his decisions, he included statements and observations from the UN and Organization for Security and Co-operation in Europe (OSCE).

I had witnessed the OSCE in Bosnia and Kosovo and knew their presence served solely as a forum for dialogue and negotiation between warring parties. They were unarmed and never empowered to intervene. However, they provided excellent information regarding the conflict.

The Serbs focused on these reports. Their accusation was not about the verbiage or reporting style, but the UN and OSCE references. They used this as the foundation for arguing his link to these organizations as a spy.

This was an impossible and implausible accusation, but Serbia was under attack by NATO and searched for any connection, even if far-reaching. Serbia was being bombed, its military decimated, and innocent civilians killed as collateral damage. Neither the country nor its police were rational; they needed to have their hands-on people to blame. Steve and Peter became the means for their revenge.

This was not an excuse for their atrocities, but it was a reason.

As the government built its case, Steve was moved from the military intelligence interrogation center to the Central Belgrade Prison. He was led to a cell approximately five meters long and one and a half meters wide, with a meshed window and a wooden bench that served as a bed. Although it was small and stark, he felt like he was on vacation. Previously, he had been chained to a wall and slept on a rough blanket on a concrete floor.

In the distance, he heard the NATO air raids, intensified since his capture. Throughout the night, he was subjected to a cacophony of cannons and machine guns firing at NATO planes. Although the sound of the jets was a morale boost, he worried the aircraft would attack the nearby anti-aircraft weapons, or that a laser-guided precision bomb would cause severe damage to his building.

On April 11, I was lying in my bed with CNN International on the television. I was reading, and the broadcast was background noise until I heard a voice I recognized. I turned toward the TV, and there sat Steve Pratt at a desk in a stark room with his hands under a table. I fumbled with my broken hand to turn up the sound. I could tell from his posture and the placement of hands that he was in trouble.

During the Vietnam War, before the North Vietnamese understood the meaning of the gesture, American prisoners forced to make televised propaganda about their supposed involvement in war crimes against the Vietnamese would place their hands on the table with both middle fingers extended. After the Vietnam War, every country learned to keep a prisoner's hands out of view of a camera.

As I could tell, Steve had been through a great deal. He had lost weight, but what struck me was how much he aged in such a short period. To say he looked haggard was a compliment; he looked like a talking skeleton. My first thought was, "My God, what have they done to him?"

In the broadcast, he stated, "When I came to [Serbia], I performed some intelligence tasks in this country by using the cover of CARE Australia. My concentration was on Kosovo and some effects of the bombing. I misused my Yugoslavian citizen staff for the acquisition of information. I realize that the damage was done in this country by these actions, for which I am greatly sorry. I always did and still do condemn the bombing of this country."[2]

Such a statement indicated that he was tortured, starved, and severely maltreated. He was a strong man who valued truth and fair treatment, and he was not a spy.

He was publicly against the bombing of Serbia from the beginning of the campaign. Because of his military background, he knew indiscriminate and collateral damage would affect innocent civilians.

---

2. Ibid.

He had always been a proponent for diplomatic solutions.

The broadcast of his forced confession reassured me he was not dead. The Serbs also reported that Peter Wallace was with him, and that Branko Jelen, a Serb who was Steve's office manager, was arrested and charged with treason and espionage. The government announced they were going to prosecute each of the men in a military tribunal.

After the broadcast, Steve was allowed several meetings with Australian officials, but his defense was to be provided by a Serb military attorney.

After nearly two months of captivity, the trial began in a closed courtroom with observers barred. Both Branko and Peter were being tried simultaneously. The sham went on for two days, concluding with Steve, Peter and Branko being cleared of espionage.

A surge of relief soared through them as the rest of the verdict was read. However, they were convicted of a new charge of passing secret information to a foreign power. Their lawyers were unable to dispute the charge because they had never been given any details of these accusations.

The judge read the terms of their conviction; Steve was sentenced to twelve years in jail, Peter to four, and Branko to six.

The punishments stunned Steve. He, Peter, and Branko were loaded into a van for their return to the Belgrade prison. Steve later recounted the guards themselves were stunned by the severity of the punishment and allowed them to converse freely. Branko had been beaten the previous night, and severe injuries covered his body. At the prison once more, Peter was moved into Steve's cell. Although it was very cramped, they appreciated each other's company. Steve requested a meeting with Branko but was denied.

After two days, soldiers arrived to tell them they would be transferred to the military prison for the duration of their confinement. They were surprised to learn the former military jail was moved to a wing of their present location at the Belgrade Central Prison. In the new area, Steve, Peter, and Branko had separate and larger cells with better food.

The most significant improvement was that Steve's wife, Samira, moved to Belgrade. On their first meeting, Steve described her, "Lumbering into the visitor's room, hugely pregnant." She was working for his freedom while carrying their second child. Steve was relieved she looked strong and healthy. Samira was able to visit him every week, and eventually allowed to bring him vegetables and fruit, which he shared with Branko and Peter.

Then the trio was moved again. Branko was taken to a separate prison about eighty kilometers from Belgrade, and Steve and Peter were transferred to Sremska Mitrovica, where he had spent his first twenty-four hours of captivity. The new jail was clean, well-organized, and surrounded by grounds and gardens. They were treated well, but the incarceration and stress of confinement gave them bouts of depression. Despite this, the mutuality of their friendship helped them cope during the worst of times.

On the morning of September 3, 1999, Peter and Steve received a visit from one of their trustees, who told them, "You are going home." They were taken to the prison governor who confirmed the news. At noon, after five months of incarceration, Steve and Peter were released from confinement to Australian authorities. Branko Jelen was held until New Year's Day, 2000. On his release, he was immediately granted Australian residency for himself, his wife and two children, and flown to Sydney.

In 2001, Steve was elected as a Liberal Member of the Australia Legislature (MLA). In 2005, Peter Wallace and Branko Jelen sued CARE Australia for negligence, alleging they were placed in danger because of the actions of senior staff, including Steve Pratt. The case was settled out of court. Steve's only comment was that he was disappointed in his former colleagues for taking legal action.

It is impossible to determine the number of people, both Serb and Kosovars, assisted by Steve's efforts.

During the deteriorating political situation, Steve did what he had in the past: he ignored the disputes and focused on the need. Turning his back and walking away from the situation was neither part of his character nor a moral option.

CHAPTER 15
THE MAN FROM ZIMBABWE

*"No work is insignificant.
All labor that uplifts humanity has dignity and importance and should be undertaken with painstaking excellence."*
—Dr. Martin Luther King Jr.

Humanitarians come in many assortments of people, personalities, and backgrounds. They might be a quiet and small woman doctor in Somalia, an old Serb woman living amid hatred in Bosnia, or a group of peasant farmers in a mountainside village in Albania.

However, few humanitarians match Colonel Lionel Dyck, the hard-nosed man I met from Zimbabwe. People either like him or hate him. He is straight-forward and plain speaking. He is never rude or unkind, but every word he speaks is the truth. Of course, it is the truth as he sees it. I first met him in a lounge at the Hartsfield Airport in Atlanta. In the late 1990s, CARE was a leading member of the humanitarian landmine removal community. We had demining projects in Cambodia, Afghanistan, Angola, Somalia, Mozambique, and Bosnia. As several nations began emerging from years of conflict, antipersonnel mines littered their landscapes. These mines would continue killing and maiming for generations.

I was responsible for overseeing CARE's demining efforts. Raising the money to maintain and increase our commitment was difficult. It was hard, but rewarding work. The difference in military demining and humanitarian mine action is in the scope of the work. While the military develops safe corridors through a mined area, clearly marking the uncleared places, the humanitarian approach has five pillars: to remove all the landmines in an infested area; to educate the people living around the minefields about the types of the ordnance and ways to avoid them; to provide physical and psychological help for victims; to advocate a ban on the use and production of landmines; and to destroy the millions of mines stockpiled by nations around the world.

On a warm, rainy afternoon, I sat at my desk in the CARE headquarters in Atlanta, still healing from the accident in Albania. My phone rang, and a man with a British accent inquired if he was speaking to Colonel Macpherson of the American Marines. It was strange to start a conversation referencing my military rank. Unlike most nations, the use of military titles after retirement from the US Armed Forces is uncommon.

I replied, "Yes, this is Robert Macpherson, a former Marine colonel." The caller identified himself as Colonel Lionel Dyck, a former colonel in the Army of Zimbabwe. I once wrote a paper entitled, "The Rhodesian War, Tactical Victory; Strategic Defeat." Consequently, I knew a bit about Zimbabwe, and a call from a man who identified himself as an army colonel was intriguing. He said he had a demining company called Minetech located in Harare, Zimbabwe. He was returning home from Guatemala where his company had completed a landmine removal project for the government. He was going to be in the Atlanta airport for a layover and asked if I could meet him.

Hartsfield is a large, crowded, and uncomfortable airport. I was on the cusp of making an excuse that I was traveling and would not be available, but I was curious. I agreed to meet Dyck.

I was familiar with Minetech. It had a good reputation and was known for introducing dogs into mine and unexploded ordnance detection. I called a colleague at the UN Mine Action Service. He affirmed Minetech did good work, and although Colonel Dyck could be tough to collaborate with, he was the industry's leading trainer of mine detection dogs, and his experience and expertise were invaluable.

Several days later I made my way to Hartsfield airport. It was hot and humid. I had left work, returned home, ate supper, and dressed in a T-shirt, sandals, and shorts. The road from Atlanta to the airport was crowded with rush hour traffic. Although it was only a fifteen-mile drive from my home, it took over an hour. At the airport, there was no hourly parking available, which meant a trip to the outer parking lots. By the time I entered the airport lounge, I was soaked with sweat from Atlanta's notorious heat and humidity.

When I entered the designated meeting area, I saw a gentleman looking curiously at me. He had a military demeanor and a short haircut. The first thing I noticed as he walked toward me was his posture and the cut of his clothes. He was older than I, but far more physically fit. His clothes were casual but starched with sharp creases. There was no doubt in my mind he was a retired member of a British inspired army. As we shook hands, I felt remarkably underdressed.

When we settled into our chairs for an introductory conversation, his sincerity and no-nonsense approach to humanitarian demining impressed me. We both agreed that after the International Campaign to Ban Landmines won the Nobel Peace Prize in 1997 companies with little experience in mine action saw an opportunity for a great deal of profit and flooded the humanitarian demining community. These companies used the traditional method of a person using a one-meter lane, lined up side-by-side with another person, probing the earth inch-by-inch looking for mines. It was a long and labor-intensive process that took years to clear an area. In contrast, Dyck employed the use of trained dogs to detect mines and unexploded ordnance. The US military had used dogs for years, but Minetech was the first commercial company whose dogs were trained to a standard that resulted in certification by the United States Department of Defense.

Dyck did not have to sell me on the use of dogs. I was more interested in him as a person, and the scope and integrity of Minetech. The mine action community was very competitive, with one company always trying to find a way to undermine the credibility of another, but Dyck refused to condemn competitors. I mentioned a company CARE was working with in Cambodia. He said, "They are well-led and honest. They have a great deal of experience in Cambodia and using them was a good move." He added that in the jungles of Cambodia there was no way to clear an area other than the traditional probing method.

I liked Dyck, but I knew enough about the Zimbabwe War of Independence and the Rhodesian War to make me curious: how could a former white officer in the Rhodesian Army transfer to the Army of Zimbabwe after a revolution winning independence from the white minority population of Rhodesia? The bitter and bloody struggle lasted for more than a decade. I asked how he made such a transition when many of the officers from the Rhodesian Army left for South Africa when Mugabe won control of the country.

He said he undoubtedly considered leaving, but in the end decided Zimbabwe was still his country and chose to remain. He also realized there would be a requirement to transform a guerrilla force into a disciplined national army. He made an appointment to see the new President of Zimbabwe, Robert Mugabe. He and Mugabe had a long chat, but the president summoned him to return several times before deciding to keep him. It was during these discussions they became cautious friends. After several months, Dyck was commissioned a colonel in the Army of Zimbabwe. It was understood he would never be promoted any further, due to the nature of politics, and the perceptions of a new nation that had just emerged from the rule of a white minority. He served for ten years in the army and is credited with being one of the founders of the modern Army of Zimbabwe.

As we parted, I thanked him for contacting me and setting up our meeting. I told him that in the future, as we developed more mine action projects, I would certainly include Minetech in the bidding process.

The mining weapons come in two types: antipersonnel and anti-vehicle. Antipersonnel is prohibited under the International Convention on the Prohibition of the Use, Stockpiling, Production and Transfer of Antipersonnel Mines, which was adopted in 1997. More than 167 countries joined this treaty. Notably, Serbia, the United States, Russia, and China did not.

Although Serbia did not sign the antipersonnel Landmine Ban Treaty, they attended the 1949 Geneva Convention. The convention set forth that when a nation uses landmines, it is obligated to mark the minefields and generate maps that depict the location of the minefield and the area of the mines within it. Additionally, mines could only be used against military combatants, not civilians.

The Serbian Army set up minefields in Kosovo and followed the Geneva conventions. When they were forced to withdraw by NATO, they turned over their maps with detailed landmine areas clearly identified to the United Nations. However, the Serb militias and the Kosovo Liberation Army kept no such records and used antipersonnel mines indiscriminately throughout the region.

Within days of the departure of the Serbian Army and the different militias from Kosovo, random antipersonnel mine explosions plagued the returning population. The number of homes and buildings booby-trapped with a variety of home-made explosive devices were just as numerous. When the soldiers and militias who occupied many of the homes throughout Kosovo retreated, they developed creative ways to inflict terror on the returning owners with these improvised booby traps.

There was an urgent need to clear the buildings and ensure the roads and fields were safe from mines to return the country back to normality. The threat of landmines would affect reengaging the economy and being able to earn a living throughout Kosovo. Many of the returning population, afraid to enter their homes, began living in tents outside of their residences. It took only one incident in a neighborhood to cause people to remain outside a house.

The threat of mines began impeding the reconstruction and revitalization efforts. Many commercial demining companies started appearing in Kosovo, but they had a limited focus and lacked strategic direction. One can look at a specific area, identify the mines and remove them. An alternative method is identifying societal requirements where mine removal would provide the most significant impact on the society and economy. For example, the first action may be to clear roadways and the grounds surrounding schools, hospitals, and factories, then clearing agricultural areas, and finally general demining.

However, in every instance, regardless of when the mines are removed, it is imperative to ensure the mined areas are marked and restricted. Unfortunately, when mines are placed indiscriminately, only a deadly explosion indicates their presence.

I returned to Kosovo in July 1999. I was well enough to return to the field and anxious to leave hospitals, doctors, and physical therapy behind. CARE decided to focus on two areas. In addition to providing direct assistance to returning individuals and families, we were going to engage in humanitarian demining as well. Our goal included removing mines, identifying infested areas, and providing mine-risk education to affected communities or regions. It was estimated more than 50,000 mines littered Kosovo. This number excluded the explosive remnants of war (ERW)—the artillery shells, grenades, mortars, rockets, air-dropped bombs, and cluster munitions left behind after a conflict ended. Throughout Kosovo, there were hundreds of thousands of these explosive munitions. The population of Kosovo then was two million people. This included approximately 800,000 Albanians who had returned to the country. The number of landmines and ERWs easily equaled one piece of ammunition for every five or six members of the population.

Early one morning, I arrived in a small hamlet west of Pristina and was told by the UN that antipersonnel mines were scattered across the fields.

When I parked my Land Rover a group of five men approached me. One of them spoke English and told me they had just returned from a refugee camp in Albania. He asked me to follow him, and we walked toward a small house on a hill. The village had no more than twenty-five homes, most of them burned or damaged. It was a farming hamlet, and my companion told me the village already lost a tractor to an anti-tank mine, and several people had been injured. There was ordnance spread all over the area. As we walked, I believed he was going to show me the area of landmine infestation. I noticed our destination was the only undamaged building in the village. During our walk, my companion asked if my vehicle was a four-wheel drive. A bit concerned that he wanted to use the vehicle in some type of mine removal, I replied that it was, and it equipped with a front-end winch with a cable.

When we reached the house, there was a group of people surrounding a well in the backyard. They stood about three meters from the wellspring and had their faces covered with their sleeves or handkerchiefs. When we got closer, the smell of rotting flesh overpowered me. The men conveyed to my companion that several women had brought them to the site. Several bodies were inside.

After most of the village departed for Albania as the Serbian militias rampaged through the country, some of the younger men went deeper into the mountains and joined the Kosovo Liberation Army. Although they had to keep their distance from their homes, they did observe what was happening in the village. The Serb militiamen who occupied the town captured seven young women. For the next month, they used this house as a prison for the women. They were guarded twenty-four hours a day and the men came and went to use the women as their sex slaves. When it became apparent NATO bombing was going to result in the withdrawal of the Serb army from Kosovo, they murdered the women and dumped them into the well to ensure they would not be able to testify against them.

We positioned ourselves upwind. The women and girls stood outside the area. The work was gruesome as we had to use a hook on the winch cable to snag a body in the well and pull it to the surface. Our desire to provide some dignity to the retrieval of the victims overshadowed our labor, but no matter how hard I tried, I could not keep the body fluids, decaying skin, and smells of death off myself. Psychologically this was very difficult. These were humans. They were women and girls who were mothers, daughters, wives, and sisters. They were captured in a ridiculous little war that no one cared about, herded into a house, and humiliated in every possible way, all for the twisted and warped desire of a few psychopaths. There was an occasional cry or sob as someone recognized a body.

I had seen all this before in Bosnia. I had seen the victims of Radovan Karadzic's rape camps. Yet, as bad as that was, it did not involve me pulling persecuted and brutalized women from a well with a four-wheel drive vehicle. Knowing that the men who did this would never be held accountable added to the misery.

The work was soul crushing.

Laying the seven bodies next to one another, two women were immediately claimed by their families and taken away. The younger men dug temporary graves for the rest. A third woman was known, but her family had not yet returned from the refugee camp in Albania. The five graves were very shallow, and the dirt barely covered the bodies. When I asked why, they told me it was so that when families from the surrounding villages came to the site, they could quickly uncover the grave to see if the body was a member of their family.

When we finished, and each of the bodies was

placed in a grave, we walked to a small river outside of the village. On the way to the stream, a woman handed me a bundle of clothes, which included a rough workman's shirt, trousers, socks, and a bar of soap. I followed the men to a secluded spot and washed. It was forty-five degrees, and the water was partially iced, but I did not notice the cold. I was in a daze and wanted the water to cleanse me of what I had seen and done.

I left the village and began my drive to Pristina. As I drove along the road, I started crying. I pulled to the side of the small dirt track and watched the dark clouds passing. As I looked across a field toward another small hamlet, I could see eleven freshly dug graves. I felt like I was at another crossroads. There was a side of me that felt I had done enough. I had given the "humanitarian stuff" my best efforts, but I was sick of it all—of scenes like today. As I pondered my future, someone knocked on the window. It scared me so badly I felt a rush to my head and thought I would pass out. I turned to see a young woman with a baby and a small girl. When I rolled down the window, she asked in sign language and very broken English if I could give her a ride to the next village several miles in the distance.

I nodded, and she got in the Land Rover. Her

daughter climbed in the back seat, and the young woman held her son on her lap. As we drove, she told me she had been in a refugee camp in Albania. The Serbs had killed her husband. She lived with her parents. It was difficult trying to understand one another, but also a simple conveyance of her story. Listening to her, I thought how, less than thirty minutes earlier, I was sitting by the roadside immersed in my own self-pity while all around me people who had experienced incalculable degrees of misery, violence, and deprivation were moving forward with their lives. I was the victim of a first-world problem: self-absorption. As the woman spoke, it was without anger, pity, or loathing; it was just a statement of facts. She could not afford to stay in her sadness because she had no safety net. No one was going to bail her out. There were no therapists or counselors for her to see. She had no time for a quest for justice or revenge. She was faced with the pragmatic recognition that life requires us to put one foot in front of the other and keep moving toward survival as individuals and a species.

When we reached her village, I reached into my wallet and gave her the equivalent of forty US dollars. There was a moment's hesitation, but as she took the money she captured my hand and kissed it. I have been humbled in my life, but seldom as deeply as in that moment. After I dropped her in front of her home, I saw her reflection in the rearview mirror. She was standing in the road holding her child while her daughter stood beside her. In the gray of a cold winter day in Kosovo, they continued to wave goodbye until I turned the final bend in the road.

For the next several weeks, I distracted myself with what a returning population requires with the approach of winter. The images of the graves in that small village lingered. I knew I had to do something about the landmines, but the day-to-day requirements of providing food, water, shelter, and sanitation for nearly a million people filled my concentration. However, when I began attending the UN meetings about landmines, I realized that what I thought was a bad situation was a horrific one. Antipersonnel mines infested the countryside.

The only reason we were not engaged in mine action was because of my inaction. The moment I decided to join the demining initiatives, Lionel Dyck's name flashed into my mind. The mine action requirements of Kosovo required clearing acres of farmland. This could not be done in the traditional probing method. It needed dogs to scent out the mines. The job would take professionalism, resolve, and determination. It would take Colonel Dyck.

It was time to call Minetech.

I called Dyck and explained the situation: I had no money from any donor to initiate a "dog-based" mine action program. It was a relatively new concept, and I would have to convince donors of its effectiveness. Thus, I had no money to provide him for the preparation, trip, and initiation of work. I would begin to write donor proposals, but it would take at least a month for the first commitments to appear in a CARE bank account. I asked him for an estimate to get him and his crew from Zimbabwe to Kosovo and cover the cost to begin work. He anticipated $90,000. I knew this was a fair cost. We discussed the number of deminers, dogs, and other details. He could field about forty staff and twenty dogs quickly. He said he would fax the total price tag to me within twenty-four hours.

With a firm number in mind, I contacted my boss, Pat Carey. Pat and I were good friends. I admired his position and respected Pat's integrity, leadership, and management skills. He and I could not have been more different. He was raised as a Quaker and I was a US Marine, but we were genuinely fond of one another. We laughed at each other's views on the same topic. Pat had multiple sclerosis, was younger than I, and needed a cane to walk. It was a life-limiting disease but never influenced his work, humor, or dedication to humanitarian work.

I told him that mine removal was one of the obstacles that needed resolution before the country could move forward from a post-conflict society to a state that could support its population. I told him I would begin writing multiple donor requests, but if he provided me with the $90,000 from CARE's unrestricted funds I could start demining efforts.

He listened patiently, then replied that the unrestricted money CARE had was not for loans, but he had a better idea. He would provide me with $250,000 from his general funding to get us started. Additionally, he did not want me working on the proposals. Instead, I should focus on the requirements in Kosovo. He would have headquarters staff begin writing and submitting the proposals. When I hung up the phone, I stared into the night and marveled at the decency of so many people.

With all the pieces in place, I called Colonel Dyck in Harare. We discussed the logistics. He said he was able to move within forty-eight hours, but I needed to do arrival preparations on my end.

Although there was not a functioning government in Kosovo, the UN was governing under an international mandate. I needed to get clearance for Minetech's arrival. I also needed to find lodging large enough to accommodate his camp, staff, and dogs. Additionally, the Pristina airport was not being used for any aircraft other than helicopters. Consequently, finding a runway in the vicinity to accommodate a cargo plane was an issue.

Dyck offered to fly to Kosovo to assist with preparations. I was grateful for his offer because, in addition to the mine action, I was still engaged with a large shelter project to get as many houses repaired before the worst of winter hit Kosovo. We wanted to solve the shelter issues first, and then focus our assistance on agriculture in the spring.

Three days later, Dyck walked through the doors of the CARE office in Pristina. He managed to build a flight itinerary from Harare to Skopje in Macedonia, and then drive to Pristina. He was a refreshing and gale-force wind of positive energy. He filled me with a renewed enthusiasm that we could make all this happen. Additionally, he was a friend that could pull me out of the depression caused by the constant exposure to death and destruction. When he saw me falling into melancholy, he would ask, "What are you about? Why are you here? Are you going to make a difference, or just think about it?" He was a man with a mission, and I was a man who felt adrift.

Dyck had another aspect to his persona: he never let anyone forget he was a professional soldier and a colonel from the Zimbabwe Army. As I knew, the humanitarian community did not trust close associations with the military and were reluctant to build any associations with its members. I downplayed my former rank and association with the Marines, but Dyck loved it. He enjoyed working with a US Marine, and it made me feel good about myself. His enthusiasm and friendship made me believe we could make a significant difference in Kosovo with dedicated mine action initiatives.

With him, we returned to the village where I had found the women in the well. I felt it was important for Dyck to see and experience this desecration before the arrival of his team. When we arrived at the little town, we were greeted warmly. I introduced Dyck to the elders. The men took us to their fields. The farmland included hundreds of acres, which were owned by individuals or as a collective of several village families. The sinister aspect of a landmine is that an explosion of one mine in an area will deem many acres unusable because of the threat. The men identified a specific area where several of their cattle were killed by a recent explosion. As we sat over tea, we heard how people were afraid to return to their fields. Kosovo was an agrarian society, and farming was the primary industry. Clearing the agricultural areas was imperative to their success.

For the next several days, we coordinated Minetech's arrival and areas of work with the UN. The United Nations Mine Action Service Department (UNMAS) had arrived in Kosovo to assign areas of engagement for the mine action companies that were coming to Kosovo. Many NGOs had a mine action component within their organizations. Several European NGOs were actively engaged in humanitarian demining as well, but CARE was the only US humanitarian nonprofit that had a large mine action program. The UN's goal was to ensure all this demining capacity was not centered in a limited number of locations while neglecting others. The tendency of demining efforts was to clear areas closer to the larger towns because of logistical ease.

UNMAS asked CARE to focus on the areas around Ferizaj, Kosovo. Ferizaj was formerly known as Urosevac, which was its Serbian name. As soon as NATO occupied the country, the population immediately changed its name to Ferizaj, the ancient Muslim name for the city. NATO assigned the US military to this area. The US Army built a facility called Camp Bondsteel to house and maintain a US ground force of approximately 1,500 men and women. The town had a population of roughly 100,000. It's an agrarian community and located in the most fertile farmland in the nation. The city also contained the Mulla Veseli mosque, built in 1891, and the St. Uroš Orthodox Cathedral. Both religious buildings symbolized religious tolerance between Muslims and Christians. Although the mosque was destroyed during WWII, it was rebuilt when the war ended. During the Kosovo War in 1999, the mosque was not damaged by the retreating Serbs because of its proximity to the Christian church.

Dyck spent several days traveling throughout the Ferizaj area looking for a place to establish the Minetech camp and interviewing people to obtain a list of mine incidents in the area. He coordinated with the US forces who were responsible for safeguarding the region, but their focus was on protection, and they had little information about areas of landmine infestation. UNMAS was doing an excellent job of collecting data, but unfortunately, at this stage of the demining activities, most of the critical information came because of mine strikes.

Colonel Dyck returned to Zimbabwe. A week later, I received a fax telling me to expect Minetech's arrival in Pristina in approximately two days. He asked me to meet him at the Pristina Airport at three in the afternoon.

The Pristina Airport had become a political dilemma for the United Nations. After NATO bombed Serbia, the Russians were excluded from a peacekeeping mission in Kosovo because they were not part of the NATO Alliance. The Soviet Union and Russia were long-standing allies of Yugoslavia and Serbia. They were determined not to let NATO have the controlling influence in Serbia.

On June 11, 1999, a column of thirty Russian armored vehicles carrying 250 Russian troops moved into Serbia. It was assumed the column was heading for Pristina and the Pristina International Airport ahead of the arrival of NATO troops as they were part of the international peacekeeping forces in Bosnia.

Upon hearing of the deployment, General Wesley Clark of the US Army, then serving as the Supreme Allied Commander Europe, ordered a contingent of British and French paratroopers to seize the airport by force. After several days of standoff between Russian and NATO troops at the airport, both NATO and the UN ceded control of the airport to the Russians. After all the political wrangling, Russian control made traveling difficult for anyone who was not a diplomat, NATO officer, or senior UN official to gain access to the airfield. After being denied entry, I parked in a shady spot and watched the military aircraft and helicopter activity at the airport.

Settling in for a long afternoon, I noticed all the aircraft flying into or out of the airport were helicopters or very light propeller planes. I speculated the runway must not be equipped to handle the weight of heavier aircraft. Then I heard the roar of a multi-engine plane in the distance. I got out of my vehicle and began searching the sky, as did the guards and everyone else. In the distance, we could see the plane approaching over the city.

It was an enormous four-jet engine transport plane. At first, I thought it was a US Air Force C-141 troop carrier, but then I heard the Russian troops cheering. When the plane made a further bank toward the airfield, I saw an Ilyushin Il-76, the Soviet-era equivalent to the US C-141. As the plane prepared to land, the sound was thunderous. I returned to my vehicle and rolled up the windows to muffle the sound. I could see a stretch of runway from the parking area and watched the plane land

The arrival of the Ilyushin was a nice break in the monotony of the afternoon. I speculated Dyck's plane may have been delayed and considered returning to the CARE office to see if I had received a fax. My cell phone rang. I heard Dyck's voice. He announced he was at the airport and asked, "Where are you?"

I was startled. "Were you in that Ilyushin?"

In his whimsical manner, he replied, "Of course we were. British Airways could not meet our schedule."

I drove to the entry gate and again attempted to make the guards understand my team had just arrived on the plane. They were adamant that I could not enter. At that point, I succumbed to something I seldom do: I pulled out a carton of Marlboro Light cigarettes. The gate opened immediately, and I was waved into the airport with a smile and salute.

After parking the Land Rover, I began walking to the terminal and heard dogs barking. For a moment, I wondered if the Russians kept a kennel of patrol dogs, then remembered the key component of Minetech's team. Inside the terminal, I saw Dyck going through an endless series of questions and demands by the Russians. Although the UN supposedly ran the arrivals, departures, and customs at the airport, the Russians controlled the process. They were asking for verification of immunization shots for the dogs and the humans, as well as demands for other documentation and authorization stamps. The rigmarole was merely an attempt to elicit bribes from Minetech.

I admired Dyck's self-control. He had a no-nonsense air about him that he should not be crossed. In the years I have known him, I have never seen him lose his temper. There is nothing frivolous about him. He does not drink, swear, or smoke, and he is not a religious person. He is self-controlled in all aspects of his life. He has two passions: his wife and his dogs.

I went outside to look at the dogs. There were nineteen German Shepherds and one Labrador Retriever. When I walked back toward the airport lobby, Dyck came out of the building and told the men and women of his group to mount the vehicles. They unloaded eight different types of carriers from the Ilyushin, including an assortment of Land Rovers configured to carry humans, dogs, demining equipment, and supplies.

As Dyck monitored the assemblage of people, dogs, and equipment, I stood next to him. He was relaxed. A Russian officer with several UN people rushed out of the building shouting, "What are you doing?"

Dyck, very much at ease, replied, "Leaving."

The Russian went into an animated proclamation that he had not been processed and his departure was not authorized. The UN staff watched in silence. Dyck looked at the UN personnel and asked if they had contacted their headquarters, as per his request. They replied no, that this was a Russian facility. He looked at the group and replied, "My documentation is in order. Both NATO and the UN Headquarters in Geneva have approved it. I am not going to pay a 'facilitation fee' of one thousand dollars. We are leaving."

The Russian said, "We will not let you leave."

Dyck climbed in the lead vehicle, and his radio operator ordered the small convoy to move. The Russian looked at me and said, "You are accountable for them. You must stop them." I smiled, shrugged my shoulders, climbed into my vehicle, and followed the convoy to the front barrier, which was a simple horizontal pole across the road to impede the flow of traffic.

As we approached the barrier, three Russian soldiers were standing behind the barricade with their Kalashnikovs pointed at Dyck's vehicle. They were young men and very nervous. Dyck stopped his Land Rover and gestured for them to lift the barrier. They had obviously been given orders not to let his convoy pass. After several minutes of the word, "Nyet," Dyck got out of his Land Rover and walked to the barricade and lifted it. His movements happened so quickly that no one anticipated his action. As soon as the pole was raised, the first vehicle roared through the checkpoint, followed by the rest of the Minetech convoy.

The Russians recovered with yelling and rifle pointing, but in a matter of moments, Minetech had cleared the barrier. I followed as closely as possible because the Russians would have hassled me for endless hours as an accomplice.

The next morning, I reviewed the NATO log of previous day's incidents that had occurred throughout Kosovo. There was no mention of an incident at the Pristina airport.

Minetech established itself in the Ferizaj encampment, and Dyck and I made our way to the UNMAS headquarters. We were greeted warmly. Although Kosovo was less overwhelmed with landmines than Cambodia or Afghanistan, each day the casualties rose, with children the most frequent victims. In the 1970s, the Soviet Union had perfected a particularly sinister type of antipersonnel mine. Its official designation is the PFM-1, but it is generally called a "Butterfly Mine." Its design is like a maple tree seedling that rotates like a helicopter when it falls from the tree to the ground. The form of the mine allows it to spin through the air when it is dropped from an aircraft. As they fall, they scatter over broad areas. They are brightly colored plastic devices containing explosive liquid, and they resemble toys. Once activated, it lies on the ground until someone kicks at it or picks it up. Then, it explodes. When handled by a child, their head, hands, or an arm is blown off. The Russians deny that it targets children, but the plastic body is molded in a variety of bright colors, contrary to the usual mines designed to blend in. The area UNMAS assigned to Minetech was infested with Butterfly antipersonnel mines.

Over the ensuing months, I watched Minetech operate daily. Colonel Dyck's encampment was set up in the style of a military bivouac site. Although the men and women lived in tents in a field, the area was kept scrupulously clean and well-maintained. The dogs were close enough to the site to be cared for, but adequately distant to allow for his staff to have proper sleep and relaxation.

Early one morning as I arrived in Ferizaj, I drove through the town on my way to the

Minetech camp. I had a habit of stopping in a local shop and buying a liter of Pepsi, which was quite a treat because it was a rarity in Kosovo. As I drove down the main street, I saw a man in the distance dressed in orange coveralls walking his dog through the village. The orange coveralls were the trademark dress of a "deminer." They are purposefully colorful to ensure everyone around the deminer knows his location. I knew Minetech exercised their dogs daily, which included some playtime. This helps to keep the dogs relaxed and focused when it is time to find the mines. The deminer was a black man from Zimbabwe. As he walked his dog, children surrounded him, laughing, talking, and petting the dog. The children were on their way to school, and it was obvious they knew both the man and his dog.

What I witnessed was why I was engaged with CARE and did humanitarian work: amid a post-conflict environment such as Kosovo, CARE brought Africans to Europe to assist with national reconstruction. The people of Kosovo were able to see black women and men from Africa differently than the typical scenes of war, famine, and strife portrayed on the evening news throughout the world.

Zimbabwe was still recovering from decades of

war. Its people had suffered under various governments and were now suffering the ravages of the AIDS virus. CARE was paying Minetech in US dollars, and that money was then sent back to help stabilize a struggling economy. The dynamics of this arrangement was one of the few things in my life I truly believed was inspired.

When I reached Dyck's camp and walked through the small city of tents and equipment, I considered the foundation of Minetech's success. Minetech did not subscribe to a racialized hierarchy of black workers and white managers. In fact, most of the primary management were black men. Later, when I was talking with Dyck about a type of antipersonnel in a specific clearing area, Dyck mentioned that most of his team were very familiar with them because they had used them during the Zimbabwe War of Independence. I realized most of his men had been members of one of the two armies of Liberation Fighters who fought against the Rhodesian government for nearly fifteen years.

Dyck confirmed that nearly all the men had been members either of the resistance, or of the Rhodesian government. Yet, here they were in Kosovo as colleagues helping to clear the land.

The complexities of war and conflict confound

me. For "causes," "justice" and "righteousness," we continue sending young men and women into combat to enforce our beliefs. Our children are armed, filled with nationalistic hyperbole, and launch weapons at the "enemy." In return, we drape their coffins with flags and medals and allow their families moments of grateful remembrances as we launch the next set of recruits into combat. What I learned as a Marine is that battles are fought by the young at the behest of the old for reasons that disappear after the last shot is fired. I suspect as I age, and as a Vietnam Veteran, I have begun to "look back" at it all with a good deal of cynicism.

During the year Minetech worked in Kosovo, they made an extraordinary impact. They cleared approximately 17,000 buildings to ensure the structures had not been booby-trapped. They removed over 1,000 antipersonnel mines from agricultural fields, school playgrounds, medical facilities, homes, and farm buildings. They cleared more than a hundred anti-tank and anti-mechanized mines from roads and tracks, or any other route that a heavy vehicle would travel.

In this process, they lost only one dog. Minetech accomplished this remarkable feat in a low-key and modest fashion. Every morning the deminers began a new day with the knowledge that a great deal could go wrong for them, but they persevered. Minetech's turnover of staff was extraordinarily low. The men and women who came to Kosovo began to know the country and its people and had an unspoken resolve to make the country a better place.

We often equate the term "humanitarian" to pictures of a young person holding an emaciated child, or of food distribution in destroyed towns, but compassion is far more profound. No endeavor during violence and deprivation can be accomplished without a dedication to humanism. A person can look at the chaos, atrocities, and destruction and turn away because it is unpleasant, uncomfortable, and potentially dangerous, or they can commit. The humanitarian begins with tentative steps, but every movement is part of a more magnificent journey: it is a pursuit for the dignity of others, rather than self.

I watched Dyck lead a group of former enemies into the fields of Kosovo to preserve and change lives. They were men with humanity that transcended wars, politics, and agendas.

Clearing unexploded munitions is a long and difficult job. Just as these munitions still infest the cities and battlefields of WWI, WWII, Korea, and

Vietnam, Kosovo still has uncleared areas because of the time involved in finding the weapons. Too often, a mined area is discovered when a child triggers an explosion while playing in a field or pasture. The most recent data states that 117 Kosovars were killed, and 459 people injured by an unexploded remnant between the end of the conflict in 1999 to December 2016.[1] It will take decades to remove all the munitions from a country the size of Rhode Island.

---

1. "Kosovo Casualties." Landmine & Cluster Munitions Monitor, June 16, 2017, accessed July 10, 2018, http://the-monitor.org/en-gb/reports/2017/kosovo/casualties.aspx.

CHAPTER 16
BATTLE OF JENIN

> *"There is just so much hurt, disappointment, and oppression one can take.... The line between reason and madness grows thinner."*
> —Rosa Parks

IN MARCH 2002, I ARRIVED IN PALESTINE to work with the CARE West Bank and Gaza office. The Palestinian territories were engulfed in the Second *Intifada* (armed uprising), and the revolt included both Gaza and the West Bank. The Palestinians were fighting to achieve independence from Israel.

Amid the violence, Palestinian CARE staff continued working. Although the main office was in east Jerusalem, their work was outside the city, and travel to Palestine required long journeys through numerous checkpoints. With each day came a new set of regulations or requirements for additional permits.

The Israelis suspected the team, even though their work was to provide lifesaving assistance to the vulnerable Palestinian populations. The Israelis felt the humanitarian aid supported the women and men initiating violence against Israel.

My assignment was to find methods to mitigate the threats and harassment our staff were experiencing from the Israeli Defence[1] Force (IDF).

However, each day the number of terrorist attacks throughout Jerusalem and Israel increased, and many of the assaults were on crowded Israeli buses. With each attack, Israel's response became more severe. Based on my experience in Somalia, Bosnia, Rwanda, and Kosovo, I knew this conflict would not end well for either side.

To accomplish my job, I had to travel with the CARE team throughout the West Bank and Gaza and experience the conditions of their work.

Our first trip was to visit our suboffice in Jenin. The Israelis had blockaded the entire area for several weeks, denying us access. We started our trip

---

1. Israel uses Oxford (British) Spelling

from East Jerusalem. My Palestinian friend and colleague, Wael, accompanied me. We passed through numerous checkpoints, repeatedly answering the same question, "What are you doing here?"

My response was standard, "CARE is here to assist the refugee population." It was not a popular reply.

In Jenin, we approached another barricade and were refused permission to continue. It was late afternoon. We needed to find a place to stay for the evening. Traveling throughout the West Bank in the dark was not an option because it was too dangerous. The driver knew the area and said he had a cousin who lived in the community of Jalqamus. It was a tiny village, but close to Jenin. After a short drive, we reached the hamlet and the driver found his cousin. They exchanged an animated conversation, then he returned to the car and pointed to a dirt track. He said it led to the refugee camp. It was open, and there were no soldiers in the area. We could see many people coming and going along the track. We proceeded and found ourselves inside Jenin and very close to the refugee camp.

We drove to the CARE office. It had been in place since the 1960s, and the camp grew around it. CARE was well-known throughout the town, and the Palestinians respected the organization. In addition to providing physical assistance to camp residents and people from the town, CARE also provided jobs. The staff knew the camp was a center for anti-Israeli operations but exercised adherence to CARE's humanitarian mandate: "To address the rights of vulnerable groups, particularly women and children, in times of crisis… CARE upholds the principle of working independently of political, commercial, military, or religious objectives and promotes the protection of humanitarian space." The staff believed in this declaration and conducted themselves accordingly to assist with the humanitarian requirements based on need rather than politics.

In the Jenin office, I met my colleague, Yousef. He had worked with CARE for many years in West Bank and Gaza. He arranged for me to stay in a small room on the top floor of the building. It had a bed, bathroom, and closet, and was designed for staff members who visited Jenin from the central office. It was comfortable, and despite the tensions in the town, I was happy to have a place to sleep.

The next day, we walked through the camp. The devastation was shocking. I had seen urban fighting in Sarajevo, Gornji Vakuf and Mostar in Bosnia, where tanks, artillery, and mortar rounds caused the destruction. In Jenin, the devastation was more calculated. The Israeli Defense Force (IDF) had used armored bulldozers to clear vast areas so their tanks could reach Palestinian positions. It was remarkable to witness the sheer number of collapsed buildings knowing there were humans who took refuge inside of them. Many people who remained in the camp during the fighting were not combatants. They were kids, women, and the infirm.

We walked to the Hawashin district. Helicopter rockets attacked the area many times, but it was so densely built and populated that the aerial attacks had little impact. Consequently, Israel deployed IDF bulldozers to systematically destroy every building and structure in the district, approximately 200 meters square. Without exception, every building was reduced to rubble. Later estimates report that during this attack fifty-three Palestinians died buried in the wreckage.

As we walked through the destruction, the flags of both Hamas and Hezbollah were flying. It was a symbolic gesture, but I was conflicted by its intent. Both Hamas and Hezbollah are labeled extremist terrorist groups by the United States, European Union, and many other countries except for Russia and China. Hamas is linked to the Sunni branch of Islam and supported by Saudi Arabia. Hezbollah is associated with the Shi'a division of Islam. Its activities are backed by Iran and Syria. Although I believed in and tried practicing the humanitarian principle of impartiality, I was also human. I remembered the October 1983 attack on the Marine barracks in Beirut that killed 241 Sailors and Marines, many of whom were my friends. It was reportedly orchestrated by Hezbollah.

The enormity of this devastation was overwhelming. Along one of the broken roads, we met an elderly man pushing his wife in her wheelchair through the rubble. Yousef knew the people and stopped to speak to them. The IDF bulldozed their home after they left to stay with a daughter outside of the city before the fighting began. There was nothing left of their home or possessions. Every remembrance, garment, piece of furniture, and utensil—gone. The old man surveyed the destruction and turned to us. In Arabic he said, "We will never yield. If it takes a thousand years, we will never yield."

During the next two days, I accompanied Wael and Yousef as they visited families in the camp. Each day, the smell from the bodies buried in the rubble grew stronger, permeating taste, and embedding itself on our clothes and skin.

The CARE staff organized to assist the refugees

with food, water, and other necessities, and the Israelis opened the roads to allow the delivery of aid. They were sensitive to the statements of condemnation from the UN. The last thing they wanted were reports that they were impeding the delivery of humanitarian assistance. Both Hamas and Hezbollah were distributing funds to families who had lost a member in the attack, had someone wounded as a resistance fighter, or whose homes were destroyed. It was surreal to be working next to Hamas and Hezbollah while distributing food imprinted with the words, "Food Gift from The People of The United States of America." The irony was that America also provided the State of Israel with the helicopters, fighter planes, rockets, and much of the ammunition used to destroy parts of Jenin.

In any conflict, nothing is entirely black or white; every side perceives a legitimate grievance. The Palestinians are a subjugated society. Their response at times is vicious. No one can condone suicide bombings and indiscriminate killing. However, what I witnessed in Jenin went far beyond the boundaries of an appropriate retaliatory response.

During the destruction, I followed a path to a high point in the rubble with a view of the area. I was alone on a rocky shelf between the Hamas and Hezbollah flags. As far as I could see, there was ruin. Every open road had people quietly moving in lines to receive aid from the NGOs or Hamas and Hezbollah.

On one side of the conflict, I was bombarded with statements about the necessity to make borders safe from terrorists and the enemies of Israel. They said the fanatics were infiltrating the state, but from where I sat, all I saw were a few flags flying over the ruins and lines of thirsty, hungry, and devastated people. I looked for the threat. With the outcry and clamor to build walls and impose restrictions, they must be lurking. This camp was supposed to be the epicenter of terrorism. Where were the terrorists? All I saw were victims. I am not naive. I knew they were here. However, the identity of a terrorist changes depending on which side of the battle one is standing.

What I saw were victims, casualties of the Palestinian movement resisting the Israelis. They were the victims of the Israelis who wanted to protect their claim to the land. They were the victims of the United States and Europeans who sold the weapons. They were the victims of Saudi Arabia and Iran who fought a proxy war against Israel through the Palestinians.

I returned to the distribution where an NGO colleague I had known for decades greeted me. Around them were hundreds of Palestinians—injured, sick, exhausted, and malnourished. In the past, I had seen terrorists and genocidal maniacs, but they were not here. These were people suffering the consequences of politics.

Surrounding me were women carrying babies, accompanied by other children. They were like all mothers, regardless of nation or culture, seeking safety for their families. In their eyes I saw fear and confusion. They were bewildered. They were carrying kids, not hand grenades. In their backpacks were the barest essentials to survive, not suicide bombs.

Wael and I had a quiet conversation. The number of CARE staff and people from other humanitarian organizations had grown. They were handling the requirements, and we felt we were getting in the way. It was time to leave. We talked to Yousef. He was grateful for our assistance and confirmed that with the arrival of additional staff, he had enough help. We said goodbye to our friends and colleagues, retrieved our backpacks from the office and loaded the car. It was mid-afternoon. It was not reasonable to depart until morning, but we wanted to leave. It was too much.

Wael had a cousin nearby Jenin with a small farm, and he thought we could stay there overnight. In half an hour, we drove down a little track between groves of olive trees, the sun sinking slowly. After the previous days, the drive was peaceful. In fact, if not for the sound of helicopters and armored vehicles in the distance, it was idyllic. Wael said he thought the land and trees we were passing might have been in the same family for centuries.

Turning a small bend, we entered a clearing with a house close to the road. Wael's cousin's family greeted us. The number of people living in makeshift shelters around the dwelling surprised me. Wael sensed my thoughts and told me that his cousin welcomed the people who fled the Jenin camp.

The area around the house was divided into family groups. There were a few tents, but most of the units were separated by lines with cloth strung from poles and trees. At this time of year, there was no concern of rain, but blue tarps were layered across the shelters to protect the inhabitants from the sun. Foam mats were spread across the ground inside each of the accommodations for people to sit and sleep on throughout the day and night. There were a lot of children and women. The men were older. There was a noticeable lack of young and middle-aged men. The absence of men in this age group did not mean they were Palestinian fighters. Most of them probably worked in Israel or other parts of the West Bank, and it was impossible for them to travel to Jenin during the fighting.

Wael's cousin walked us to an opening under an olive tree. He told us this was where we could rest. He assured us we could stay as long as we wanted. Later, when we walked around his house, the people in the small encampment greeted us. Several boys brought us two sleeping mats and blankets.

Along with the boys, two older women brought tea, hummus, and bread. I was hesitant to take the food because I did not want to make others do without, but Wael assured me there was plenty. In Jenin, we had Humanitarian Daily Rations (HDRs)[2] that we carried with us in the vehicle, but they were gone after two days. The hummus and bread felt like a Thanksgiving feast.

It was a pleasant night. I pulled my mat from under the olive tree and watched the stars. There

---

2. Humanitarian daily rations (HDRs) are packets of food intended for people in a humanitarian crisis. Each ration contains approximately 2,200 calories.

were no clouds, and the moon was in its waning phase with almost no light. I saw the Milky Way spilling across the heavens from one horizon to the next. Some meteorites flashed across the sky, and airplanes crossed the horizon at such heights they looked like distant stars. I fell into a deep sleep.

I woke once and thought I heard movement in the brush. I hoped it was an animal and not an IDF patrol. I was too exhausted to care but did not want to spend the night being questioned and transported to an internment center.

In the morning, Wael told me he wanted to visit his father's youngest brother to ensure all was well with the family. He lived outside the small town of Jalame. The house and olive groves were approximately six miles apart. I agreed. I was not ready to return to the normalcy of American life. The intensity of Palestine was still too raw.

Although both of us had cell phones and chargers, there was no signal in our area. The networks were interrupted throughout most of West Bank. I knew CARE in East Jerusalem and Atlanta would be concerned, but Wael was confident our well-being and location were known. I had seen these casual means of communications across Africa and had no doubt they were just as effective in the West Bank.

I reflected on the landscape's natural beauty surrounding us as we drove. I caught sight of Wael's uncle's home. It was a block building with stucco siding painted pale blue and nestled on a gentle slope. The house and its surroundings were peaceful. There was one notable exception: two hundred meters behind the home was a wide span of denuded land that led to an electric fence with a road on the far side. The lane allowed the IDF to patrol the barricade efficiently. The fence was the precursor to a solid wall, which would eventually surround his property.

After greeting Wael's uncle, we walked to the fence. Wael translated his uncle's comments about the cattle grazing in fields on the other side of the barrier. The land was his, but the cattle were not. They belonged to Israeli settlers. His uncle's family had owned the acreage for more than 200 years. The Israeli government assured them they would still own the land despite the fence, but they broke their promise. The only way his uncle could maintain the property was to drive or walk seven kilometers to a checkpoint and cross, but the journey was futile. The settlers had quickly appropriated the land and filed a petition in an Israeli court for ownership by claiming it was abandoned.

We stayed with Wael's uncle for the night. The

next morning, we began our journey to Ramallah. It took most of the day. There were numerous checkpoints with the same questions regarding who we were. Why were we traveling in West Bank? Where were we coming from? What is CARE International? Who do we help? The repetition, open hostility, and the knowledge the wrong word or attitude would put us into endless hours of interrogation was debilitating.

Along the way, Wael and I stopped speaking to one another. It was not from anger. Days of witnessing the destruction, death and violations had taken its toll. We were numb. The state of Israel controlled everything. We shuffled along the road with the knowledge that we did not matter. We were expendable. I had a passport. I would go home. I saw the misery, but this was not my place. I did not have to endure it, but next to me was a man who could not leave. His family had lived here for centuries, but now they were outsiders. As we made our way to Ramallah, desperation seized me. How could a nation grown from the most brutal and inhuman treatment in modern history allow itself to inflict this type of violence on others?

As evening approached, we entered Ramallah. There was evidence of the uprising throughout the city. The IDF patrolled the town, and the checkpoints had increased to every two blocks. Still, the city felt like an oasis. By turning down any side street, parking the truck and walking, we could enter the alleys and connecting courtyards to avoid the military presence. However, traveling like this through the city could generate another set of problems if we were caught by the IDF. We decided to abide by the barriers and cross through the center of town to the hotel.

I spent two days at the City Inn Hotel. It was a quiet sanctuary free from the violence. Cell phone coverage was intermittent, and instant access to the internet was still in the future. I was alone and needed time to process what I witnessed. From my room, I could see the wall surrounding the city. I measured the makings of a great nation. It should not be founded on walls and escalating violence, nor the continued onslaught of suicide bombs and retaliatory helicopter attacks. Great nations are made of brave men and women on both sides who say, "enough." I saw this in Rwanda. It takes courage to make the first step, but amid this violence I witnessed the deepest expressions of tolerance, hope, and humanity. Yousef and Wael were courageous Stewards who risked a great deal traveling and remaining in Jenin. They did this because they knew they were part of a more significant effort.

The CARE West Bank and Gaza staff are a brilliant light in a dark place. As a group, they embody a universal principle of nonviolence using engagement, compassion, and dignity as their guidelines. The team are primarily Palestinian women who set themselves above the politics and focus on the humanitarian requirements of shared decency. They are not for or against anything other than the delivery of aid. They face many obstacles assisting the population, but they persevere. When told no, they find different ways. In their office, I witnessed a group of women and men building collective solidarity to peacefully face insurmountable obstacles and persist in the name of humanitarianism. By doing so, their efforts sowed the seeds of justice and freedom throughout Palestine.

Before my departure, I met with a group of the West Bank Gaza staff. We discussed the complexities of the problems in Palestine. One woman said, "There has to be a new way of thinking. It must be based on mutual respect. To change the current patterns of behavior, the starting point should be respecting each other. Only then can we discuss how to overcome the violence. Because when we respect each other, the idea of who came first—and questioning each other's capacities and capabilities—becomes irrelevant. The question is, how can we make this land a better place with the authenticity of each of us individually? We all bring something valuable. Each of us has a lot to give."

That statement has stuck with me for nearly two decades.

CHAPTER 17
THE ESSENCE OF COURAGE

"I won't live my life dictated by fear."
—Margaret Hassan

THE KIDNAPPING OF HUMANITARIAN workers is a longstanding problem. In the eyes of a local criminal group, the aid worker represents a wealthy western organization. While the international media notes the abduction of foreign staff, most of the seizures are national workers and the issue gets quickly resolved with a cash payment or transfer of goods. These incidents resembled a business transaction. The kidnappers wanted money and had no intention of harming the victim.

Beginning in Somalia and Bosnia in the 1990s,

the parameters began changing and the violence increased. If the negotiation took too long, the victim was often killed. Although it was still a rare event, the humanitarian community began training their staff to mitigate the threats of violence and kidnapping.

NGOs realized paying a ransom encouraged other abductions. Thus, most of the humanitarian community adopted a no-ransom policy. This was more than a casual declaration; it was a code that had to be followed. When an NGO publicly announced, "We will not pay for the return of a staff member," it was a declaration without equivocation and worked for a time. Abductions decreased as criminals realized there was no profit in a kidnapping.

The respite changed after 9/11 with the invasion of Afghanistan and Iraq and the rise of international terrorism. The kidnapping of an aid worker became a political proclamation. No one was prepared for the sight of a man standing in front of a kneeling victim and slitting their throat. All the informal codes that helped safeguard humanitarians were swept aside. Kidnapping and publicly slaughtering an international aid worker in front of a camera was an easy way to gain attention and proclaim a group's cause via the evening news. Such carnage met the fundamental criteria of terrorism. What better way to spread universal fear than slaughtering the most innocent party in a conflict whose sole purpose was assisting those in need?

Before Iraq, I spent a decade helping whole communities. Whether in a refugee camp or a blockaded city, my responsibility was finding the means to assist the greatest number of people in dire need. Iraq changed that. For the first time I learned that sometimes humanitarian assistance must focus on saving one person.

I met Margaret Hassan in Amman, Jordan, in early 2003. Although she was the Director of CARE Iraq, she moved her administrative staff to co-locate with the CARE Jordan office because conducting business in Baghdad became too difficult in the buildup to the Iraqi war. The international communications systems inside Iraq were shut down, and CARE Iraq needed to communicate with international donors to manage, solicit, and report the use of millions of dollars of grants and donations. Margaret, though, decided to remain in Baghdad with her husband, Tahseen Ali Hassan, an Iraqi citizen, to continue overseeing CARE's humanitarian projects still operating throughout the country. She and Tahseen met when he was studying engineering in the United Kingdom. They married, and she moved to Iraq with him in 1972.

Margaret attempted to visit the Jordan office every three weeks. At the time, there were no commercial flights and few UN flights connecting Amman with Baghdad. The NATO military attack on Iraq was imminent. No one knew when the invasion would start, but by the size of the assembled forces in the countries surrounding Iraq, it had to be soon.

A trip from Baghdad to Amman was an eleven-hour journey, with frequent stops at Iraqi checkpoints. Although Margaret had lived in Iraq for more than three decades, was fluent in Arabic, and a citizen, her Gaelic features caused her undue attention.

Before the NATO invasion of Iraq, I traveled to Jordan to join several other humanitarian groups to form a coalition to coordinate our responses with NATO governments after the attack. Although the concept had merit, it was not productive. The most significant value of the shared engagement was to allow NGOs to plan and coordinate amongst ourselves and then attempt to engage the militaries for post-conflict reconstruction.

The pending assault unsettled me with memories of the Vietnam War, where nearly 60,000

American servicewomen and men died and approximately 1,300,000 north and south Vietnamese soldiers and civilians were killed.[1] I had a bias, shaped from that era. In my mind, I saw people sitting in plush government chambers, remote and safe from conflict, making politically expedient decisions about sending our youth to war.

As the case was made for the invasion, I listened carefully to a man I believed would not send my nation down another rabbit hole of pointless conflict. I had faith in General Colin Powell, a Vietnam War veteran. He would not advocate sending Americans into war unless it was a clear danger to the United States.

I listened to his presentation to the United Nations on February 3, 2003, alleging Iraq was hiding weapons of mass destruction from the U.N. Monitoring, Verification, and Inspection Commission.

He failed to convince me.

I knew several members of the U.N. investigation teams charged with finding them. They were professional and competent women and men. I had served two with of them in the U.S. military. They

---

1. *America in Vietnam*, by Guenter Lewy, Oxford Univ. Press, 1981, pp. 442–443.

knew what they were searching for and would not hesitate to announce the presence of these weapons.

Also, the NATO strategy of armed containment of Iraqi forces within specified longitudes and latitudes worked. I was not a pacifist but realistic about war. In the end, it never seems to be the children of the strongest proponents for conflict who are sent home in body bags.

There was another reason for my reluctance to be in Jordan and Iraq. Regardless of the estimated timeframe, we planned to engage in the humanitarian response, it was always far longer than anticipated. I remarried in September 2002. My new wife and I shared a common experience in humanitarian work in Africa in the early '90s, followed by Bosnia, and understood the consequences of too much time in a war zone. We met after I moved to Atlanta. Although we worked in different divisions at CARE, we were eventually brought together by a common elevator bank on the 4th floor.

Early on March 3, 2003, concerned about another unnecessary war and prolonged separation from my wife. I walked across an open field toward the CARE office from the small hotel where I stayed. I saw Margaret and her driver loading the vehicle for their trip back to Baghdad in the distance. When I reached them, I helped carry supplies. After the SUV was loaded, I shook hands with her driver and walked to the passenger side to say goodbye. We had tears in our eyes. Margaret was returning to a city that was going to be bombed and attacked by the most well-equipped military force in history. Any sense as to whether such an attack was right or wrong was overshadowed by looking at this anxious woman who only wanted to hear someone say, "It will be alright." I spoke the words, but we both knew no one could guarantee her safety. Margaret regained her composure, straightened her back, got in the vehicle, and went to war. There was never any discussion about her and Tahseen moving to Amman until the conflict ended.

On March 19, the bombing began; all communications with Baghdad were cut off. We hoped our satellite phones would work, but they were blocked. Watching CNN and BBC, we saw the aerial bombings and the assurances by NATO that their attacks were supported by precision strikes. However, the bombs could still cause collateral damage—code words for killing civilians.

I was afraid, not only for Margaret, but for the world. This war was needless.

Throughout the fighting, we heard about

Margaret from refugees arriving in Amman. They assured us that she, her family, and the CARE staff were well.

After NATO moved into Baghdad in April I flew to the city on an ICRC plane. Approaching Baghdad, the pilots used the "spiraling method" to land, the tactic used to avoid being shot out of the sky by a surface-to-air missile. During the final approach, the plane tilted to such a degree I could see the landing gear lock into place under the wings. The aircraft began spiraling like a corkscrew. Landing took about ten minutes, but the constant twirling and bumping from wind shears tested my stomach.

Once on the ground, I went through a very casual immigration process. The most striking observation was the number of well-armed private security company (PSC) men and women guarding the airport. The guards were wearing uniforms of various PSCs and were older than the average soldier. I did not see any NATO active-duty military.

Two CARE staff greeted me. Driving into the capital, I was surprised by the amount of traffic. There were many military vehicles, but in no sense was this an occupied city. In fact, it was the opposite. The numbers of Iraqis going about their lives obscured the military presence. I saw minimal destruction. There was none of the wholesale obliteration of cities, towns, and villages I had seen in Beirut, Kosovo, Somalia, and Bosnia.

As we made our way to the office, we passed several shopping districts. I was impressed with the number of products being loaded into cars. People were purchasing everything from satellite television dishes to washing machines and refrigerators. Every other building had a restaurant or café doing brisk business. This was not a city struggling to get back on its feet.

For the next several weeks, there was an ambivalence by the Iraqi citizenry toward the coalition forces. NATO was not welcomed as a liberator in the fashion I saw in Kosovo, but there was no sense of resistance, rage, or violence. Most people were merely glad the fighting was over. In retrospect, I realize it was a brief interlude of peace while dissidents organized, and sectarian partitions regrouped.

The political dynamics of the Saddam Hussein government made it difficult for CARE Iraq to attract international donor assistance. The United Nations sanctions put in place at the end of the Iraqi War in 1991 included many prohibitions on importing medicines and medical equipment. Margaret did a remarkable job of working around these restrictions. Her principal focus was enhancing the medical infrastructure in Iraq through sanitation, health, and nutrition. By 1998, she had legally obtained and transported leukemia medicine to child cancer victims.

Minus the administrative staff in Amman, she had approximately twenty people in her Iraq office, and the amount of work they accomplished was remarkable. In tandem with Margaret's focus on children and young people, CARE built and equipped a new Children's Spinal Care Wing to a Baghdad hospital. This was the only center in Iraq designed to treat the several hundred children who suffered spinal cord damage each year. Before opening, only parents with money and connections could send their children outside the country for treatment. It was a significant accomplishment for anyone, but to manage this during the United Nations sanctions was an incredible feat.

Traveling through the country, I witnessed several new efforts, but Margaret kept her focus on health and sanitation. The programs included assistance with replacing and building new sewage systems throughout Baghdad and repairing water treatment plants. During my trips, we saw few soldiers. Most of the population wanted a return to normalcy.

Paramilitary soldiers continued arriving. They had some degree of training, but generally lacked discipline and were aggressively arrogant. I was driving by a US government facility and saw a man in his fifties guarding the entrance. He was one hundred pounds overweight and had bandoliers of ammunition crisscrossing his chest. He was smoking a cigar and wore a bandana of the Confederate flag over his head. I was dismayed this man represented my country, but his assault rifle and degree of authority troubled me more.

The number of paramilitaries increased each day, and soon there were more armed civilian contractors than service members in Baghdad. Although the majority were from the United States, South Africa, and Europe, there were many former Gurkha soldiers from Nepal. They were the most well-disciplined and professional. The entire composite of PSCs became quite a sight, and all lines of authority seemed to rest inside these individual private security companies. Their employees had varying degrees of training, unknown levels of self-discipline, no indication of their psychological stability, and seemingly no restrictions regarding their use of alcohol or drugs. Into this mix, NATO disbanded both the Iraqi military and police forces. The country was stripped of judicial authority, which resulted in Baghdad being run by thousands of older foreign men racing through its streets in heavily-armed vehicles.

There is a term used in NATO doctrine called, "Rear Area Operations." It is defined as, "operations, [which] protect assets in the rear area to support the force. Rear area operations encompass more than just rear area security... rear area operations provide security for personnel, equipment, and facilities in the area..." At the end of the war, there was a requirement to ensure the stability of Iraq and provide security to the rear areas, but there were not enough trained soldiers to accomplish both tasks. Consequently, active-duty military secured the countryside, while private soldiers protected Baghdad.

In the following months, I could not discount the feeling that the paramilitaries in Baghdad helped fuel the Iraqis' loss of confidence in NATO forces and the United States. Although some women and men did professional and courageous work to protect the Iraqi citizenry, there were too many episodes of abuse and misappropriation of power and funds that destabilized a society already weakened by entrenched sectarian divisions.

NATO invaded Iraq, freed the country from a ruthless dictator, ended years of economic boycotts, and was beginning to initiate billions of dollars of humanitarian and development aid to assist the Iraqis in building a viable and democratic government. This should have led to positive change.

However, in the ensuing months, the security situation in Baghdad collapsed because of the depth of sectarian separations in Iraq. The removal of Saddam Hussein after decades of suppressed rage between the Shi'a majority and the Sunnis erupted into open conflict. Added to this was NATO's failure to recognize the emergence of Al-Qaeda as a Sunni-based terrorist organization. Nothing prepared America for the type of terrorism that appeared in Iraq, particularly under the direction of Abu Musab al-Zarqawi.

Sitting in postwar Iraq, it was easy to see the ineptitude of the planning from the moment the bullets stopped. The Pentagon oversaw reconstruction. The US military is an extraordinary war-fighting mechanism, but it is not a humanitarian and development organization. On the cessation of hostilities, Lieutenant General Jay Garner, United States Army, was selected to lead the post-war reconstruction efforts. He became the DoD Director of the Office for Reconstruction and Humanitarian Assistance. However, the US government already had an organization with a professional reconstruction workforce of approximately 24,000 women and men: The United States Agency for International Development (USAID).

The reconstruction money came from billions of Iraqi oil dollars held by the United Nations because of the embargos. The US would oversee elections within ninety days, and with the reinstatement of a centralized and freely elected government, the coalition would redeploy some of its troops to provide a stabilization force while the new government rebuilt a viable army.

However, without an existing Iraqi police system, Baghdad rapidly collapsed into a rampage of lawlessness with widespread looting, revenge killings, and general chaos. The infrastructure of the country collapsed, government ministries were broken, and official records destroyed. The only bureau protected by coalition forces was the Ministry of Oil. General Garner was given an unviable mission.

During this violence, Margaret continued rebuilding her programming activities. After years of CARE's efforts, she felt the organization had gained the respect of the Iraqi people and that acceptance would safeguard them, but traditional protection for humanitarian workers was about to change in a manner no one anticipated.

On the afternoon of August 19, 2003, a terrorist bomb exploded at the Canal Hotel, the converted headquarters for the United Nations Assistance Mission in Iraq. The attack killed twenty-two people and wounded more than one hundred. One of the dead was Sergio de Mello, the UN High Commissioner for Human Rights.

Abu Musab al-Zarqawi, the leader of Al-Qaeda in Iraq, claimed responsibility for the blast. Zarqawi asserted the specific victim of the attack was de Mello because he assisted East Timor to become an independent state in 2002. Zarqawi stated de Mello had participated in the illegal secession of the area from Indonesia and was a war criminal.

A second attack, a suicide bombing, took place two months later at the compound of the ICRC. Again, Zarqawi took responsibility. He publicly declared war on humanitarian organizations and considered all of them pawns of the UN and the United States government. Thus, in a short period, a little-known former criminal from Jordan moved center stage in the complexity of Baghdad and quickly became a world figure.

In the increasing violence, my focus shifted to

staff safety and security. As Margaret wanted to increase CARE's levels of assistance, we started disagreeing over the dangers to her and her staff who would travel the country implementing and overseeing the programs. Margaret dismissed any threat to herself and believed that by using her Iraqi team to manage the projects, and restricting the international workers to Baghdad, she could mitigate the risks.

After the attack on the Canal Hotel, there was a great deal of collateral damage. One of the areas destroyed was the Children's Spinal Cord treatment center that CARE had established. Within hours, Margaret began the effort to rebuild the clinic. Her work was tireless, but I worried about her public persona. People started referring to her as "Mother Margaret of Iraq." She disliked the reference to Mother Teresa out of genuine modesty, but her face began appearing more frequently on television. Her name cropped up in the newspapers as she advocated for more international donor assistance for humanitarian aid. She was becoming too visible and notable.

Every day, the kidnappings of internationals increased, and Margaret represented an aid group that terrorists identified as an American organization. I believed she was becoming a potential victim.

When we discussed this, she was incensed. She said she was an Iraqi doing charitable work, and that combination would keep her safe. When I persisted, she told me I was overcautious and getting in her way. I was an outsider who knew nothing about Iraq, its culture, or how it worked. I had appeared in her office one day and become an obstacle to her programming activities. What angered her was that I had the authority to force critical decisions when I determined the office could not or would not take appropriate actions to mitigate threats to its workers. She began to resent me.

My dilemma was that she was involved in critical work. Without her efforts, people would die. I did not want to start a process to suspend CARE's activities in Iraq. However, we had to find a balance between too much attention to staff security and too little, but Margaret was a hard woman to deal with when she believed she was right.

At my recommendation, CARE's leadership agreed the Baghdad office was in a precarious location and forced her to move. She rented a large villa in a safer locale and, with the agreement of her immediate neighbors, CARE erected precast concrete security barriers on the three streets leading into the neighborhood. The barriers were unmanned but positioned to slow vehicles as they weaved their way through several rows of the blocks.

When I visited Margaret at her new location, she was polite but not enamored with my presence nor my recommendation that caused her to move to the new site. She continued insisting there was no security issue because CARE's presence in Iraq consisted of an office primarily staffed by nationals. I persisted that Zarqawi was targeting all foreigners, regardless of their association with governmental or non-governmental organizations, and her European background made her a target. She was very direct in telling me she had been in Iraq long enough to be considered an Iraqi. That was the end of the conversation.

On November 25, 2003, the CARE office was attacked at approximately eleven o'clock at night. The neighbors reported that a single car stopped in front of the site. Two men got out of a vehicle, each armed with an RPG-7, a rocket-propelled grenade used as an anti-tank weapon. It can penetrate ten inches of steel, and the concrete villa was not an obstacle. They fired three rockets. One hit a palm tree in the front yard, and two of them struck the building. Fortunately, there was no one in the structure, and there were no injuries.

The office closed, and the international staff relocated to Jordan while CARE management reviewed the security situation. Margaret's team believed the concrete barriers in the street caused several disgruntled neighbors to instigate an attack to drive CARE out of the neighborhood. Meanwhile, terrorists proclaimed CARE an instrument of the west and a Christian occupation force.

Margaret moved back to the original office and re-opened operations. The attack reinforced her belief that she should not have relocated from the original site.

Once she settled into the old office, I departed for Afghanistan where CARE's work was rapidly expanding, but the security situation for the staff in Iraq and Afghanistan was deteriorating. I spent several weeks with the CARE team looking at ways to mitigate the threats, then I returned to the CARE headquarters in Atlanta in the spring. Throughout the summer and fall, I traveled to Kenya, Zimbabwe, and Burundi where security conditions were worsening as well.

On October 19, 2004, I received a call from Jon Mitchell, the CARE Regional Director for the Middle East. He told me that at 7:30 a.m., as she was en route to the CARE office in Baghdad, armed men abducted Margaret Hassan.

There were three routes from Margaret's home to the CARE building. Her driver alternated them daily. However, all the roads converged onto one street that served as the only entrance to the site. As her vehicle turned onto the single lane, a car obstructed the way. A second auto appeared from the rear. One kidnapper, armed with a rocket-propelled grenade launcher, took a position to guard the remaining escape route. Margaret was pulled from the car, hooded, and pushed into the backseat of the rear vehicle. The driver was released unharmed, and the entire event took less than sixty seconds. The precision indicated a well-planned and rehearsed event.

The neighbors alerted the office. The CARE Iraq staff spent several hours canvassing the neighborhood trying to gather information in hopes of determining who kidnapped Margaret to negotiate her release, all the while traumatized that their friend and leader was in grave danger. After several hours, they alerted the police and the British Embassy. Although notification of the authorities would typically be the first act in a kidnapping, this was Baghdad, and the police force was corrupt and inept.

After explaining the situation, Jon asked me to meet him in Amman, Jordan, and fly to Baghdad to assist him in the effort to gain her freedom. Within hours, I climbed on a plane from Atlanta to Heathrow, and onward to Amman. I had a twelve-hour layover in London, and CARE booked me into a small hotel so I could sleep. I turned on the television to follow the story about Ken Bigley. Zarqawi's group had kidnapped him and his two American colleagues. Bigley was a British civil engineer working for the Gulf Supplies and Commercial Services, a Kuwaiti company working on reconstruction projects in Iraq.

Within seven days, Zarqawi beheaded both Americans in front of a camera and mailed the decapitation films to Al Jazeera. With Bigley, Zarqawi used the media to gain notoriety, develop his perceived status as a terrorist, and experiment with how much attention he could achieve by keeping Bigley in front of the cameras. Zarqawi released several videos of him pleading for his life and begging Tony Blair to save him. The British press accused Blair of not doing enough to help.

Blair made a statement to the media as he was leaving a meeting. There were accusations that Blair's government had refused to talk with the kidnappers, which resulted in Bigley's murder.

Blair responded to the camera, "We will never negotiate, but we will talk to anyone at any time to gain someone's freedom." At the time, my interest in the statement was casual, but in the following years it disturbed and unsettled me. This statement informed our actions in the ensuing months with Margaret's kidnapping.

The next morning, I boarded a flight to Amman and landed late in the evening. By the time I reached my hotel, it was nearly midnight. At the desk, I had a message telling me I was scheduled to depart for Baghdad at six in the morning on an ICRC flight, and there would be a pick up at 3:00 a.m. I walked to my room, brushed my teeth and collapsed into bed. At three o'clock, I met Jon Mitchell. He looked exhausted. He had been working and traveling nonstop for days. He said we would be staying at the Swiss Embassy in Baghdad.

The departure airport for military, UN, and NGO flights to Iraq was an old airfield in the city of Amman. The terminal building was a structure that had not received any repair in years. Jon and I made our way to a long stretch of wall, put our backpacks down and stretched out on the floor. At 4:30, a member of the ICRC told us the flight was delayed until 1:30 that afternoon due to rockets that hit the Baghdad airport. When the time came to leave, I was surprised at how precise the departure procedures were. Customs officials inspected our luggage and passports, documented, and stamped. We loaded into a small ICRC jet that seated ten passengers and left.

As we approached Baghdad, the plane began a gradual climb to start its corkscrew descent. It seemed we climbed to a higher altitude before the final approach than in previous visits. Thankfully, after fifteen minutes, the runway appeared, and we made our final approach onto the tarmac.

We hurried into the main terminal. In the past, this was a relaxed and casual stroll. Now, there was an urgency to get people out of the open as quickly as possible. I noted all windows and entry points were heavily sandbagged to protect from shrapnel in the event of an explosion. After Jon and I cleared customs and immigration, we stepped into the main terminal and looked for someone with a sign from the Swiss Embassy. While scanning the crowd, two men with black military combat uniforms, black flak-jackets, dark sunglasses, and AR-15 automatic rifles approached us.

One of them asked if I was Colonel Macpherson. I had not been referred to as Colonel for some years, and particularly not as a humanitarian worker in a complex environment like Iraq. I nodded. The man responded he was to escort Colonel Macpherson and Mr. Jon Mitchell to the British Embassy. I looked at Jon and said, "So much for the Swiss."

Jon responded, "Maybe we have to check in with the Brits before we meet the Swiss?"

We showed the men our ID, and I asked to see theirs. Their documents identified them as members of the private security company Control Risk.

While loading our gear into the armored vehicle, the guards received a radio message. There was a suicide car bomb explosion on the road to Baghdad, which had become known as the "Highway of Death." A road heavily traveled by civilians, and a major route for military vehicles, it experienced multiple attacks daily.

In half an hour, we were authorized to make the trip to the city. Driving along the corridor, the number of scorched and destroyed vehicles on both sides of the highway stunned me. The entire four-lane road had become a series of potholes blasted by explosions. The blasts may have come from suicide bombers or roadside explosives known as IEDs (improvised explosive devices) hidden in a discarded sack or animal carcass, or from a barrage of mortars or rocket-propelled grenades. Along the highway, the coalition forces had placed armored vehicles with machine guns every 300 to 400 meters. They lined both sides of the road. Military armored cars patrolled in both directions. Despite this, the rash of bombings and attacks continued. The last time I was in Baghdad it was a dangerous place. Now, it looked like a city from a science fiction movie.

Entering the Green Zone, which was the common name for the International Zone of Baghdad, we relaxed. The zone was approximately four square miles, and the center of the coalition authority in Iraq. Concrete blast walls surrounded the entire area, ranging in height from ten to sixteen feet. US forces guarded the limited entry points.

Inside the area were numerous embassies, hotels, and apartments for the civilian members of the coalition occupation. There was a US Army hospital and headquarters for the private security companies. Although the sector was called a "safe area," mortar and rocket attacks were continual, like rain. In the past, I refrained from going near it. Now, I had to enter to meet with the members of the British government.

After clearing the barrier, we went to meet with

the UK Ambassador to Iraq. Jon and I assumed we were going to the British embassy. We were surprised when we pulled into the driveway of a small home.

While unloading my bag, I noted a sign on the side of the drive, saying Kroll Security—a private security company. Inside were half a dozen people, several members of the British embassy, and three men from Kroll. The senior person was the UK Deputy of Mission. He apologized that the Ambassador was unable to greet us but would brief us himself on the status of their efforts to free Margaret. The discussion revealed there had been no communications with the kidnappers. The embassy arranged with Kroll to house and support us during our stay and recommended we remain no longer than a week. The British were concerned that Jon and I would become targets for kidnapping, and we agreed with them.

When I told them, we had planned to stay with the Swiss, he replied that her majesty's government thought it best for us to remain closer to their embassy because they had taken the lead to gain Margaret's release. Within twenty-four hours, the British government co-opted us.

This was the last thing I wanted. We were members of an impartial humanitarian organization and needed to project an image of independence from the coalition forces. Now, we were housed and controlled by a private security company as we worked for Margaret's release. Kroll was another firewall to ensure Jon and I did not get "too far out of the box." We were in a corner, but knew we needed rest before we addressed the situation.

The next morning, the head of Kroll showed us around his building and offices. I paid closer attention to him. His name was Paul Wood. He was tall and lean, and carried himself with the demeanor of a soldier. He had been a commander in a British parachute regiment. I wanted to dislike him but saw that he had a genuine concern about Margaret. He became a friend and mentor to Jon and me.

When we entered the common area of his offices, he guided us to two desks. Each had a laptop and telephone. We had brought our own laptops. Both computers were hard-wired to the internet. I knew we had no choice about internet connectivity, but I was reluctant to use computers provided by the British embassy. I did not want to feel like a government wholly controlled us.

We entered an adjacent room that housed the weapons locker. It contained a dozen Kalashnikov AK-47 assault rifles and an equal number of pistols. He said all the residents of the house kept a pistol and Kalashnikov in their bedrooms and asked if we wanted a weapon. Jon immediately declined. I pondered the balance between the neutrality of a non-governmental organization and the threat level of our current environment and realized there were enough weapons in the house that if I ever needed one I could find it. I declined the offer.

During the tour, I asked Paul, "How did we end up at Kroll?"

He said he had received a call from the British Embassy asking if he would house two people from CARE for a week while they were in Baghdad to engage with CARE staff after the kidnapping of Margaret Hassan. I asked if Kroll worked with the British government. He said they did not, but he knew many people in the embassy, and when they could not find lodging for us they asked him.

Jon and I went to the British embassy for our initial meeting. The embassy was two miles from our lodging, but the trip wasn't something you could hop in a taxi to accomplish. Every visit required an armored vehicle with two armed guards. The logistics of the journey required extensive coordination to schedule a pickup and drop off. CARE had some vehicles and drivers, but they were not allowed in the Green Zone. Jon and I contemplated moving to the CARE compound, but the staff was adamantly against such an action. They felt it would put us and, by association, all the CARE team in extraordinary danger.

When we arrived at the embassy, we were escorted to the badging room and provided an authorization pass. It allowed us more access throughout the building. I was surprised by the casualness of the certification process. We had our photos taken and affixed to a badge to gain entrance to the embassy. There were no fingerprints, forms, passport identifications, or briefs. we had been vetted before arriving. I was impressed with their sophistication and ability to react so swiftly while we were en route to Iraq.

After receiving our credentials, we met with Ambassador Edward Chaplin. He was polite and expressed his country's concerns for Margaret Hassan, pledging to do all he could to gain her release and welcoming us as partners. I was impressed with his sincerity.

Departing the Ambassador's office, the senior member of embassy security issued Jon and I a cell phone with pre-programmed embassy numbers. They were simple Nokia mobiles, but the thought crossed my mind they may be equipped to monitor my conversations. I smiled at my paranoia. This was Iraq in the middle of a war. There were probably more US National Security Agency satellites than I could count aimed at the Middle East to monitor phone conversations and email traffic.

Of course, my communications were monitored!

In his office, the security officer updated us about what the embassy knew about the kidnapping. Mostly, they had nothing. The UK government was attempting to discern who had abducted her, but they knew so little it was impossible to speculate. They mentioned Zarqawi. Privately, Jon and I guessed her abduction was a criminal and not a political act. Our fear was that if they kidnapped Margaret for money and the UK government became too strident in their proclamation about "paying no ransom," that the kidnappers would just kill and discard her.

At Jon's request, the Iraqi CARE team began quietly broadcasting that Jon and I were in Baghdad seeking to contact the kidnappers. CARE had a strict "no ransom" policy, too, but the British government believed CARE would negotiate a settlement, making the process more manageable. It took time for the British to accept that CARE would not pay. Although payment never became an issue, it was an emotional concern for me. I understood the pragmatic reasons not to pay a ransom, but I was plagued with worry over how to negotiate with criminals in a civil war toward a solution that did not end up with Margaret being killed.

That night, we had our first meeting with the three-person crisis response team from MI5. They were impressive while providing a survey of their background and experience. The British had sent their best. The group emphasized they could not engage in ransom demands. Still, if that became an impediment, they would advise Jon and me without entering the negotiation process. At this meeting, Jon and I quickly understood how deeply we would engage with the actions to free Margaret. In addition to handling the negotiations, we would become the "face of CARE" in Iraq. Coordinating with the British Embassy, the Government of Iraq, NATO forces, Margaret's family, and CARE staff. Without reservation, we were in the country for the duration. At the end of the meeting, the MI5 team suggested we meet daily for updates in a shared space.

The team worked on a rotation basis. The plan was to spend two weeks in Baghdad and rotate to a different location when another three-person group relieved them. In a kidnap negotiation, the standard procedure is to stagger a team's departure by having one person remain a week longer. When two people rotated back to the UK, there was always one member of the team on hand to greet and brief the incoming members. This did not happen. As the weeks passed, it was left to Jon and me to spend several days introducing ourselves to the new members and discussing the nuances of the effort. When the second team arrived, we discovered they had completed the official crisis response training but in effect were merely on call for such a mission. After the first month, the degree of professionalism declined to a point from which we never recovered. The longer Margaret's kidnap lasted, the less professional the British government's response.

When the first kidnap film aired on October 19, on Al Jazeera television network, it showed Margaret sitting with her back against a wall. There was no audio. Her arms were tied behind her back. She was shaking. The camera zoomed on her Iraqi national ID card, her CARE identification, and a credit card. The video was intended to show proof of capture and life.

Three days later, a second video aired on Al Jazeera. Margaret was pleading for her life and relaying the kidnapper's demands. "Please, please I beg of you, the British people, to help me. I don't want to die like Bigley. Tell Mr. Blair to take the troops out of Iraq and not bring them here to Baghdad. That's why people like myself and Mr. Bigley have been caught. Please, please, I beg of you. Please help me, this might be my last hour." The tape did not identify nor show any of the kidnappers.

In response, CARE issued a statement stressing Margaret's humanitarian work to serve the poorest in Iraq and appealed for her release. The British Foreign Secretary issued the following statement: "The video of Margaret Hassan, which has been released by her kidnappers is extremely distressing. I have the greatest sympathy for what her family is suffering. Margaret Hassan has spent more than thirty years working for the Iraqi people. We hope all Iraqis will join us in calling for her immediate release."

The next day, CARE received information and advice from Un Ponte Per (UPP), an Italian NGO, on possible negotiation channels via a local businessman. In a spirit of cooperation, we passed the information to the British. Several days later, the British government advised us not to pursue these channels. An Australian media interview with Sheikh Taj El-Din Al Hilaly, the Mufti of Australia, followed soon after. It appeared another negotiation channel emerged. Again, the British advised us not to pursue this opening either. When we asked for their reasons we were told the information was classified. When we asked what was being accomplished by the British to open lines of communications with the kidnappers, we were told it was classified. When we pressed the issues, we were pointedly told to keep our distance or be excluded from the UK government's actions. Jon and I pondered, "What actions?"

Five days after the second video, Al Jazeera aired the third film. Margaret appeared unharmed. She relayed demands from the kidnappers, "Please, please, don't send the soldiers to Baghdad. Take them away. On top of that, please release the women prisoners in prison. Please, please, I beg you. And CARE must close. You must close CARE, please, please."

For the first time, there was an achievable demand: closing CARE in Iraq. All the advice we received from the CARE Iraq staff supported the closure. Jon and I knew the ability to withdraw coalition forces and release women prisoners was beyond our capacity, but we could demonstrate good faith by suspending our program activities. It was not a hard decision. Out of concern for our team's safety, we had earlier ceased operations and sent the staff home.

CARE supported the closure of the Iraq office based on the advice of the Iraqi staff. Yet, we had to mitigate the impact of the decision on the staff. In a joint meeting, we collectively decided to continue their pay for three months and reexamine the decision at the end of ninety days. It was a good choice, and I was proud of Jon Mitchell. The next day, we made a public statement, which directly responded to the kidnapper's demand to close the office. It read, "CARE has closed down all operations in Iraq. Please release Mrs. Hassan to her family and friends in Iraq." The statement was also read in Arabic by a female CARE spokesperson in Amman.

From the beginning of this event, one of our primary concerns was to avoid CARE Iraq staff working on the investigation. They wanted to be involved, but we were afraid of deadly reprisals against them. One fact clouded our decision: the British police and intelligence services claimed to have no "on the ground" means in Baghdad to gather information. I did not believe them. The British were in the middle of a civil war. It was impossible to believe they did not have operatives on the streets of Baghdad who could help with this crime. They referred to their association and work with the Baghdad Major Crimes Unit (MCU). However, when we discussed this with our CARE staff, they were adamant the MCU was not to be trusted. In fact, they could easily be part of this problem rather than a solution.

To further complicate our relationship with the British, they speculated that a CARE staff member was involved with the kidnap. When we pressed for information, they claimed there was no substantive proof, but they continued investigating one of our CARE team members. It was an obvious answer and one we did not want to dismiss. He knew all the details about routes, routines, and vehicle use. Both the British and the MCU were anxious to find a quick resolution to the crime. After they revealed the person to us, we encouraged him to take a lie detector test. He did, and it exonerated him, but they delayed the test for weeks, which cost us valuable time.

During the next few weeks, we worked with Margaret's husband, Tahseen. The logistics of meeting him were significant, requiring two armored vehicles and six armed guards. It was not prudent to pick him up at his home because the arrival of British government cars and a security detail would link him to NATO rather than a humanitarian organization. He drove to a specified place a significant distance across Baghdad. At the rendezvous point, he transferred to a guarded convoy that the British required for his entry into the international zone. This exposed him to the possibility of bombings and attacks on private security company vehicles as he navigated to the pickup point.

Additionally complicating matters, the meeting times were regulated by the British embassy. Throughout October and November daylight hours became shorter. If he had a scheduled meeting at 1:00 p.m. inside the International Zone, he would leave his home at 7:00 that morning. To ensure he was not traveling in Baghdad after dark, we had to have him out of the International Zone by 2:15 p.m..

We developed a routine, beginning with a general meeting with the crisis team. Following that session, Tahseen met privately with me and Jon. He wanted reassurance on issues involving media strategies, government requests, and offers for outside assistance. As practical as these talks appeared, they were debilitating because of our emotions. Tahseen demanded honesty regarding whether or not we believed they would kill Margaret, and it took a toll on all of us. We always told the truth, but it could be brutal. In the beginning, we were mechanical. We reviewed passports, proof of life issues, and a host of other related subjects, but as the crisis deepened, our interactions became personal and intensely private.

As the situation progressed, Jon and I were confronted with the reality that the most relevant information about Margaret's kidnapping was coming from CARE staff on the streets attempting to secure her release. Regardless of what Jon said, they continued searching for her. They passed their information to Jon, and he relayed it to the embassy crisis team. The British wanted us to cut ourselves out of the process and have CARE staff report directly to them. We refused to comply because it was a one-way street. All the information went into their system, and they never provided us with an analysis of the data. Jon and I spent every waking hour working on the kidnapping. Any relevant information was being gathered by our staff at considerable risk, and still we were excluded from full engagement with the government.

Our team discovered that Margaret was transferred to a second car, close to the site of the kidnapping. After giving the information to the embassy, no one attempted to locate the second vehicle. CARE staff identified a used car lot where it was dropped. This interaction demonstrated how little we could depend on the MCU or the British government. CARE staff again canvassed the neighborhood where the kidnapping took place. The MCU had not done this.

The daily visits to the embassy became more frustrating. While Jon and I provided information, we sat through updates that included nothing of substance in return. However, there was one tool CARE possessed that could rival any government: the ability to influence public opinion. Jon did an extraordinary job of building a mechanism to coordinate CARE initiatives with national and international media. The British government never supported his work in this area.

As Jon developed the CARE "Influence and Media Strategy," he identified key elements of a consistent message. The emphasis was to portray Margaret as an Iraqi and a humanitarian. In line with this depiction was a localization strategy, which engaged Iraqi and Arab publicity by working through local media channels. Our hope was that engaging Iraqi public opinion would pressure the kidnappers to release her. Jon targeted domestic and international Arabic support, with interviews by Tahseen and coverage of public demonstrations in support of Margaret.

The second leg of Jon's work was identifying and contacting influential people in Iraq who could directly sway public opinion. Jon worked with Muslim clerics, tribal leaders, Iraqi civil society partners, and CARE's partners. Several communications between Tahseen and Muslim clerics provided significant public assistance. Additionally, several clerics worked behind the scenes making direct appeals to Abu Musab al-Zarqawi. Since the kidnappers had not been determined, Zarqawi was the principal focus. However, the clerics began to believe Zarqawi was not the culprit. These men had more knowledge about the political and religious situation in Iraq than any foreign government. Jon and I were presented with a dilemma. If not Zarqawi, then who? We passed the information to the British government; it went behind a closed door and disappeared from our view.

On October 23, we received information and advice from UPP, the Italian NGO, which had two women abducted a few weeks earlier. The group holding their women never engaged directly with them and had both political and economic motivations. They determined the kidnappers were probably from Ramadi and affiliated with Salafit and Wahlabit religious factions.

UPP said this group was highly sensitive to

Islamic influence and advised us to energize all Islamic assistance. The Italians used several organizations, including the Ulaamas of Baghdad, the Fallujah Center of Human Rights, the Sheikhs in Ramadi, and the Zafarania mosque. They stressed that contacting these centers had to be made by CARE without any government involvement. They also counseled patience. The kidnappers made their own inquiry about the UPP women's work and decided to free them based on their anti-war and non-governmental profile.

We passed this information to the British and asked for their recommendation and reminded them of the request. They never responded. Over the next several days, Jon made a herculean effort to engage prominent Islamic representatives worldwide. On October 26, in an Australian media interview, Sheikh Taj El-Din Al Hilaly, the Mufti of Australia, claimed to have contacts with influential clerics in Iraq who would help negotiate Margaret's release. CARE drafted a letter for Tahseen to send to the Mufti asking for his assistance.

While working to open a line of communication with Margaret's kidnappers, a situation arose that Jon and I never imagined. Canon White, an Anglican priest associated with the Iraqi Institute of Peace, contacted the British embassy, on

October 27 with an offer to assist. They were enthusiastic about him joining the effort. Jon and I were reluctant to engage because we did not want to inflame Islamic fundamentalists with an impression of partnering with a Christian cleric.

The British embassy encouraged us to accept the assistance and explained a partnership between White's Coventry Cathedral in the UK and an organization called the Iraqi Institute of Peace (IIP). Both the British government and the US Institute of Peace (USIP) funded the IIP. I was familiar with USIP. It was a respected, credible, and non-aligned organization. The IIP was valued in the Muslim community and operated with the blessing of key religious leaders. Its primary focus was to facilitate inter-ethnic and inter-religious cooperation to build the foundation necessary for transforming Iraq into a liberal democracy.

On October 29, I received a call from the head of the IIP. He explained the role of his organization and the scope of their possible assistance. They were very active in the Ken Bigley case and purported to have passed useful information to the British. We requested their help to establish a community hotline. He was happy to help by providing volunteers to man the phones. When we met, we learned they had a team of twelve investigators. Human Rights organizations often use investigative teams to verify incidents of rights violations.

On November 3, the IIP held a press conference publicly launching the Margaret Hassan telephone hotline. This was accompanied by newspaper advertisements with telephone numbers and CARE staff handling the calls and sending information to Jon and me by email. By this point, Margaret Hassan had been in the kidnappers' captivity for sixteen days.

The IIP routinely met with us to provide updates on their investigative work. We started becoming uncomfortable with our relationships—between CARE staff's street investigations, the IIP's efforts, and the hotline, Jon and I were running an intelligence gathering operation in Baghdad. This had never been our intent, and it evolved for different reasons. When I asked the IIP why they were not passing their information directly to the British, I received obtuse answers. However, I was willing to make a deal with the devil to gain Margaret's freedom. The IIP reported they were focusing their efforts on the Dora neighborhood in south Baghdad as a place where she may have been held.

My concerns about the IIP were balanced by

their media savvy and their ability to coordinate with the religious community. In this area, their assistance was invaluable. However, their involvement with our efforts started unnerving us. They had a different perception of their role in the Iraqi crisis.

At our next meeting, the IIP head announced his team was investigating terrorist leads throughout Baghdad. He asked for several VHF radios, maps, and GPS devices. To maintain a balance with the assistance they were providing with media and contacts, we provided them with maps and three cell phones from CARE's supplies.

Several days later, an IIP representative approached us with information regarding a dentist. He was a Syrian with Iraqi nationality and described as a major terrorist with links to the people who kidnapped Margaret.

As Jon and I considered what to do with the IIP, on November 4, we were distracted by the fourth video received by Al Jazeera. They were not going to air it, but the British Ambassador in Doha watched the tape. Tahseen, Jon, and I were only given a brief message that the video was received and seen. There was no information as to what it contained.

Late the next day, its contents were released to

us. The tape began with a view of Margaret in a plain room with no furnishing, banners, or insignia. She spoke in English in a quivering voice: "Please, I beg of you to help me, help me to get out of here. Please help me, please." She then falls to the floor in a faint. The camera pans over her head and upper body. Someone's hand appears with a tin can and pours water over her face. Margaret recovers, gets up, and sobs into a tissue. The video cuts to the figure of a man, standing against a white wall. He appears to be in the same room. He is stocky, and his head is swathed in a large white scarf that conceals his features. He is wearing a gray sweatshirt with a white band around the chest and holding a Kalashnikov rifle across his stomach. He speaks in a thick Baghdad accent difficult to understand. He quotes a verse from the Holy Quran, "Fight them, and God will torture them by their own hands." Then he continues, "Britain has not kept its promises. It has not withdrawn its troops and has not released the Iraqi women prisoners. Consequently, we have decided to call upon our brothers in the leadership of Al Jihad Wal Tawhid (JTJ) or the Ussad Alla brigades to come and take her away with the documents of her interrogation in 48 hours from now, so that they execute God's judgment on her, if Britain still had not accepted our demands."

The British Embassy believed the video strengthened their view that the abduction was criminal. There were no banners in the picture, the group remained unnamed, and the man in the video was dressed in western street clothes. There were no black uniforms or hoods. The speaker used the old name "JTJ" for the group that renamed itself "Al Qaeda of the Two Rivers" (AQTR) several weeks earlier, which indicated they were not part of the political terrorist network. The British considered the film a signal of intent to sell Margaret to another group or to CARE. It was also considered an attempt to up the ante and her price. The kidnappers believed Margaret was a valuable commodity and were unlikely to harm her.

We speculated that if the AQTR, Lions of God, or another terrorist group wanted Margaret, they would already have her. Her sale would be difficult. The kidnappers had to establish contact with other groups, find a faction interested, and manage the logistics of a handover. The 48-hour deadline was intended to raise our stress in preparation for a ransom demand. An alternative theory was that if the kidnappers were motivated by politics or ideology, the purpose of the video may have been to establish their credibility with hardline terrorist groups. However, Jon and I believed we would soon receive a ransom demand and needed to continue the localization strategy to increase public support for Margaret.

As we waited for contact from the kidnappers, the IIP man reported his team no longer believed the dentist was involved in Margaret's abduction but was a significant terrorist threat. He had pictures of Bin Laden and Abu Musab al-Zarqawi on the wall of his apartment. Investigators broke into his residence to photograph the images and gave the evidence to the CIA. The IIP contact explained that clandestine intelligence gathering and counter-terrorist activities were the primary reason for the existence of the IIP.

By November 5, I realized involvement with the IIP was unreasonable. Additionally, we had legitimized Canon White's association with Margaret's kidnapping. Our relationship with the IIP was displayed on the United States Institute of Peace website. USIP is a good and honorable organization. However, for any Jihadist group, the words "United States" in front of "Institute of Peace" was the only evidence they needed to condemn it as a US government agency.

If the IIP were identified as an anti-terrorist

group, supported by the British government with a public association with CARE, it would lead to an extreme response against Margaret. After sketching these thoughts into a visual image of intersecting circles on a yellow legal sheet, my final graphic contained the words, "CARE had become the perfect front for clandestine anti-terrorist activities." Men and women who trusted my organization's humanitarian principles were being used to collect intelligence on the streets of Baghdad that was then fed to the NATO governments.

The next day, I met with the British Ambassador. Usually, this process involved a series of scheduling requirements and details concerning the purpose of the meeting. When I told his executive secretary I wanted to discuss the United Kingdom's association with the Iraqi Institute of Peace, she excused herself and walked to his office. When she returned, she told me the Ambassador would be available at 2:30 that afternoon.

At the appointed time, I entered his office and found two additional men who never spoke. I relayed my discussions with the IIP and ended that either the British government did not know the extent of their activities, or they knew and intentionally involved CARE to legitimize IIP's anti-terrorist operations. I added that I suspected the latter. The Ambassador and his colleagues were mute. After an uncomfortable minute of staring, the Ambassador said he would, "Look into the matter."

After the meeting, I reflected on Jon and my own presence in Iraq and was baffled about how bizarre this situation had become. Jon and I arrived in Baghdad to provide information to the British government about Margaret Hassan, and about how CARE works in Iraq. Now, we had CARE staff on the streets holding clandestine meetings to obtain information we then provided to the British. CARE had established a media plan to facilitate public support for freeing Margaret. We assumed all associations with Margaret's husband. We had become the central conduit between a purported peace group, associated with the Anglican church, sponsored by the British government, and the United States Institute of Peace, which had just outlined their association with the CIA to gather intelligence and "other activities." Meanwhile, the British continued to withhold relevant information about Margaret from Tahseen, Jon, and me.

We never heard from the IIP again.

CHAPTER 18
SOME THINGS NEVER LET US GO

*"You've faced horrors in these past weeks…
I don't know which is worse.
The terror you feel the first time you witness such things,
or the numbness that comes after it starts to become ordinary."*
—Tasha Alexander

AT 9 P.M. ON NOVEMBER 5, TAHSEEN received a call from a man stating, "I have Margaret." He immediately contacted me and asked, "What should I do?" He said the call came from Margaret's cell phone number and appeared to be genuine. The caller said Margaret had confessed to working with the British government. Tahseen replied, "That is not true. It is impossible.

I am her husband, and I would know such a thing. She is forced to say something like that." The caller said he had her statement on a disk.

The man stated he wanted to meet with someone from the British Government to negotiate her release. Tahseen said that was impossible because the British government was not involved.

The kidnapper replied, "I would speak to British or Irish, whatever."

Tahseen stated he did not want to involve any governments, and he could bring in someone from CARE.

The caller said this would be all right, but he wanted to know the plan when he called again on Saturday evening to arrange a meeting.

Tahseen replied that when he called back he wanted to speak to Margaret to ensure she was okay.

The caller assured Tahseen that Margaret was well and being treated humanely. Tahseen said this is not what he was seeing on the news.

When I ended the call with Tahseen, I walked to the courtyard of the house where I was staying. In the distance I heard rifle fire. Above me, helicopters and jets roared across the sky, and mortars and rockets landed and exploded in the Green Zone. I was standing at the epicenter of a war. I watched an explosion in the distance and felt the full weight of the question, "What in the hell am I doing here?"

I wanted to be a peacemaker.

Is that asking too much?

I went to war too many times and needed to find a way to balance my own acts of violence within myself and the universe. Now, as an aid worker, I was at the center of a bizarre world where I dealt with kidnappers, spies, assassins, terrorists, ambassadors, and a man shattered by the prospect of never seeing his wife again. Every day, I asked the women and men of CARE to venture into the middle of this violence to meet people who called the hotline and supposedly had information about Margaret. Jon and I had to decide the credibility of each caller and respond accordingly.

As I pondered this, I thought back to the light I saw in the vehicle when I went over the cliff in Albania. The events that moved me from a Marine in Somalia to a humanitarian in the middle of Baghdad were beyond my understanding.

Fear I would fail weighed on me. Margaret represented everything I wanted; she was a peacemaker. I could not make a mistake. I was there for the sole purpose of bringing this woman home, and the thought terrified me.

After discussing the call with the British crisis response team, they believed it was a genuine contact. Tahseen was advised to handle future calls based on a localization strategy. If there was a demand to speak to a government official, he was advised to reply, "Why? She has nothing to do with them. Any of them! Please, give me back my wife." Regarding a request to talk to CARE, Tahseen would reply, "You told them they had to shut down. They did. They are gone. I have asked for their help, but they refused." He would maintain he was raising money from family and friends; to support this claim, he had announced he was preparing to sell his home and business if required to pay a ransom.

Jon and I confirmed with the British that in the event the kidnappers insisted on speaking with a government official we assumed their full participation until there was a ransom demand. While they posed no objection, they never provided a name or number of a representative with whom the kidnappers could speak.

On November 6, Al Jazeera released a statement from Zarqawi: "We call on those responsible for Margaret Hassan's captivity to release her, unless she is proven to be a collaborator with the US occupation forces." It continued, "The kidnappers are obligated to release any proof they might be holding against her." Zarqawi harshly criticized Hassan's kidnappers for saying they would turn her over to his group. If they did so, "We will release her immediately unless she is proven to have conspired against Muslims." The communication proceeded, "It's meaningless to try to outbid us as others have attempted by saying they would turn the captive Margaret Hassan over to us within 48 hours unless their demands are met. Those using this captive as a bargaining chip do not truly know our religion, which states that women not involved in combat should not be attacked."

The impact of having the most notorious and brutal killer in Iraq become an ally in the quest to free Margaret was unnerving. The only thing I felt was the gut-wrenching truth that an innocent person was being used and abused by every party.

I wanted to believe Zarqawi, but for the first time I allowed myself to speculate that Margaret's fate was doomed. Whoever took her had crossed a point of no return. Before this moment, the kidnappers moved with impunity throughout Baghdad. Neither the US nor the British would put the resources on the streets to find her. The city was in anarchy, and the kidnappers thrived in the chaos. Now, they were confronted with an element that was organized, ruthless, and able to operate with universal protection and a constant flow of intelligence and information. While the coalition forces were helpless inside the city, Zarqawi's group was free to operate and hunt them.

After the announcement, Jon and I inquired what the British thought about Zarqawi's statement. Was it a good or bad thing for Margaret? They never answered. However, the Margaret hotline was inundated with telephone calls. The majority were sincere and offered information or supposed sightings. We faithfully turned the reports over to the British, but we were losing faith in what they did to verify or assist. With some of the calls, CARE staff held private meetings with people who offered to help. In each case, we notified the embassy to ensure our staff member was not caught in an ambush or became implicated as party to the crime.

Each day the Embassy asked Jon and me the same question: did any CARE staff have contact with people other than those who called the hotline? It took us several days to realize the British were primarily interested if any of our people were communicating directly with Zarqawi's group, al-Tawhid Wal-Jihad, and could lead them to him. Once again, Margaret was being used as a pawn.

During the evening of November 7, Tahseen received two calls from Margaret's cell phone. The kidnapper asked if he had the phone number for a contact at the British Embassy. Tahseen replied he contacted them, but they told him they were not interested in helping. The kidnapper said, "Typical, don't expect any help there." He then asked for the phone number for the head CARE person in Brussels. This was Secretary General Denis Caillaux, the leader of the international federation of CARE organizations.

The request stunned me because I had worked hard to consider every possible question and demand associated with this contact. Yet, something as simple as Denis' phone number got away from me. It was not programmed into the mobile I used in Iraq. I thought for a moment to use my own phone number, but the specificity of his request informed me that he understood CARE's organizational structure and probably knew that Denis was French. I could not pass as a Frenchman. I was numb. Tahseen said he did not have the number and the kidnapper hung up.

The caller phoned a short time later. He said he tried the CARE number in Amman, and no one answered. It was an old emergency contact, which was no longer used. He stated he would call back within twenty-four hours to get the number of the head CARE person in Brussels. He said he needed to negotiate with someone. Tahseen immediately called us, and we gave him Jon's Cairo cell phone as the preferred number.

The next day we developed detailed negotiation guidance, including proof of life questions for Tahseen and any CARE staff who might be contacted. The British offered a tape recorder to fit Tahseen's phone. It was a cassette with a suction cup. This was 2004 when we had digital listening devices, but their recorder was technology from the 1960s. Jon and I went to the American PX in the Green Zone and bought a digital recorder with a direct attachment for his phone. We sat next to the phone all night awaiting the call. No one called us or Tahseen.

My fears grew. I was baffled by the British government's response. Every time the kidnappers contacted Tahseen, they used Margaret's cell phone. The phone was equipped with a GPS chip. The British knew her number. The National Security Agency (NSA) had to be monitoring every phone call throughout Iraq and the Middle East to identify and capture terrorists and interrupt their plans. It was inconceivable they were not intercepting the calls from Margaret's phone to determine where the signals were originating. If the GPS chip in her phone was disabled, there was a basic procedure used since WWII to triangulate an electronic transmission that was well within the capability of the coalition forces.

The kidnappers said from the beginning they wanted to speak to the British government. They never said they wanted to negotiate with them. This did not mean that once they had a government representative on the phone they would not make a ransom demand. However, from the beginning of Margret's kidnap, the British were adamant they would not speak to the kidnappers. When I mentioned the Prime Minister's statement that the British government would speak to anyone, but never negotiate, all I received were blank stares and silence.

The third tier of the British crisis response team arrived. They were well-meaning but totally unprepared for dealing with Margaret's kidnap. Two of the three members lasted four days before returning to Great Britain because of the stress of the daily rocket and mortar attacks.

On the morning of November 10, Jon and I sat in the embassy common meeting room. We were twenty-five minutes early for the routine gathering. I noticed someone walking into the crisis response teams' working center. The door was affixed with a sign that said, "Stay Out–Restricted Area–Authorized Personnel Only." The door closed and it struck me: the person had opened the door and walked straight into the office. There was no key or cipher lock, or camera to monitor access.

Jon sat across from me reading a document with his back to the hallway. I stood, walked across the hall, opened the door, and entered the heart of Her Royal Majesty's government response to Margaret Hassan's kidnap. I found a sparsely furnished area with several desks, a few chairs, and a whiteboard with random notes. There was one computer monitor and one telephone. The single item of interest was a map of the City of Fallujah. At a table, one of the responders was drinking tea while watching a game of chess between two of his colleagues. The head of the team turned and said, "You're not authorized to be in here." It was one of those moments when you wish you had an insightful or cutting retort. However, all I could say was, "Sorry." I walked out, but the image of the map of Fallujah remained with me. There was no reason for it to be displayed.

I found the small garden in a quiet corner of the embassy. Sitting on a bench, I thought about Fallujah. Is that where Margaret was located? If so, why not share the information with Jon and me? I felt a flush of anger but contained it; emotions would not free Margaret.

I thought about combat as a Marine. I tried separating fear and terror and finding a place inside from which to pull calmness, logic, and intellect. I did this to keep my Marines alive and persevere in battle. I had to employ that strategy here and accept the reality of working with the embassy. I did not like it, but I had to remove any negative energy that distracted me from bringing Margaret home.

The next morning at 1:30 Al Jazeera broadcast a "confession" video from Margaret. She was wearing a black shirt with white markings and sitting on a green blanket on a bed. She looked tired and stressed, but calm. She was well groomed, and there was no sign of physical injury. When she spoke, it was under duress and prompted by a male voice. She said, "I admit CARE worked with the occupying forces and worked with them in many places. We worked on water pipes, water treatment plants, repairing hospitals, primary health care centers, and hospitals in the governorates of Qadisiya, Misan, Babel, and Al Anbar. We also worked to provide water for the airport. I admit we worked with the occupying forces and we worked in many places in the airport. We provided the occupying forces details of where we were working, so they knew what was happening in those areas."

The British thought the video was another step in the negotiations, but it may also have been providing evidence to the Jihadists of Margaret's cooperation with the occupation forces. We expressed our concern that communication channels with the kidnappers were being closed. Our only contact with the abductors was through Al Jazeera videos. Jon and I were uneasy that the efforts to personalize Margaret to the Iraqi people were being obstructed by the embassy. Jon remained the sole originator of the strategy. The embassy had a complete public relations group, but they did not engage. One member of their team assisted, more from a sense of guilt rather than direction from the embassy. The British wanted to keep Margaret's kidnap at a low profile.

Jon and I were exhausted. I tried to get five hours of sleep each night, but Jon was operating on four or less. At every turn, we seemed to be forced to deal with the British without making headway. We were surviving on coffee and calories from processed foods of cake, candy, and biscuits. Both of us smoked four packs of cigarettes a day. Every three days, we visited the American PX to buy two cartons of Marlboro Lights each. We agreed our association with the British was becoming useless.

The only direct link to the kidnappers was through Tahseen. He could engage in negotiation and keep the British informed. If the British were monitoring the calls from Margaret's phone and identified a location where she was being held, we knew none of us would be notified before a rescue attempt.

We had to focus on the CARE media strategy. We would continue dutifully passing information to the British but remove ourselves from the association with the embassy that took up nearly seven hours a day. For the first time in weeks, Jon and I felt we had a plan. We had a glimmer of hope and resurgence of energy now that we had extricated ourselves from the British politics.

It was short lived.

That afternoon, Jon and I were notified that a vehicle from the embassy was dispatched to bring us to their facility. When we arrived, we were escorted to a conference room with only the Ambassador and his deputy. He told us he had received news of a sixth video, which purported to show the execution of Margaret Hassan.

The ambassador recounted a strange story. The film was supposed to be part of the "confession video." While an editor at Al Jazeera was reviewing the tape, he received a call at his desk. Engaged in conversation, he inadvertently let the video continue for several minutes. After a blank interlude, another tape began. The nature of the killing indicated her murder was accomplished by professionals.

I could not believe it. Why kill her? Everything she did was motivated by humanitarianism and decency. She was tough to work with, not because of self-promotion or ego, but because we were not moving fast enough to assist people. Even Zarqawi saw the decency in this remarkable woman.

I needed to see Tahseen. The prospect of visiting him was a difficult venture if I followed standard protocols. I could walk to a Green Zone access gate and take a taxi. I knew all the reasons not to do this, but I needed to get to him. This was not an occasion for armored vehicles and guards. Several hours later, I arrived at Margaret's home.

Tahseen was waiting for me. His first words were, "Do you believe she is really dead?" The British had already contacted him. I hung my head and answered, "Yes." I told him what was purported by Al Jazeera and the British. He said he just received a phone call from Margaret's siblings in Europe who conveyed the same message. The

British told them Al Jazeera would not release the film but would allow a family member to travel to Doha to view it to confirm her identity. Margaret's brother was going to make the trip. I told Tahseen that Jon contacted Al Jazeera and asked them to release the disc to the UK for analysis in London. They told Jon the British already had the video.

Tahseen asked, "Why have the British made all this so complicated?"

"I have no idea." None of their actions seemed reasonable.

Tahseen bowed his head, waited for a long moment, then looked at me with overwhelming grief in his eyes and face. His look still haunts me. "Why did they do this to Margaret? She was a good person, only trying to help. If they killed her, can't they just deliver her back to me and let us rest?" The sun had set. In the night, I could hear a mosque's call to prayer. We sat in the dark and let the sounds of prayer and explosions fill the emptiness.

It was too late to return to the Green Zone. Tahseen showed me to a small bedroom where I spent the night. Lying in bed, waiting for sleep to overtake my sadness, I could hear the distant boom of rockets and mortars. None of the explosions were close to Margaret's home. The aggression was focused on the Green Zone and the coalition forces.

In the morning, I said goodbye to Tahseen and made my way to the Green Zone. I got out of the taxi and waited with the day workers to be allowed into the area. Inside the zone, I received a call from a member of the crisis response team. He asked if I could come by for a discussion. When I entered the embassy, Jon and the spokesperson for the crisis response team were waiting. We were escorted to the Ambassador's office. He told us the British government was confident the murdered woman in the video was Margaret Hassan. The film was reviewed by a few people, including her brother. They all agreed it was Margaret.

I asked the obvious question, "Who killed her?"

He shook his head and quietly replied, "We just don't know."

Soon after that meeting, I wrote the following in my journal:

> I have just completed my final visit with Tahseen. Too often, we use words like dignity, honor, and compassion with such frequency they become trite. Over the past months, I learned the true meaning of these words through Tahseen.
>
> It is not only difficult, but impossible, to

accurately describe what kind of man he is. What he possesses is integrity and moral courage.

Tahseen still has hope. Until a body is found, he will not give up. He told me, he is not 'un-accepting,' but wonders why he should relinquish hope until he knows for sure that she is dead. He said, there will be a time when his heart will let him know. He promised it would not take the rest of his life. He made me promise not to give up what I do at CARE. He told me if I value Margaret I owe it to her—not to back away from my work because of this tragedy.

In Tahseen's heart, he wants to believe Margaret is still out there. He has been pushed by families and the British government to accept her death, but he will not. He received a bouquet from Reuters with a condolence note. He tore it up and disposed of the flowers. Not in rage, but in a reasoned fashion. He will accept it when he is ready, in his own time.

Margaret was tough. She possessed a backbone forged in titanium. I seldom agreed with her, but I respected and admired her. She made a difference in people's lives. The same uncompromising passion that upset me was precisely the trait that made her remarkable. She embodied the fundamental principle of humanitarianism through her words, "Human suffering must be addressed wherever it is found. The purpose of humanitarian action is to protect life and ensure respect for human beings."

In that pursuit, she was unbending.

She made me a better person by knowing her.

There are inevitable demarcations in life. The key to moving forward is finding the truth and looking for an element of reason. I attempted to do this, thinking that her kidnappers were frightened. The coalition forces continued to search, and Zarqawi threatened them not to harm her. They needed a safe place to hide, but my speculation ended with that thought. I did not know Iraq well enough to consider such a spot.

Suddenly, one night in a dream, I saw the image of the map of Fallujah on the wall of the British crisis response team's office. I woke up, stared at the ceiling, and the pieces of my conjecture finally came together.

At the time of Margaret's kidnap, Fallujah was a magnet for Iraqi resistance fighters, but not political terrorist groups.

It was the perfect place to hide her.

The kidnappers did not know that in late October 2004, the coalition forces would blockade the city. The US Marines appeared and warned the residents of a pending attack, encouraging them to leave. Numerous checkpoints surrounded the town ensuring that only civilians and non-combatants were departing. Yet, it was easy to smuggle a CD-ROM with the videos of Margaret's pleas for mercy through the military inspections and then pass the disk to Al Jazeera.

However, it was impossible to smuggle a Caucasian woman through a control point of coalition forces. The kidnappers had to do something with her before escaping the city. I suspect it was at this point they killed Margaret Hassan and fled Fallujah before the attack commenced on November 8.

Meanwhile, Jon and I were led to believe by the British that Margaret was held in Baghdad. We attended endless meetings, engaged the women and men of the CARE office, who risked their well-being to locate her as we worked on leads from the hotline. All this time the British knew she was in Fallujah and were aware of the pending battle long before the blockade of the town. I also suspect they knew precisely where she was in the city because of her phone GPS.

I still wrestle with what I may have seen on the Fallujah map. Did it have a red circle identifying

Margaret's location, or is that something I wanted to see and over the years started imagining?

If the coalition knew her position, why not send a team of SEALs or commandos to rescue her? The reason may have been that no one could confirm her presence in a building, so an assault would not accomplish a rescue but merely risk unnecessary casualties.

This scenario also explains why the British government started to use the bottom tier of their crisis response teams. There was no need to engage their primary responders when they already knew where she was.

Everything about Margaret's location was designated as classified information because of the military's preparation to attack Fallujah. Jon and I were aid workers, not government or military officials. In military parlance, we did not have a "need to know." Why trust us with the truth?

For a moment, I examined this hypothesis, but then I pushed it as far away as possible.

It frightened me. Margaret became an inconvenience to everyone—the kidnappers, the coalition forces, and the British government—so she became expendable.

I still dream about it, and when I do my heart pounds, and I'm drenched in sweat.

I am with Jon in a room in Baghdad, looking at the video of Margaret's death. Around us are exploding mortars and rockets. I can hear them, and see people roaming the streets with weapons and armaments. They are clinically and pathologically insane; as I turn, I see unblinking eyes staring at me.

They are black.

They are more than an image.

They are real and surround me.

I have seen them too often.

They hold my gaze and pull me into the senselessness of it all.

CHAPTER 19
AFGHANISTAN

"There's no better system than our own morality, not law, not science, not religion… just decency."
—Rebecca McNutt

DURING THE LATE 1970S, MANY LOOSELY aligned opposition groups rebelled against the pro-Soviet Democratic Republic of Afghanistan (DRA) government. In 1979, at the request of the DRA, the Soviet Union crossed the border into Afghanistan to come to the aid of the Afghan government. The collection of resistance fighters became known as the Mujahideen. The term originally applied to Afghan fighters who resisted Great Britain's push into Afghanistan throughout the 1800s. Throughout the ensuing struggle with the Soviets, the Mujahideen inflicted severe casualties against the invaders. In 1989, the Soviet Union withdrew from Afghanistan.

For the Afghans, it was a painful victory. Throughout the decade of fighting, more than a million people were killed, and an additional five million became refugees or were internally displaced. With a population of approximately thirteen million, 50 percent either died or fled the fighting. In the wake of the political chaos following the Soviet departure, the fundamentalist group known as the Taliban seized power in Kabul in 1996, imposing an austere version of Sharia law. They took control of all of Afghanistan except for the north, where they were resisted by Ahmad Shah Massoud until his assassination in 2001.

When the Soviets invaded, all but a few international humanitarian organizations withdrew from the country. CARE remained, continuing to aid people through the worst of the fighting.

After the Taliban seized control, they were extremely suspicious of international humanitarian organizations. They maintained the perception they were spying for foreign governments. It was impossible for them to accept that the United States would give assistance to an NGO and not use its staff to gather intelligence.

Eventually, CARE had to withdraw its foreign staff from Kabul and maintain an administrative headquarters in Peshawar, Pakistan. During this period, CARE made a strategic move, allowing them to continue operations and achieve a compromise with the Taliban. They began employing former Mujahideen men in office positions.

These men were respected by the regime. Although they were not Taliban, they had associations with them from their days of resisting the Soviet invasion. It was not a comfortable relationship, but the leaders in the CARE office knew how to work within the parameters of the new system.

In June of 2000, I landed in Islamabad, Pakistan, from Atlanta, and found a local bus to take me to Peshawar. It was a three-hour trip and brutally hot. When I reached Peshawar, I got a taxi and went to a small hotel where CARE had reserved a room for me. I noted the thermometer on the outside wall of the building. It registered 47 degrees Celsius, approximately 116 degrees Fahrenheit. My room had a working air conditioner, and the hotel had a backup generator. The city's power supply was intermittent, but the generator kept the air conditioner working.

For the next several days, I visited the Afghan administrative office to become acquainted with its programming activities. CARE Afghanistan had several implementing partnerships with the US Office of Foreign Disaster Assistance (OFDA) in the US Agency for International Development. It was an interesting relationship. While the US government and the Taliban had no diplomatic relations, and the US accused the Taliban of supporting international terrorism, the American government was willing to look beyond political animosities and support the humanitarian needs of a desperate people.

The people of Afghanistan had endured nearly two decades of war. There was no infrastructure. Most of the country was arid, and every dam, reservoir, or irrigation system was destroyed. Agriculture was at a subsistence level. The only viable export was the opium poppy, and its farmers were paid a bare minimum for the product. Outside of Kabul, there was no electricity. Both food and water were scarce, and the warring parties consumed most of those resources. Several million people were without basic provisons.

CARE started programs to build dams, spillways, and irrigation systems to assist farming. They employed Afghans to construct or repair roads throughout the country and implemented a forward-thinking initiative to use solar panels to bring electricity to rural villages.

I was asked to visit the office in Kabul to monitor the progress of the existing OFDA programs throughout the country and to provide any suggestions regarding risk mitigation for staff as they worked under the Afghan government. I found it extraordinary, both as an American and a former US Marine, that I was about to embark on a trip into the midst of the Taliban.

My colleagues in the CARE office in Peshawar had tried getting me a seat on the UN flight into Kabul, but they were unsuccessful. With an apologetic note, they told me I was going to have to travel to Kabul by road. It was an eleven-hour trip, but I was excited. I was looking forward to seeing the country from the ground. I was also anticipating a break from the heat and humidity of Peshawar since Kabul was nearly six thousand feet above sea level.

At four the next morning, I met my driver. The Land Rover was filled with administrative supplies and a few items of food. The vehicle was old but sound. The driver did not speak English. As dawn appeared, we approached the Khyber Pass. Soon we stopped at a military base and I walked into small office with the driver. The

Pakistani authorities required us to have a soldier with us until we reached the Afghan boundary. Although the Khyber Pass was well traveled, there were still incidents of ambushes and robberies when there was a foreign national in the vehicle.

When we reached the border, it was surrounded by a bazaar. It seemed to stretch for miles. The driver pulled to the side of the road. The soldier departed, and the driver indicated we would leave in two hours. He motioned it was okay for me to walk through the myriad booths. There were a number of eight by twenty-foot steel shipping containers or Conex Boxes serving as workplaces. All the shops involved skilled labor, such as welding or metal fabrication. These places were followed by other craftsmen who built beds and furniture. I turned a bend and found rows of structures with washing machines, refrigerators, computers, televisions, and stereo sets. Behind each of the buildings were small vans, Toyota pickup trucks, or SUVs. All of them were being loaded with different appliances. Despite the Taliban, there was a thriving appetite for black-market goods. As I walked deeper into the bazaar, I found different sections selling dry goods, clothes, toys, medicines, bicycles, motorbikes, beer, wine, and alcohol. The shops seemed to serve one purpose: to supply these goods to smugglers.

The last group of stalls was the most shocking. Each of the small shops displayed an array of weapons. The majority were Soviet-era Kalashnikov rifles. They included the AK-47, AKM, and AK-74. In addition to the rifles there were endless displays of pistols. Many of them I recognized as NATO or Soviet-issued .45 and 9 millimeter firearms, while others seemed to be from WWII. There were open trays of hand grenades, Claymore, and antipersonnel mines displayed like fruit in a farmer's market. Most of them were standard US military ordnance. At one shop, I asked the price of an AK-47. I was quoted one hundred US dollars. As I walked away, he shouted, "seventy-five dollars!" to bargain with me.

I could buy a US military M-67 hand grenade for $2, a Claymore mine for $10, and a Soviet rocket-propelled grenade (RPG) for $150. It was not merely the availability of this weaponry, but the amount. There appeared to be more than a hundred small shops and containers. It was impossible to determine where all this ordinance came from, but the size of the market stunned me.

Returning to the vehicle, the driver indicated I needed to accompany him with my passport to the checkpoint. I had visited a small office in Peshawar that represented the Taliban and received my visa to enter the country. I also had additional papers I was instructed to present at the border.

Approaching the small building, there was a horizontal wooden pole across the road. It served as a barrier separating Pakistan and Afghanistan. We were the only people at the structure. There was a man reclined on a bench on the small porch who indicated we should follow him to a desk inside the office. He looked like what I imagined of the Taliban; he was dressed in black, had a long beard, and wore a black headdress. I presented my passport and papers. He looked at the visa, looked at me, stamped my passport and gestured for me to leave.

The driver and I went to the border crossing. The agent lifted the pole, and we entered the Islamic Emirate of Afghanistan. In front of us was an open and barren plain of rocks and desert. I noticed the number of vehicles racing across the fields on small tracks from the bazaar to our road. There were neither Afghan nor Pakistani controls at the border, so smugglers entered and departed Pakistan at will. They had open access to Afghanistan. I had seen buses laden with people in the bazaar. I assumed they would make a proper crossing at the official checkpoint, but they did not. The buses followed the same worn paths across the plains and joined the road in front of us.

The main road was two lanes. At some point, it had been blacktop, but it was now worn and pitted. The vehicles around us began a free-for-all dash to their destination, speeding across the cratered roadway. I could see the springs of the vehicles bouncing like a child's jack-in-the-box. As we made our way to Kabul, I felt like I was being punched in the stomach at each hollow in the highway. This was not an occasional track of the bad road. It was nearly 150 miles.

When we reached Kabul, it was dark, and there were few lights. The city sits on a flat plain surrounded by mountains, and the way we came brought us to the top of a hill and then descended into the capital. There were few cars and no people on the roads or sidewalks. It was approximately 8 p.m. and the city appeared deserted. An occasional bus or Toyota pickup truck was speeding down a street with a 50-caliber anti-aircraft machine gun mounted in the bed of the truck.

We turned onto a broad street, lined with old oak trees. It was peaceful and idyllic. It was hard to believe we were in the center of Taliban Afghanistan. All the stone walls surrounding the dwellings had an additional twelve feet of black cloth rising from the top of the walls, making the eight-foot walls stretch twenty feet in height. The additional height ensured that the homes of foreigners, who could have uncovered and unmarried women living with men, were shielded from the sight of any passersby.

As we progressed down the avenue, we made an abrupt turn into a small entryway. The driver stopped, got out, and pounded on the steel door. When it opened, I marveled at the sight of a spacious lawn in front of a large home. We drove to the front where a young man who spoke superb English greeted me. He said, "Welcome Mr. Robert. I have saved an evening meal for you." I picked up my backpack and walked into the hallway of a beautiful home. As I stood in the foyer, my host told me the house had been the residence of the Danish ambassador before he departed the country. I followed my host up the staircase, and he showed me to my room at the rear of the dwelling. It was modest but had its own bathroom and was isolated from the usual noise of the building.

I walked downstairs to the dining room of the CARE guest house and found a meal of chicken and potatoes with a salad and bottled water waiting for me. After supper, I toured the home. The living room had a satellite TV and a DVD player with a good selection of movies. There was a bookcase with several hundred books.

I went to my room and slept for the next twelve hours.

The next day at noon, a small Nissan car took me to the CARE office. As we traveled the short distance to the headquarters, I noticed there were few cars or buses on the streets. Most of the people traveled by foot or on bicycles. All the men were dressed in a long black outer garment, kept their hair long, and had beards. Only men were riding bikes. Of the few women I saw, they wore light blue burkas that covered their entire bodies. There was a small, oval fishnet material over their eyes allowing them to see. They were not to travel outside their home without a male family member. If they were in a car or bus, they had to sit in the rear.

The office was in a large compound surrounded by a ten-foot wall, and the interior of the complex was approximately two acres in size with two large buildings. I learned it was the old site of the US Embassy. Inside the main building was the CARE office. It housed several office spaces, and all of them were occupied. I was impressed with the number of Afghan women working there. They were all in western clothes, but their full-length blue Burkas hung on the walls. The moment they stepped out of the compound, they would have to be fully covered and accompanied.

In the country director's office, I met Nazhand for the first time. He was a large man with a flowing white beard. He wore conservative Afghan clothing but favored a lighter white or tan color robe. His English was perfect. He said he had learned to speak English in school as a young man. He was educated as a civil engineer, and many of his textbooks were in English.

In 1992, while the fighting in Kabul and throughout Afghanistan raged, CARE had hired Nazhand Abdul Raouf. He was a former Mujahideen fighter with a reputation for bravery and suffered severe wounds during the resistance. He became the de facto head of the CARE office.

I noticed his eyes first. They radiated intellect and kindness. But as our friendship grew, it was his brilliant humor that astounded me. He was the image of a conservative Muslim, but I began re-examining my preconceptions in getting to know him. If I passed him on the street in London, he would not frighten me, but I would perceive him as a Muslim fundamentalist. I was wrong; he was simply a man from another culture. Nazhand was truly funny, not merely humorous, but side-splittingly, laugh-out-loud funny. He would recount stories about his days with the Mujahideen, or a trip to Bangkok, or his interactions with the Taliban, and I would laugh until I cried. All his accounts were at his own expense. He never spoke ill of anyone or any group. He was a religious man, but his spirituality was tolerant, accepting, and open. His demeanor was calm, and I knew his strength came from a deep belief in Allah.

His reputation as an extraordinary leader began in 1995 when CARE had two of its international staff kidnapped in the Tribal areas of North Waziristan in Pakistan. Every attempt to engage the government of Pakistan to help obtain the staff's release failed. However, Nazhand reached out to village elders, mullahs, and extended family members in the area to secure their release. In the same year, he saved the CARE suboffice in the city of Khost from an attack and looting by a group of angry and disaffected tribal people, and he normalized CARE's relationship with them.

Amid the continuing chaos and fighting throughout the country, a group of thieves hijacked 200 tons of food en route to starving people in the Spera Valley of Zadran in the Khost province.

Again, using his own contacts, he located the food and intervened to retrieve the food and deliver it.

By 1996, it was obvious the Taliban would gain control of Kabul. Nazhand initiated contact with their forces who surrounded the city. With several other CARE staff, he crossed the lines and met with their leadership. He convinced them of the necessity to continue humanitarian aid and the legitimacy of CARE as an independent and impartial organization. Although this was a remarkable achievement, he also signed an astonishing protocol, which was honored until the day the Taliban fled Kabul in 2001.

The Taliban believed educated and working women were counter to the teachings of Islam and as such were unholy. Nazhand reached an understanding with local Taliban officials who agreed that in the provision of humanitarian assistance to all Muslims, he could maintain a staff of fifty-four women in a suboffice in Ghazni.

In his office, as we reviewed my reason for being in Afghanistan and talked about how I should conduct myself with the Taliban, he told me I should never be without my passport, always ensure my shirt sleeves were rolled down, always wear socks, and never appear in public in a pair of shorts or a T-shirt. If I was stopped, I should present my passport to the Taliban and tell them I worked for CARE.

Nazhand suggested spending several days in the main office reviewing the projects, meeting with staff members, adjusting to the Afghan time zone and Kabul altitude, and catching up on my sleep from jet lag. After that, he and I would take a journey for ten days to see the work CARE was doing and meet with his teams in the suboffices. I was grateful for the break and looked forward to engaging with his staff.

I would be required to meet with a government official who worked in the Ministry of Culture and Information. He was responsible for the oversight of the humanitarian organizations. I asked Nazhand if that was a problem. He told me if I stayed in Kabul, there would not be a requirement to meet, but since we would be traveling throughout the country, I needed to get his authorization to obtain the necessary travel document.

The next morning, with Nazhand, I arrived at the headquarters of the Government of the Islamic Emirates of Afghanistan. I was hyperaware of walking into the heart of the Taliban, armed with my US passport, and accompanied by a former member of the Mujahideen. As we approached the front of the building, I was surprised—there were no guards. We just opened the door and walked into the headquarters.

Nazhand knew his way to the proper office on the second floor. The building was bustling with men. All of them had beards, long hair, and black clothing—the trademark look of the Taliban. There were no women. Everyone ignored us. Earlier, I noticed Nazhand carrying a ream of computer paper and a box of standard blue Bic pens. I found this curious but did not know him well enough to ask his reason.

We entered the office of Amir Khan Muttaqi, the culture minister of the Taliban. It was bright and open, with a row of tall windows allowing light to spill into the workplace. It also allowed the heat to build in the rooms. It was stiflingly hot. A young man appeared to ask Nazhand his purpose, and after a short discussion we were instructed to sit. I was prepared for a long wait, but within moments we were escorted into the Minister's office. He gave Nazhand a warm greeting. It was obvious they were well acquainted.

The Minister indicated for us to sit on a couch, and he moved his chair to face us comfortably. There was a small table between us, and his assistant entered with a tray of green tea, grapes, and sugar cookies. Nazhand and the Minister began discussing our trip. Nazhand would stop on occasion and give me a short update on their discussion.

Finally, the Minister looked at me and through Nazhand's translation, asked me about my purpose for being in Afghanistan. He asked how long I had worked with CARE and what I did before I joined the humanitarian organization. I reckoned he already knew what I had done, but this was a different reality to sit amid the Taliban and say I had been a career member of the United States Marines. He stared at me for a moment and then broke into a loud laugh. He said, "That is good, because Nazhand probably needed the help of an American Marine when he traveled." With that, he rose and graciously escorted us to the door.

He spoke to his assistant, and we concluded the interview. Nazhand talked to the young man for a moment and handed him the ream of computer paper and box of pens. He indicated I needed to present my passport. After we sat on the couch, Nazhand told me that computer paper and pens were now so scarce that when CARE needed to come to a government office for official documentation the staff had to bring the paper and pens.

As we waited, we were given more green tea. The tray of tea had small sugar cubes to sweeten the drink. It was an acquired taste I still enjoy today. After an hour's wait, Nazhand was presented with several documents with many signatures and stamps, and my passport was returned. He handed me a paper, which was written in Dari, the official government language of Afghanistan. The only writing I recognized was my own name. Nazhand told me this was my authorization to travel anyplace in Afghanistan other than the north. I was to keep the paper and my passport on me at all times. Although I had a visa, this paper was my official acceptance to be in Afghanistan, authorized for three months, a length which surprised Nazhand.

When we returned to CARE, Nazhand escorted me to an office in the rear of the building. It was bright, comfortable, and hot. Nazhand said he would be out of the office for several days and I could work in this space. I was appreciative for his assistance, and thankful for the abundance of bottled water in the building. I settled into reviewing CARE's humanitarian projects and spent time talking to the staff and learning about CARE Afghanistan.

The next day, as I sat in my office, I was repeatedly startled by loud pounding on a large steel door that served as the rear entrance to the compound. I was on the second floor, and the door was beneath me. The hammering occurred several times an hour. When I questioned one of the women in the human resources office next to my workspace, she told me it was the "widows." In the Taliban's interpretation of Islam, if a widow was begging it meant she was not under the care of a male relative. Since she was not supervised by a male, her presence was unacceptable. Her begging was sinful. If caught, she would be subjected to a severe beating, or worse. Although the Taliban provided no assistance to widows, including war widows, they were not permitted to work. Without a husband they could easily starve to death with their children.

Nazhand recognized the enormity of this travesty. He initiated an action, which put him in direct defiance of the Taliban. He established a system where any widow or orphan throughout Kabul who needed food or water could make their way to the rear door of the CARE compound, pound on it, and be given enough food and water to survive for several days. They were encouraged to return. Nazhand's stature in Kabul and Afghanistan was a buffer to keep the religious police away from the building or lurking in the vicinity.

My residence was about one mile from the

office, and I asked my colleagues about whether it was okay for me to walk to and from the headquarters. They assured me it was acceptable. The following days, I would leave at approximately 7:30 a.m. and walk to my workplace. I was warned not to initiate contact with anyone, to never give money to a beggar, and always present my passport if stopped by the Taliban. As I walked, there were few people on the streets, an occasional car, but always many bicycles. Nearly all the storefronts were boarded. There was no music, or idle chatter from people lounging on the sidewalks. There was no use of tobacco and certainly no alcohol for sale.

When I became more familiar with the area, I realized there were several side streets I could take to avoid the main road. I began exploring different routes. While I walked by the walled and gated homes, I could hear children laughing, crying, and playing inside of the compounds, but there were no children on the streets.

Along the way, I noticed women curled in the doorways of vacant buildings with a small bowl in their hands. They did not speak or gesture toward anyone. Many were cradling babies, or had small children sitting next to them. I noticed two men walking in front of me reach into their pockets and seemingly examine their change. When they casually put the coins back into their outer garment, the change accidentally fell to the street. They continued to walk, not noticing. Instinctively, I was inclined to tell them, but did not want to draw attention to myself. It finally struck me. This was not a random event and always occurred within two or three meters of a woman sitting in the doorway.

One evening, I stayed in the office until seven o'clock. It was not dark, but well into dusk. I started to walk to the residence. It was a clear night, and I was thankful the weather had cooled. As I turned a slight bend on the side road, two men started walking toward me. Although they were unarmed, they had the demeanor of authority. They shifted their path to confront me. When we reached one another, the older one spoke in Dari. I shrugged my shoulders, pointed to my mouth, and said, "English." They conversed with one another for a moment, and the younger man said, "Where are you from?"

"America."

After a quick look at one another, the man said, "Passport."

I handed him my passport and the Minister's authorization. He looked at the documents while giving the paper to his companion. The older man scanned the document and started an intense conversation with his companion, who also reviewed the authorization from Amir Khan Muttaqi. During their discussion, I heard the name CARE mentioned numerous times.

When the younger man returned my documents he asked, "What do you do?"

I made a quick decision not to get into a long discussion about humanitarian aid. I replied, "I am a water engineer."

That seemed to satisfy him. They returned my authorization paper and indicated I should leave. It was not a confrontational event, but as an American stopped by the Taliban on a dark street in Kabul in the year 2000, I was grateful for my association with CARE.

One of the highlights of CARE's work in Afghanistan was water and sanitation. I was surprised by this effort, because water was not one of CARE's primary concentrations. The British NGO Oxfam was the leading non-profit specializing in large-scale humanitarian water and sanitation projects. When Oxfam was forced to withdraw from Afghanistan by the Taliban, CARE assumed most of their projects. One of the most notable was in Kabul. Much of the city's water infrastructure was destroyed. As a result, there were few sewers to connect sinks, showers, and toilets to the wastewater treatment plant. Many of the 2.3 million people in the metro area used outhouses, and much of that waste ended up in canals, ditches, and other unsanitary dumping grounds, where it contaminated the drinking water and spread disease.

CARE began laying more than sixteen miles of water and waste pipe throughout the capital. The scale of the work was impressive in itself, but more impressive still the effort was done by hand. Because of war and international embargos, there were few earth-moving machines in the country. There was no capability other than the picks and shovels of manual labor.

Every day before dawn, groups of men assembled around the city to begin digging the trenches required to lay the pipe. There were hundreds of men moving with the steady rhythm of picks, shovels, and wheelbarrows to channel the earth. These conduits were not superficial troughs that only scratched the surface. Often, they were six to eight feet deep and ten feet wide. All the channels were constructed to international engineering codes and standards, but it was done by hand. For several days, I accompanied different groups of CARE engineers throughout the city. I marveled at how much excavation they accomplished each day.

The workers were paid a decent wage, which sustained their families. In return, their efforts were focused and direct. The weather was cool, but I could see the sweat soaking their clothes. There was little talk. They had a silent dance—when the man with the pick stopped, his partner shoveled the dirt into the wheelbarrow, and the man with the cart moved the earth from the ditch. It was a movement repeated by scores of men.

The piping came from Pakistan. It was cast iron and had to be manually placed into the trenches. Small wooden structures made of wood, rope, and props lined the ditches. They were quickly moved from one position to another to lower the pipes into the ground. The process was remarkably functional and ingenious. I was from a culture where mechanization assisted every aspect of living. There are machines to help with everything from washing dishes to building a skyscraper. Here, I watched men successfully reverting to the practices of a previous century.

Throughout the next decade, when I returned to Kabul, I could still envision the men who built the water and sanitation systems that continue flowing under Kabul.

When Nazhand returned, he told me we would journey to some projects throughout rural Afghanistan. We would visit the provinces of Logar, Paktia, Khost, and Ghazni. Most of the work in these areas involved education, light road building, and irrigation. I asked if we would be part of a team, but he said no, it would just be the two of us.

For the next week before we left, I accompanied him around Kabul as he worked with the local projects. He was tireless. His days began before dawn and continued well into the night. There were many evenings when he would drop me at my residence at eight o'clock and return to the office to catch up on administrative requirements. I marveled at his stamina and constant cheerfulness. I never saw him angry or dismissive, and he was well-known throughout the city. If we were stopped by the Taliban, they quickly waved him forward once they saw his face. His large white beard was unmistakable.

In the early morning on the day of our departure, I threw my backpack and sleeping bag into the rear of an old Toyota Corolla. The trunk had several cases of bottled water and many bundles and containers of administrative supplies for each of the suboffices. At dawn, we started the old car and headed to the province of Logar. The suboffice was approximately a one-hour drive from Kabul. The road was one of the few maintained two-lane blacktop highways in Afghanistan. Yet, at this time, the term "maintained" had a special meaning. During my cross-country drive from the Afghan border to Kabul, I noticed young men and boys sitting at the side of the highway with a shovel. Occasionally, they threw some dirt into a gaping hole in the road. It was a nice gesture, but the roads were so bad their efforts seemed inconsequential. I did not think about it again until we were on our way to Logar.

I asked Nazhand if the men and the boys were paid by the government to maintain the road. He told me they were people who lived close to the highway and did not have any other means to make a living. They spent days trying to fix the road in the hopes that an occasional passerby would throw a few coins from the window of a car or truck. It was a thankless job. There were few vehicles, and most of them were driven by men trying to survive on their own minimal resources. However, after our discussion, I noticed coins being dropped from vehicles, mostly from buses.

In Logar, we began a routine that lasted the

rest of our journey. When we arrived at an office, there were introductions to the staff. After the formalities, Nazhand would hold a series of group or individual meetings, and I was paired with several junior project managers. The men always spoke English. We spent days visiting the different CARE initiatives throughout the province.

It was at this time that I was introduced to the Kochi people. "Koch" is a Persian word for migration. The Kochi are Afghan nomads. I saw them walking next to the roads or camped with their tents in the distance. They were often herding goats and sheep. If they were moving from one area to another, donkeys and camels carried their tents and equipment. As the women walked along the roads, they wore bright red or blue dresses, and were adorned with brilliant silver necklaces and bracelets. Some of them wore minimal headscarves or were uncovered. They had flowing black hair and walked freely with the men. When they camped, the women set up the sites. Their tents blended with the brown and arid earth of the desert and sustained the high winds of dust storms.

Although the Kochi were nomadic, they were a strong and influential culture within Afghanistan, and fierce warriors. The Taliban did not want to inflame their resentment by forcing their tenets of fundamentalism on them. Thus, they tolerated their dress and liberal attitudes toward women.

As we continued our journey to Ghazni, I witnessed a remarkable series of projects, which spoke to the courage of Nazhand and the women of Afghanistan. Nazhand had developed an arrangement with the Taliban to allow girls' education and schools throughout the province. On its own, this was an amazing accomplishment, but the CARE suboffice he established to oversee the work was led and staffed by women. There were male drivers, mechanics, and day laborers, but the professional work was done by women. Their efforts were not minor—they traveled by themselves and interacted with the beneficiaries to monitor the projects as head of the various initiatives. They created a score of well-organized and effective schools.

One of the most notable schools was in a small but well-heated and well-lit building in an adjacent village. There were approximately twenty girls and young women who arrived each day shortly after dawn, and attended reading, writing, and geography classes. At eleven, the students engaged in play or sport. At noon, they were served a meal and rested for a short period. Afterward, they adjourned to weaving rooms. Each of the young women was also learning a skill that would assist her family. I asked Nazhand why the local Taliban allowed this type of schooling. He told me the farther we journeyed from Kabul, the more liberal the attitudes of Taliban leaders toward women and girls. With a smile, he said, "It helps that some of the young women in the schools are also their daughters."

Throughout the remainder of the trip, I noticed most of the women in the rural areas routinely walked and worked without a head covering, and I seldom saw women in burkas.

In Ghazni, I was staying in a small chamber with a row of windows overlooking the desert. From my room, I watched the evening slip into darkness. In the desert, there is very little humidity, and dusk passes very quickly. It feels like daylight one moment and solid black the next. As far as I could see, there were no lights, buildings, roads, lamps, or signs of humanity. There was just blackness. It took time for my eyes to adjust. As I stood in the room surrounded by comforting darkness, I saw a flash in the sky. I thought it was a light from a passing jetliner, but realized it was a meteor plunging to the earth.

However, it was the sight of the heavens that made me open my window, sit on my bed, and stare in awe. I had never seen such a view. I walked outside and away from the small compound into the adjacent field. I put a blanket on the ground and lay on my back. I knew I may never see such a vision again. For the first time, I saw the stars suspended low over the desert. There was no moisture, dust, or barriers of any kind. It was the clearest air I had ever encountered. I could see the Milky Way displayed with such beauty my throat constricted with emotion. I was overwhelmed. The cosmos was filled with unnumbered points of brilliance. The stars were enormous. They dropped into a horizon where the earth seemed to end. In the east, the cosmos ascended from dunes of sand that defined the borders of my sight. Toward the west, heaven merged into the black emptiness of the desert. It was so beautiful. I held my breath in fear any sound would make it all disappear. I continued star gazing every night we were in the country.

As Nazhand and I continued to Paktia and Khost, we visited projects with every form of irrigation. Nazhand initiated work involving small dams, reservoirs, spillways, culverts, irrigation conduits, small bridges, and siphon tubes. With each project, he included the means to protect the environment from erosion. There were walls, stones, terracing, and other methods to preserve the habitat.

I was impressed with the number of reservoirs being built around small villages. These were isolated hamlets amid an arid desert. All of the lands were surrounded by a range of mountains with peaks well over 12,000 feet. Fields of snow and ice capped each crest. The goal was to move the water from the melting snow into reservoirs for irrigation and daily use by the people in the communities. The basins were dug in a grove of Eucalyptus trees, which grow to an enormous height, providing the pools with shade.

On a hot afternoon, Nazhand and I were with several engineers who had just completed a reservoir. It was in Sra Kala village of Khogyani valley, the district of Ghazni province. The basin was approximately six by eight meters wide and one meter deep. As we walked around the basin, I kneeled and put my hand in the water. It was frigid. Nazhand said it would be a good day for a swim; I laughed. A moment later I felt a small push and fell into the pool. It was a severe shock, but my body quickly adjusted. Around me my Afghan colleagues were laughing like a group of schoolchildren. I hooted and walked to the edge of the reservoir, extending my hand for Nazhand to help me out of the water. When I had a firm grip, I fell back into the basin and pulled him with me. When he came to the surface, he started laughing until he had tears in his eyes.

We quickly scrambled out of the pool, and my companions removed their outer robes to the full set of clothing they wore underneath. We spent the next half hour splashing, laughing, and playing like we were at summer camp. In those moments of abandonment, we let go of our pretenses and cultural restrictions and biases. We became one. We were not Afghans, Americans, Christians, or Muslims—we were just people enjoying one another's company and having fun.

After three days, we made our way back to Kabul. I started the trip with a colleague and returned with a friend. I had other obligations with CARE and had to depart the country, but I kept track of Nazhand and his work. He continued to advocate for women and girls' rights and education. After 9/11 and the subsequent invasion of Afghanistan by NATO forces, CARE's international staff returned to Kabul, and Nazhand reverted to his role as the field administration manager and director of human resources.

Over the next several years, I made brief trips to the country as the security situation for the humanitarian community deteriorated. Nazhand was concerned about the resurgence of the Taliban and the direction of humanitarian assistance. The country was flooded with international experts who made rapid evaluations without engaging the Afghan people for their opinions. CARE was fortunate because most of its staff were Afghans who guided the integration of international desires with local requirements.

The country director was Paul Barker, a remarkable person who valued his national staff and allowed them to take the lead in deciding the direction of the organization's efforts. He was fluent in Dari and lived in the Afghan community in a small house several blocks from the office. Often, I saw him walking or riding his bicycle to and from headquarters. I liked and respected him, but it was his unpretentious humility that inspired me. He epitomized the personality, conduct, and actions of a person who engaged in humanitarian work for the sake of individual rights and focused assistance. He forged a trust between CARE and the Afghans. His actions set the standard for inclusive cooperation between the international community and the people of Afghanistan.

Yet, as more commercial companies began to implement US government development projects, there was a gradual breakdown in Afghans' trust of commercial corporations. As the violence grew and the foreigners retreated into walled compounds protected by an array of security companies, the Taliban began representing itself as champions of an oppressed people. As history has shown, the Afghans do not do well on bended knee.

Nazhand's role as the human resources coordinator became increasingly important, but his informal role as an intermediary with the different warring factions was a crucial factor in allowing CARE staff to safely operate throughout the country. Yet, as Afghan security forces focused on the violence enacted by numerous anti-government elements, another group started to flourish. There had always been criminals in Afghanistan, but the government's attention on counter-terrorism allowed the rise of organized criminal gangs.

In May 2005, six months after the death of Margaret Hassan, I received a call from Jon Mitchell telling me a CARE international staff member was kidnapped in Kabul. Her name was Clementina Cantoni. She was Italian and had been in Afghanistan since 2002. She was the project manager of CARE's Humanitarian Assistance for Women of Afghanistan. Clementina worked with thousands of Afghan widows and their children who had no family or support system. The project supplied them with clean water, food, medicine, and clothing. Additionally, her team created job opportunities to provide widows with a chance to become self-sufficient.

At approximately 8:45 p.m. on May 16, Clementina was kidnapped from a CARE vehicle. The driver was immediately released. The head of the criminal gang, Timor Shah, announced through public media he had kidnapped her and provided a video of her sitting on a floor with a man pointing his Kalashnikov rifle at her.

She looked terrified. Shah made several rambling demands, which included a ban of a local radio station that broadcasted a Wednesday night youth program. He wanted a crackdown on importing and selling alcohol, and greater government attention to Madrasa (religious schools). Privately, he sought the release of his mother from prison. She was convicted of being an accessory to the murder of an Afghan businessman.

After the kidnap of Margaret Hassan, CARE's executive level learned its lesson from the tragedy.

My role was to coordinate with professional kidnap negotiators who were part of the group's special insurance policy. When I arrived in Kabul, I was greeted by a host of different individuals. The most prominent was an experienced kidnap negotiator from Great Britain, who was to represent CARE. After my recent experience in Iraq, I was grateful for his presence and expertise.

The Afghan government took the lead during the initial contacts with Shah.

However, the negotiations became convoluted as numerous people from different governments, and their departments, became involved in the discussions. Each evening, I attended a meeting at the Afghan Ministry of Interior. The large room was filled with representatives from different departments of the Afghan government, the British, Italian, and US governments, members of the Afghan police, representatives from NATO, crisis negotiators and other internationals who were intelligence operatives. Most spoke English, and for those who did not there were several translators.

After the general meeting, a smaller group adjourned to a private conversation. It was clear that different organizations and people were vying for control of the event. Although the meetings were organized, there was little revealed that was not already being reported in the media. Increasingly, Shah became more erratic and at one point announced he would kill Clementina within forty-eight hours. His demands were inconsistent but the result of too many people contacting him and negotiating their own agendas.

Ultimately, it became clear that Shah wanted his mother and several men from his gang released from prison. He also demanded a ransom payment. Although the Afghan government initially refused, they agreed to free his mother. They were not willing to make a deal about his gang members. Justifiably, they feared that such an exchange would generate a cycle of additional kidnappings to free more criminals.

The negotiations stalled. The evening meetings were repetitive discussions by different parties speculating about the next moves Shah might make. To this point, there was one critical asset missing from the discussions: Nazhand. The Afghan government was determined to show they had the power to resolve this incident. Their allies wanted to demonstrate to the international community the Afghans were in charge and could protect other foreigners in Afghanistan. Everyone had an agenda to keep the negotiations under the control of the national government. The last thing they wanted was help from a former Mujahideen who worked for an international charity.

After days of inconclusive governmental efforts, Nazhand contacted his network of clan chiefs, clerics, former Mujahideen, Taliban, and other secular and religious leaders. Both the government and anti-government elements knew where Clementina was located. The dilemma was how to free her without an armed confrontation. Nazhand's associates applied pressure on Shah to ensure her safety and modify his demands to achievable actions. There were two sides to these informal discussions. One appealed to Shah's humanity. The other made it clear that if he harmed Clementina or did not quickly resolve this event, he would not be able to hide.

Within a day of these informal discussions, at approximately 9 p.m. on June 9, I received a call from a man with an Afghan accent. He told me to go to the Afghan Interior Ministry. Clementina was going to be freed. I was hopeful but cautious. I did not want to leave my compound at night and become another kidnap victim.

I called Nazhand. He said he was just about to contact me. He had been told Clementina was going to be exchanged for Shah's mother that night. The exchange site was guaranteed by NATO, the Afghan government, and anti-governmental elements. With the additional pressures from the Taliban, Shah had cut the best deal he could. He would receive his mother, and the Italians were paying a very small sum of compensation for money he claimed was stolen from him.

I went to the Interior Ministry compound. The scene reminded me of the mayhem of a Black Friday sale at an American mall. There were people, media, journalists, spotlights, and soldiers all jostling with one another to enter the building. The guards were trying to maintain control, but everyone was ignoring them as they shoved one another through the door. My driver signaled for me to follow him. We walked to the far end of another building and entered an unguarded passage. I followed him to the second floor and proceeded down a long hallway.

At the end was a door into a common area. He opened it, and we walked across a small bridge to the second floor of the Minister's building. We ended in a room outside his office, where the driver nodded toward the door. I showed the guards my CARE credentials and was allowed into the Minister's hallway, which was full of media and government officials. The Minister was talking to local and international journalists.

Clementina had been held for three weeks, and the first act after her release was orchestrating a media circus praising the Minister's efforts under the guise of celebrating her freedom. As I looked around, I saw numerous Afghan officials and representatives from the US, British, and Italian governments.

In the middle of the crowd, I saw Clementina sitting in a chair, staring into space. No one was talking to her. They were eating, chatting, drinking, and dropping their food crumbs on her. She might as well have been a lamp. I was heartsick. In the front of the room, the Minister of the Interior sat at a table introducing an endless number of people who he claimed helped secure her release. It was an enormous episode of self-congratulation. When I saw the Italian ambassador in the distance, he looked miserable. I'm sure he was conflicted but wanted to let the Afghans have their moment.

I pulled a chair in front of Clementina and told her I was with CARE. She focused her eyes on me and asked if I could arrange for her to speak to her parents. I was stunned. She was made a prop for the media before even being allowed to talk with her family. I made my way to the Italian ambassador and relayed her request. He spoke to his assistant, who quickly disappeared.

Clementina was clearly exhausted. As I talked with her, I continued scanning the crowd for Nazhand. His presence would help her relax and introduce a modicum of dignity to this spectacle, but I could not find him. I thought he had been held in the hallway or stairwell where a host of others were waiting for a glance at Clementina or to snap a photo of her. She asked me about her driver. I assured her that he was well and unharmed. She expressed gratitude to all the CARE staff who she knew were concerned. The only emotion she showed was shock when she said how sorry she was to have caused so much trouble. I tried to assure her this event was not her fault.

As we talked, I could see a multitude of mosquito and bug bites on her arms and face. She told me she had not changed her clothes or bathed in weeks.

Finally, I saw the Italian ambassador with his assistant moving in our direction. Clementina had not yet received a physical exam, and no one could ascertain whether she was assaulted.

The Italian ambassador had apparently had enough of the spectacle and was taking her under his control. He told me his vehicles were waiting outside and asked if I would accompany her to his car. When we opened the door to the hallway, there was a rush of people shouting questions, and bright lights from cameras. It was chaos. Fortunately, the ambassador's personal protection group began clearing a route to the vehicles. They led Clementina to a van, and the entourage sped into the night.

I walked to the parking lot and found the driver who had brought me to the Ministry. I asked him if he had seen Nazhand. He told me he had not. We started walking to the compound gate. There was a line of departing vehicles. I thought about calling Nazhand, but it was nearing two in the morning and I did not want to disturb him. As we left the car park, I glanced to my right and saw Nazhand standing by the wall. He brightened when he saw me and waved. I exited the vehicle and asked where he had been. He told me he was denied access to the complex.

I was incredulous. He was the man who was instrumental in obtaining Clementina's release, and he was excluded from meeting with her. I apologized to Nazhand and told him he should have called me, but he laughed and said it was a minor issue. He wanted to know how Clementina was and praised Allah for her release. I looked at Nazhand and knew the praise he expressed was precisely what he meant. His belief in God, and working for the common good of others rather than himself, were the guiding principles of his life. I never heard him talk about his beliefs, but he constantly lived them.

The essence of friendship, especially one that crosses so many cultural and societal norms, is what you learn from one another. Amid a war, terrorism, and competition for ideological claims and intents, I met a man who based his entire life on a moral compass founded on his Islamic faith. While my country riled against the Islamic world, Nazhand negotiated with the Taliban to ensure humanitarian assistance to his countrymen. He was a strong advocate of women's rights. It is impossible to understand the risks he took to confront the Taliban as a member of an international organization with its headquarters in the United States.

I have been privileged to associate with many honorable, brave, and dedicated people throughout my life, but rarely have I encountered a person whose principles have been guided by such a steadfast understanding of what it takes to do the right thing, and then—without concern for his personal safety—act toward the common good regardless of politics, culture, or religion. Nazhand Abdul Raouf embodied every principle of servant leadership. For nearly a quarter of a century with CARE, he put the needs of others ahead of his own and worked to empower people regardless of gender, position, or culture.

His efforts were heroic in every sense of that word.

EPILOGUE

"Life will let you get away with something for a while, but [eventually], you will pay the price. Everything you do in life causes the effects that you experience. When you get the bill, be prepared to pay."
—Iyanla Vanzant

Writing this book enabled me to record the stories of extraordinary and selfless women and men. These individuals crossed the margins of race, religion, age, and gender. Yet, out of necessity, I was limited to specific events. It was impossible to capture the sum of their contributions to humanity.

They lived in extreme settings of deprivation, worked long hours, and were surrounded by high-risk conditions. Violence, kidnapping, assault, injury, and death have made humanitarian work one of the world's most dangerous professions. Attacks on aid workers have tripled in the past decade.

It's important to note most of these victims are not international staff, but those assisting in their own country, working closest to their own population. Humanitarian assistance is not the domain of the west but a global movement. The national aid workers who have made the ultimate sacrifice testify to this fact.

But for both national and international staff, how did the profession affect them?

I spent decades with some of them. Others, I knew only during our time working together. I was uncomfortable with the answer because I saw it in myself. As my colleague, Romeo Dallaire, writes, "[It is the] moral injuries that ravage our minds, our souls [and repeated] assaults... our most sacred and fundamental values and beliefs."[1]

A survey conducted by the Guardian newspaper reported a shocking statistic. After considerable research, it found that approximately 80 percent of

---

1. Romeo Dallaire, *Waiting for First Light: My Ongoing Battle with PTSD* (Toronto: Vintage Canada, 2018).

aid worker respondents from the Guardian Global Development Professional Network said, "They had experienced some sort of mental health issue, with almost half declaring they were diagnosed with depression. Previous research... indicated that 30% of those deployed on field assignments report symptoms of post-traumatic stress disorder [PTSD] after returning home."[2]

The Antares Foundation found this 30 percent more significant when compared with the numbers reported by the US Veterans Administration (VA) of women and men who served in the Afghan War. The VA found that 11 percent of these veterans have been diagnosed with PTSD.

Many aid workers engage only in a single humanitarian event and return to their former life. For many, it is daunting. After returning home, even from a short period in the field witnessing so much trauma, they felt detached and could not fit into their former lives. They were changed in ways their friends and family could not understand.

In addition to short-term staff and volunteers,

---

2. Holly Young, "Research Suggests Mental Health Crisis among Aid Workers," The Guardian, November 23, 2015, accessed June 28, 2020, https://www.theguardian.com/global-development-professionals-network/2015/nov/23/guardian-research-suggests-mental-health-crisis-among-aid-workers.

there are approximately 450,000 professional aid workers throughout the world, many of whom move from one emergency to another. They self-medicate for stress by immersing themselves into an increasing number of crisis events. It is an easy solution to remain in the company of people who share similar experiences. There is a common refrain, "You get addicted to this work, and it's hard to settle back into normal life."

How do I start to convey the issue of PTSD within the humanitarian community?

It is with an admission: I suffer from post-traumatic stress disorder. Who admits to having a mental problem? Indeed, not someone who's been raised in a family of stoic Highland Scots and spent nearly three decades as a US Marine.

As I tried unraveling the diagnosis, I wandered down inevitable paths and questions:

"Why me?"

"How did this happen?"

"What did I experience to cause it?"

"I know so many people who have seen and experienced a lot worse than me. They seem okay. Why am I not?"

But the cruelest voice in me said, "I'm weak."

PTSD doesn't just rob you of your happiness and capacity for joy. It crushes your soul. In the place of joyfulness, it pulls you into fear and chaos.

The Veterans Administration gave me a place to go with my condition, and I had a group of professionals assisting me. The team consisted of a psychiatrist, psychologist, physician, licensed clinical social worker, and a fellow veteran. They provided me with a 24-hour telephone number, and each step of the treatment was personalized. In the beginning, I was skeptical. I thought I would just be a number, but that did not happen, and it was overwhelming. These people really cared about my well-being.

As I started to get my life together, and my mind slowed down, I could focus on things bigger than myself.

I had become a person who had to think about every engagement in life. Going to a restaurant, movie, church, workshop, airplane trip, or grocery store required conscious preparation for an exposure to crowds. At times, I was not able to make the journey or visit, and I just couldn't cope. Even though my wife quietly and gently accepted it, my inability to do ordinary things increased my guilt and feelings of shame and inadequacy.

My wife often visited a new location like a restaurant, church, or meeting hall before suggesting a trip. She looked at the seating arrangements, size of crowds, best place for me to stand or sit. She never told me what she was doing, but I noticed when we went through the door of a new location she often knew exactly where to sit or stand. I could not believe how far I had fallen. I was angry, I could not sleep, and I was becoming more reclusive. Yet, I never realized what this was doing to my family.

My lingering fear is that I will fall back into the abyss where I lose my dignity, self-respect, and sense of worth. It is a place of total blackness; it presses down on me like a giant boulder. I'm being crushed and cannot escape. But even in this complete darkness, I sense others who can navigate life, and I cannot. I hear a voice repeating over and over, "You're weak, you failed so many others and they died, you're a fraud and do not deserve to be here."

It is a terrifying place.

But now, for the first time in decades, I feel alive. I am living my life, not hiding from it, and I can focus on things other than my own survival.

I wrote *Stewards of Humanity* throughout my treatment. Working on the book, I realized how many of the *Stewards* not mentioned had died by suicide, direct and indirect violence, or were suffering other forms of trauma.

As a group, humanitarians commit themselves to assist amid dark and tragic events and places, they witness horrific and senseless actions. Their trauma intensifies as they try to understand the viciousness because in doing so they relive the horror. They blame themselves for being unable to resolve the conditions of the victims and are burdened by both guilt and feelings of responsibility.

As aid workers' mental health problems manifest, they have severe consequences on the individual's personal and professional life. Humanitarians have begun to speak out about their difficulties and expressed an urgent need for help on public forums, such as the Facebook groups "Fifty Shades of Aid" and the "Secret Aid Worker" series, and published articles by The Guardian.[3]

While more humanitarian organizations have begun addressing the problem, and increasingly understand that the compromised mental

---

3. Secret aid worker, "Secret aid worker: when your dream job ends in depression," The Guardian, July 19, 2016, accessed March 7, 2019, https://www.theguardian.com/global-development-professionals-network/2016/jul/19/secret-aid-worker-when-your-dream-job-ends-in-depression

well-being of their workers impacts organizational effectiveness, there remain significant barriers to implementing impactful mental health support services. Assistance is mostly insufficient, and donors are unwilling to support funding for staff well-being projects.[4]

Humanitarian aid workers are identical to other members of the first-responder profession, which includes the military, police, firefighters, and emergency medical staff, but with one exception: they enter the chaos of desperate situations without the degree of organizational support of other immediate responders, and many of their mental health problems are intensified by issues particular to the humanitarian community. For example, aid workers do not benefit from being part of a well-trained, tightly knit team with a clear command structure. Additionally, their training, particularly about psychological issues, is generally inadequate. This is particularly pertinent for aid agencies that

---

4. World Humanitarian Summit, "Humanitarian effectiveness and staff wellness: Summary report of the online consultation event," International Association of Professionals in Humanitarian Assistance and Protection, July 30, 2015, accessed November 23, 2017, https://phap.org/PHAP/Events/OEV2015/WHS150730.aspx?EventKey=WHS150730

use volunteers with no previous experience as aid workers.

Humanitarian workers have committed themselves to a needed calling, and their service must be recognized in a manner worthy of its importance. Aid organizations must realize it is their responsibility and be held accountable to support staff mental wellness and not use abstract rationalizations—such as the deficiency of funding from donor groups—as an excuse for lack of adequate attention. Said another way, if an agency can't provide proper mental health support for their staff, they should get out of the business.

In most western nations, there is a precept known as "Duty of Care." It is described as, "Legal obligation imposed on an organization requiring they adhere to a standard of reasonable care while [staff] [engage in] an act that presents a reasonably foreseeable risk of harm to [themselves]." Consequently, by law, it is incumbent on organizational management to ensure staff is aware of the risks they are being asked to face and to define precisely what the organization will do to assist with mitigating the dangers. Aid agencies must have adequate redress measures in place, including health, disability, injury and death, and loss of income insurance, payment of damages, and post-incident treatment to compensate an employee who has suffered damages.[5]

The most impactful support agencies can provide their workers is assistance before they begin suffering from the cumulative effects of traumatic stress. Staff need to be treated for PTSD at its first signs, and humanitarian organizations must anticipate the need for care and not wait until an aid worker is desperate enough to ask for help. This requires training for all staff to recognize the indicators of stress in the field and, most importantly, have the backing of the organization to assist when they believe a team member needs help.

"Aid workers feel the support options offered… are either inadequate (time-limited or inaccessible), ill-fitting (the available clinicians or [programs] offered don't understand or tackle the issues faced) or unsafe (they fear that a call for help could result in professional blemishes on personnel records)… Others believe support offered,

---

5. Edward Kemp, and Maarten Merkelbach, "Can you get sued? Legal liability of international humanitarian aid organisations towards their staff," Global Interagency Security Forum, November 1, 2011, accessed April 11, 2017, https://www.eisf.eu/library/can-you-get-sued-legal-liability-of-international-humanitarian-aid-organisations-towards-their-staff/.

like a list of self-care tips or brief rest and relaxation, is too simple."[6]

An additional problem is that both management and aid workers don't recognize trauma symptoms and are unaware of what is happening as they chase the next crisis in hopes of recreating the feeling of satisfaction they initially experienced when they signed up to do the work. When this happens, workers stop responding to human suffering, which impacts the validity of the support they're providing.[7]

For many aid workers, this operational stress becomes a repeated attack on their fundamental values and beliefs. Although the physical consequences of their exposure to war and terrorism can be fatal, PTSD is a moral injury that affects their minds and souls. The ethical and moral quandaries that confront them become cumulative. No matter how hard they try to handle it, their exposure to death, starvation, and mayhem affects their belief in justice, goodness, and human rights as every personal and professional value is under assault.

---

6. Rich McEachran, "Aid workers and post-traumatic stress disorder," *The Guardian*, March 2, 2014, accessed June 14, 2019, https://www.theguardian.com/global-development-professionals-network/2014/mar/03/post-traumantic-stress-disorder-aid-workers.
7. Ibid.

Presently, PTSD is considered an individual problem, but it should not be—it must be shared. A single humanitarian's descent into this form of mental illness is a tragedy and needs to be treated with the same care that is given to a war veteran. When PTSD becomes a shared condition, individual health becomes part of a collective response.

In 1999, a group of representatives from several aid agencies met to discuss the rising threat of physical violence against aid workers around the world. As a result of that meeting and many that followed, humanitarian organizations adopted Minimum Operating Security Standards known as MOSS. Based on these principles was a requirement for all aid agencies to certify their compliance with funding donors. MOSS served as the benchmark for protecting the physical safety and security of humanitarians.

Now, there is a requirement for a comparable industry-wide program to address the moral injuries associated with aid work, including mental health and psychosocial needs. There are many good programs throughout the community, but they are individualized and dependent on the interest and willingness of each organization to fund mental health programs.

Working toward this goal would provide a means for a shared effort between the NGOs, donor organizations, and governments to create movement toward prioritizing the response to mental health. The structuring and functioning of psychosocial and wellness management would be recognized in the same fashion as training and intervention for crisis mitigation. Such an effort would level the playing field between aid agencies and donors regarding funding. In addition, this movement would establish minimum standards for more objective analysis of organizational preparedness regarding policies, performance, and post-incident management. It would introduce a measure of needed regulation to the community's activities. This call to support the much-needed mental health requirements of aid workers is essential.

I want us to end this journey by remembering the extraordinary work of all Stewards, undertaken often at great personal cost.

Robert F. Kennedy, said,

"Few will have the greatness to bend history itself, but each of us can work to change a small portion of events. It is from numberless diverse acts of courage and belief that human history is shaped. Each time a [person] stands up for an ideal, or acts to improve the lot of others, or strikes out against injustice, [they] send forth a tiny ripple of hope... crossing each other from a million different centers of energy and... those ripples build a current [to] sweep down the mightiest walls of oppression and resistance."

You and I traveled into some of the darkest events of the twentieth and twenty-first centuries; along the way, we witnessed the efforts of remarkable people. Some of these tragedies are resolved, but Somalia, Afghanistan, the West Bank and Gaza, the Democratic Republic of the Congo, and Iraq continue. Others have been added—Syria, Sudan, South Sudan, Myanmar, Yemen, and the Tigray region in Ethiopia. In each of these places are the Stewards.

Although the faces have changed, they all have similar characteristics founded on their willingness to step outside the bounds of normalcy and walk into the worlds of disaster, violence, and deprivation. In the chaos, they forge solidarity with others by listening to the heartbeat of humanity. Wading into horrific situations, armed only with their willingness to confront rather than retreat from injustice, there is no deliberation that some are worth saving while others are not—all lives have value.

Their commitment is not to friend or foe, religion, country, nor creed. It is from that freedom, when the night is darkest, their light manifests to bring forth the dawn.

ABOUT THE AUTHOR

Robert Macpherson has been a writer, aid worker, and career infantry officer in the U.S. Marines with service in Vietnam, Iraq and Somalia.

After retiring as a Colonel, Robert enjoyed a second career with the humanitarian organization CARE, where he directed global risk mitigation for staff and vulnerable populations and led humanitarian response missions worldwide. These efforts often required engaging with foreign governments and the United Nations, and as frequently with non-traditional actors such as the Taliban in Afghanistan, warlords in Sudan and Somalia, local militias and kidnappers.

Stewards of Humanity is his debut book. He lives

in Charlotte, NC with his wife and service dog, Blue.

Connect with Bob at:
rsm@robertseamusmacpherson.com

THANK YOU!

Thank you for reading! The team at Torchflame Books hopes you've enjoyed this book and might consider leaving a review on Amazon, Goodreads, BookBub, The Story Graph, or anywhere else you like to track your recent reads. Alternatively, you could post online or tell a friend about it. This helps our authors more than you may know.

Additional Large Print books are available for purchase at torchflamebooks.com/large-print or may be requested through your local library.

- The Team at Torchflame Books

www.ingramcontent.com/pod-product-compliance
Lightning Source LLC
Chambersburg PA
CBHW021825220426
43663CB00005B/132